THE REPUBLIC
OF LETTERS

Edited by
WILLIAM ROSE, M.A., Ph.D.

THE REPUBLIC
OF LETTERS

Volumes Ready

VOLTAIRE	RICHARD ALDINGTON
PUSHKIN	D. S. MIRSKY
GOGOL	JANKO LAVRIN
GOETHE	J. G. ROBERTSON
RICHARDSON	BRIAN W. DOWNS
HEINE	H. G. ATKINS

Volumes in Preparation

DRYDEN	MONTAGUE SUMMERS
STENDHAL	T. W. EARP
CASANOVA	G. D. GRIBBLE
CALDERON	J. B. TREND
FROISSART	F. S. SHEARS
DANTE	T. S. ELIOT
MONTAIGNE	RICHARD ALDINGTON
JOHNSON	RICHARD CHURCH
CHAUCER	J. ISAACS
BALZAC	BONAMY DOBRÉE
DIDEROT	FRANCIS BIRRELL
NOVALIS	WILLIAM ROSE

From an original oil painting in the possession of
Sir Israel Gollancz

HEINE

HEINE

By

H. G. Atkins

*Professor of German in the University of London,
Fellow of King's College*

With a Portrait

NEW YORK
E. P. DUTTON & Co., Inc.
1929

PRINTED IN GUERNSEY, C.I., BRITISH ISLES,
BY THE STAR AND GAZETTE COMPANY LTD.

CONTENTS

		Page
Preface		VII
I Heine's Youth in Düsseldorf		I
II Youthful Sorrows		26
III Student Years		37
IV Heine on the Heights		65
V " Buch der Lieder"		79
VI Last Years in Germany		93
VII First Years in Paris		119
VIII Gathering Clouds		151
IX "Neue Gedichte"		182
X Illness and Turn of Fortune		193
XI "Romanzero" and Last Poems		230
XII Conclusion		249
Chronological List of Works		262
Bibliography		265
Appendix (Translations of Poems quoted in the Text)		276
Index		287

PREFACE

All great men, and peculiarly all great poets, belong not to the country of their birth alone. The Germans are entitled to their own Shakespeare, and the facet they see differs in many respects from that which he presents to us. Equally we are entitled to our own Heine. There are many German Heines, coloured by various prepossessions, social, political and religious. He is a rock of offence to many, a problem to all.

We in England are not divided as critics into Gentiles and Jews, into religious and political camps. Much that is of interest to German readers is somewhat remote to an English public ; his relations to less-known writers, the details of political movements and intrigues, and other things. We are interested, it is true, in Heine the ironic philosopher and the wit, and are especially attracted by his candid and not too flattering opinion of ourselves. But with us the lyric poet stands more clearly in the foreground than with the Germans, and we are on the whole less concerned with the study of Heine as a specifically Jewish poet, or as a cosmopolitan thinker, or as a Liberal reformer.

One of our chief sources of information, especially concerning Heine's parentage and the conditions of his early life in Düsseldorf, is to be found in his own writings. He early planned a work which was to be a *Dichtung und Wahrheit* on an even more comprehensive scale, but of which we possess to-day only a mutilated fragment published after his death, in 1884, his *Memoiren*. The plan accompanied him from 1823 to the end of his life, when he re-wrote the part which we now possess. As he said to Campe in a letter of 1st March, 1837, when there was a question of writing his autobiography as an appendage to his collected works, he was planning to write " not a short, dry summary, but a big book, perhaps of several volumes, which should form the conclusion of the Collected Edition, and should comprise the whole history of my Times, in whose great moments I have played a part, along with the most notable people of my day, the whole of Europe, the whole of modern life, German conditions up to the July Revolution, the results of my sojourn in the lobby of the political and social revolution, the fruits of my most costly and painful studies, the book that is very specially expected of me."

His Confessions (*Geständnisse*), which were written in German, but first appeared in French in the *Revue des deux Mondes* in 1854, were regarded by him as a precursor and a study for the *Memoirs*. We possess in addition a brief three page sketch of his life in French, sent in 1835 to the French critic Philarète Chasles and published in the *Revue de Paris*, and a still briefer Latin *curriculum vitae*, addressed to the Dean of the Faculty of Laws on the occasion of his candidature for the doctorate in 1825. To these must be added the second volume of the *Reisebilder*, *Das Buch Le Grand*, with its fascinating account of his boyhood years.

All biographers draw, and rightly draw, very largely on these sources, but it must all the same be borne in mind that they are often unreliable in points of fact, and that they tend to place the position and fortunes of the family in altogether too favourable a light. The *Sketch* in particular gives entirely the impression of the " correct " education of a youth of good standing. " Mon père était négociant et assez riche: il est mort. Ma mère, femme distinguée, vit encore, retirée du grand monde." If one took it literally, one might perhaps write, as did the author of an article which appeared not long ago in one of our leading Monthlies : " He had highly eligible parents. He went to good schools, the best universities. The most distinguished houses were open to him." Quite an Eton and Christchurch touch ! We shall have to get away from such a conception, and also generally to discount the picture presented by members of this family, in which the aristocratic bent was so strong, and in which later on titles blossomed so luxuriantly, if we wish to understand the actual setting of Heine's youth.

However serious the loss of the *Memoirs* may be, we have another first-hand source of information which is even more direct and spontaneous than they would have been— his Letters. They are now available in three large volumes, edited by Friedrich Hirth, which contain 1,180 letters from and to Heine. They form an indispensable source for the study of the poet's life and personality, and are, with their notable introductions and their 50 portraits, comprising an almost complete iconography, one of the most important Heine publications of recent years. They are natural, unadorned communications, written with no eye to publication, and so much the more valuable for that reason.

Anyone familiar with the intrigues that have raged round Heine's letters, and with the attempts made, especially by members of the family, to give them to the world in a form that would redound most to the credit of the parties concerned, will realize what is meant by this complete collection, which spares no one, and the poet himself least of all. Other publications have been intended to show him as the tender son and brother, or to improve the reputation of someone or other, but here we get Heine for better or worse—often for worse—but at any rate a full and undistorted picture of one of the most complex and sensitive of modern souls.

Finally there may be mentioned another even more recent volume, which through most of its 997 pages forms fascinating reading, the *Gespräche mit Heine*, collected and edited by H. H. Houben. A good deal of what it contains was already known, but it gathers together in one compact and handy volume the testimony of a host of witnesses who knew Heine and have left their impressions of him.

The portrait of Heine here reproduced is from an original oil-painting now in the possession of my colleague, Professor Sir Israel Gollancz. The picture is thought to be by Friedrich August Elsasser or Julius Elsasser, and belonged formerly to Fräulein Mathilde von Waldenburg, from whom it was acquired by Mrs. Frida Mond in 1906.

The translations, both in prose and verse, are throughout my own.

H. G. ATKINS.

University of London,
King's College,
June, 1929.

HEINE

Chapter One

HEINE'S YOUTH IN DÜSSELDORF

Heinrich Heine was born at Düsseldorf in the year 1797, and he spent there the first eighteen years of his life. In the same year there was born not far away, at Hülshoff near Münster in Westphalia, the greatest German poetess, Annette von Droste-Hülshoff, and an interesting light might be thrown on Heine's place in German literature by a comparison between him and this aristocratic, orthodox, Catholic contemporary.

Any lover of Heine proceeding in simple good faith to Düsseldorf to-day would, no doubt, expect to find abundant outward and visible signs of Heine in this city of his birth. How great would be his surprise ! In the shop-windows he would find pictures of all sorts of celebrities, but rarely, if ever, one of Heine. Of public monuments to Heine there are precisely as many as in London ; the tablet in Craven Street is matched by a tablet on the house where he was born. It requires, it is true, little search to discover two further traces of him—a " Gedenkecke " in an inn in the Bolkerstrasse, the Goldene Kessel, with a bust of Heine by Emil Jungblut of Düsseldorf ; and most important of all, the " Heinezimmer " in the Landes-und Stadt-Biblio-thek, containing, apart from its invaluable collection of books, various Heine relics, including the death mask, the bust by Adolf Schmiedings, the original portrait of 1828 by Gottlieb Gassen—and Mathilde's famous parrot! Monuments have been erected to Heine in New York, in Corfu, two now in Hamburg, even one in the Forests of the Congo ; but when proposals have been made for a public monument in Düsseldorf, nothing has come of it, or the plan has been definitely rejected, as was the case in 1893 with that favoured by the Empress of Austria, one of his most fervent admirers. The reasons are not so much a lack of interest, as a conflict of views. And Düsseldorf is herein a microcosm of Germany as a whole.

Düsseldorf is to-day a large and flourishing town with a population approaching the half million. At the heart of it lies a beautiful inner circle rich in public grounds and parks and gardens. It prides itself especially on being a "garden city," as well as a great industrial centre. The most striking feature is the Königsallee, one of the finest streets in Europe. Down the middle runs the old moat, which with its bridges and grassy banks and overhanging trees reminds one of the Cam in the Cambridge backs. This again is flanked by avenues of chestnut-trees, beyond which on either side are streets of fine shops, hotels and banks.

The Hofgarten, the Hyde Park of Düsseldorf, was founded in 1773 and enlarged under Napoleon in 1810. Now, as in Heine's youth, it is not only the favourite promenade of the elders, but a happy playground for the children. The "Napoleonsberg" is its mountain, an artificial mound some twenty feet high, made of the excavations of the harbour. Standing upon it Napoleon is said to have declared Düsseldorf to be a "Little Paris," that highest badge of honour, which more than one German city has claimed for itself. Many place-names, and the language one still hears in the streets, bear witness to the fact that Düsseldorf stands on Low German soil.

The Düsseldorf into which Heine was born was a small Rhine town of 15,000 inhabitants, of whom 2,000 were Protestants, 300 Jews and the rest Catholics. It was "erzkatholisch", and had not even the 28 per cent of Protestants of the present day. The handful of 300 Jews did not live in a ghetto, as they did in other larger towns of Western Germany, and probably Heine did not in his boyhood have the consciousness of his race brought home to him in any very marked fashion.

Heine's youth coincided with an ebb-tide of Düsseldorf's artistic life. The brilliant time had just passed when the Jacobis gathered round them in their beautiful country house at Pempelfort, on the outskirts of the town, many of the most famous men of the day, Goethe (1774 and 1792), Hamann, Lavater, Wieland, Herder, the Stolbergs, and others. The garden can still be seen, and the house has been since 1860, as the "Malkasten," a club for the Düsseldorf artists. The days of the Elector Johann Wilhelm (1690-1716), the Jan Wellem of popular fame, whose bronze equestrian statue by Grupello stands in the centre of the market-place, were long gone by. He had made Düsseldorf famous as a centre of art, and his successor Carl Theodor (1742-93) had increased its fame by founding the Academy, and had drawn many famous artists to the town. But the European upheaval had ended this state of affairs, and the days had not yet come when Cornelius and Schadow, Mendelssohn and Schumann, Immermann and Grabbe, were to raise its artistic fame once more.

Heinrich Heine was a member of a family which has counted many able people among its members, but of which he and his uncle Solomon were, in their very different ways, the only really big ones.   Heinrich alone possessed any marked artistic sensibility—a sport in this family of ambitious, rather snobbish, successful people.   Heine's father, Samson Heine, was the second of the eight children of Heymann Heine, a small Jewish trader of Bückeburg, who later migrated to Hanover, and died in the eighties of the 18th century.   His real name was Chajjim Bückeburg, since Jews had then no surnames, but were known by the name of their birthplace.   It would appear that he changed Chajjim to the more familiar sounding Heymann, and took from this Heymann or Heinemann the first part Heine as a surname.   The name is therefore one of the abbreviations of Heinrich, which appear variously as Heine, Hein and Hehn, and the name Heinrich Heine really a doublet such as we frequently find in Wales.   Heine tells us in the Memoirs that his father, in reply to a question of his, gave half humorously the curt reply, "Your grandfather was a little Jew with a big beard."   There was no great family tradition there, and it required a good deal of building up afterwards.

All the six sons of Heymann prospered, with the exception of Samson.   The great man, the Rothschild of the family, was Solomon, who settled in Hamburg, and became in a comparatively short time a multi-millionaire in marks. Samson had nothing of the grim tenacity of the great banker, and nothing of his strength of character, though he appears to have been an attractive ne'er-do-well, and a favourite with both sexes.   His heroic age was the time spent as commissary with the army of the Duke of Cumberland, the future King Ernst August of Hanover, at the outbreak of the French Revolution, in which capacity he took part in the campaign in Flanders and Brabant.

In the *Memoirs* Heine goes out of his way to refute the insinuations of his " enemies " that in his biographical writings he had a great deal to say about his mother's family, but nothing of his father's relations, and so practised a vain reserve similar to that shown by Goethe, who often spoke of his mother's father but never mentioned his paternal grandfather (Heine, strangely enough, reverses the rôles). But the truth is that Heine, for all his disclaimer, did throw a romantic glamour over the whole of his family, and suggests that the " little Jew with a big beard " who married the " extraordinarily beautiful only daughter of a Hamburg banker " was far from an ordinary person after all. That is no doubt true, and it was from the paternal side of the family that the unusual qualities, the genius, came, and not from the clever, respectable, Geldern side. The emergence of such a wonderful personality as that of Heine is a problem of the greatest interest, and we follow his account of the various elements of the family, however cautiously, with no less interest than Goethe's famous lines on his paternal and maternal legacy.

Very well known is Heine's description of his father—of his somewhat delicate, characterless, almost feminine beauty, which contrasted so strongly with the regular features and manly beauty of his brother Solomon. That Solomon himself was a handsome man we know from his portraits, and that he had a beautiful wife, and that their children were " all without exception enchantingly beautiful," a " schöner Menschenblumenstrauss," we are quite prepared to believe. Beauty was a gift in this family—for the poet a tragic gift, and for an understanding of his life it is one of the things to be taken seriously into account. The passages in the *Memoirs* in which the poet at the end of his life speaks of them all is one of the most touching to be found in his works : " I loved all these children so much, and I loved their mother too, who was also so beautiful, and passed away early, and all of them have cost me many tears. At this moment I find it necessary indeed to shake the bells on my fool's cap in order to drown all tearful thoughts."

But to return to his father. The account Heine gives of him as a dandy, a Beau Brummel in miniature, a favourite of the Duke, who, in the manner of princes, forgot his former plaything, has doubtless little relation to fact. His father may well have told the story so often that he came to believe it himself, and Heine doubtless accepted it as a boy, and never checked it by the critical faculty of later years. The whole picture of his youth has probably this subjective truth—that it portrays indeed the inner world in which he lived as a boy. Only in this sense can we believe in the dashing ex-officer, with a passion for dogs and horses and ladies of the theatre. " On his arrival at Düsseldorf, where, out of love for my mother, he established himself in business, he had brought twelve of the finest horses with him," he tells us. No less highly-coloured is the picture given of him later as an officer of the civic-guard, and of the rivers of wine which flowed in the guard-room when he was in command—an extravagance which not only his purse, but also the military regulations, would have forbidden.

He was, as Heinrich tells us, a great child, filled with the joy of life, and of all human beings the one he loved most on earth. When he speaks of him it is in real earnest and " he seeks in vain to drown his melancholy by the tinkling of his bells "—the same simile once more! Heine is in many respects the heir of his father's qualities, of his boastfulness, his love of making a figure and cutting a dash, his irresponsibility in financial matters, his swagger and quarrelsomeness—and his personal charm.

As a matter of sober fact, Samson was quite poor when he arrived in Düsseldorf, so poor that the Jewish community was at first unwilling to receive him, and it was a great rise in the social scale when he married, on the first of February, 1797, Piera van Geldern, the daughter and sister of Jewish doctors. Her father, Joseph van Geldern —Heine in the *Memoirs* and elsewhere renders the *van* by *de*, and the family generally made of it a particle of nobility —was a well-known physician in Düsseldorf, and her brother court-physician of the Elector Palatine. Of her grandfather, who had been court-factor of Karl Philipp of Jülich-Berg, an old great-aunt used to tell wonderful stories, which "sounded to him like *The Arabian Nights* —of the great palaces and Persian carpets and heavy gold and silver plate which he owned in the days when he was in high favour at the Court, and which he later so grievously lost."

His uncle, Simon van Geldern, a strange oddity of a man, whose life was devoted to private study and the painful elaboration of ineffectual and obscure literary works, and the memory of his great-uncle Simon the "Morgen-länder," who had lived in North Africa as chief of a Bedouin tribe, filled the romantic imagination of the impressionable child. In connection with this great-uncle Heine makes a confession of the greatest interest for the problem of multiple personality. He tells us that old Simon and his wanderings and exploits made such a deep impression on his mind that often, even in broad daylight, he was seized with the uncanny feeling that he was himself his great-uncle and was living a continuation of his life, while at night in his dreams he identified himself entirely with him and walked securely in places he had never seen, and conversed in languages he had never heard. "This uncanny state lasted a good year, and although I attained again complete mastery of consciousness, hidden traces remained in my mind. Many an idiosyncrasy, many fatal sympathies and antipathies, which are not in accordance with my nature, even many actions, which are contrary to my way of thinking, I explain as after-effects of that dream-period when I was my own great-uncle."

Heine's account of his mother, no less than that of his father, has to be received with caution. He tells us that she had received a learned education, was a student of Rousseau, and an intelligent admirer of Goethe, and knew Latin, French and English. No doubt she was intellectually and by education her husband's superior, but his picture of a cultured woman of the world, a *grande dame*, is not borne out by the facts as we know them. We possess letters of hers which are far from being in a correct German, but show just those very faults, confusion of accusative and dative, of strong and weak forms of the adjective, which are characteristic of Heine himself, especially in his youth. They are written in German with Jewish letters, and contain Jewish slang expressions, such as we find in Heine's own letters when writing to his family, and particularly to his mother towards the end of his life, when they were a kind of baby-talk used by the home-sick ailing poet under the influence of childish memories. In fact the German spoken by Heine's parents was probably no better and no worse than that spoken in other similar houses at the end of the eighteenth century. How they pronounced it we cannot tell, though according to Heine he enjoyed the great advantage of hearing from his father " the dialect of Hanover, where the best pronunciation is to be found, and not the horrible jargon of the Lower Rhine, as spoken in Düsseldorf."

Piera, or Betty as she was commonly called, was a realist, the product of a rationalistic philosophy, and her aims and ideals in life were of an entirely practical nature. The rôles of the two parents were almost exactly the opposite of those of Goethe's parents; it was here the mother who provided the foresight and prudence, while the father had the merry heart and lively imagination. Moreover, she was not, like Frau Rat, a girl of eighteen at her marriage, but was already twenty-five, a mature age for those times, and especially for a Jewish girl. She could not say, as Goethe's mother did, that she and her boy had been young together. It was the father who might have said that— the big Peter Pan who never grew up, and to the end loved to play at soldiers and other games.

When Samson and Betty married on 1st February, 1797, she was twenty-five and he was thirty-three. Their eldest son was born on 13th December of the same year and given the name of Harry, in honour of the business friend in Liverpool from whom his father got the velveteen which was one of his favourite wares. Harry he was called in the family and among his friends and neighbours, and he liked to the end of his life to hear this pet familiar name. He answered in his life to the German, English and French forms, for in Paris he was translated into Henri, and even the whole name into Enrienne, as one can still hear to-day.

The year of Heine's birth has been variously given. He himself tells us in the *Confessions* that he was born in the last year of the eighteenth century. In the *Sketch* he gives the year of his birth as 1800, while in the oft-quoted passage in the *Bäder von Lucca* he says: " I, Signora, was born on New Year's Night, 1800," to which the Markese adds: " I have already told you: he is one of the first men of our century." Elsewhere, in one of his *Gedanken*, he says : " Around my cradle played the last moonbeams of the eighteenth century and the morning dawn of the nineteenth." He felt himself, and rightly, as one of the men of the new age, and shared in the hypnotic effect that the start of a fresh century, artificial division though it be, exercises upon men's minds. His niece, the Principessa della Rocca, quotes Heine's date of New Year, 1800, but says that according to his mother he was born on 13th December, 1799. The point is elaborated to show how unreliable Heine's own statements and those of his family are on matters of fact. There is little doubt to-day that the actual birthday was 13th December, 1797, though the old date of 1799 still lives on in guide books and on memorial tablets. The reason for the later date was probably to enable the boy to escape Prussian military service in 1815, or perhaps to facilitate his reception into the Lyceum, and it was rendered easier by the slender build and the unusually youthful appearance of Heine during the early part of his life.

The second child, Charlotte, was probably born in October 1800, and though she and Harry were separated by some few years, the difference was not great enough to prevent them from being playmates and close associates. They hung together somewhat as Goethe and Cornelia did, but Charlotte was a universal favourite, and far from finding the world the uncomfortable place that Goethe's sister did. The other two children were so much younger —Gustav was born in 1805 and Max in 1807—that they hardly counted during the earliest formative years, and the bonds that were forged between the two eldest during their

first childhood were never loosened. One of Heine's
best known poems, written in 1823 or 1824, has preserved
all the freshness of these childish associations :

> " Mein Kind, wir waren Kinder,
> Zwei Kinder, klein und froh ;
> Wir krochen ins Hühnerhäuschen,
> Versteckten uns unter das Stroh.

> " Wir krähten wie die Hähne,
> Und kamen Leute vorbei——
> ' Kikereküh ! ' sie glaubten,
> Es wäre Hahnengeschrei.

> " Die Kisten auf unserem Hofe
> Die tapezierten wir aus,
> Und wohnten drin beisammen,
> Und machten ein vornehmes Haus.

> " Des Nachbars alte Katze
> Kam öfters zum Besuch ;
> Wir machten ihr Bückling' und Knickse
> Und Komplimente genug.

> " Wir haben nach ihrem Befinden
> Besorglich und freundlich gefragt ;
> Wir haben seitdem dasselbe
> Mancher alten Katze gesagt.

> " Wir sassen auch oft und sprachen
> Vernünftig, wie alte Leut',
> Und klagten, wie alles besser
> Gewesen zu unserer Zeit ;

> " Wie Lieb' und Treu' und Glauben
>   Verschwunden aus der Welt,
>   Und wie so teuer der Kaffee,
>   Und wie so rar das Geld !———
>
> " Vorbei sind die Kinderspiele,
>   Und alles rollt vorbei,——
>   Das Geld und die Welt und die Zeiten,
>   Und Glauben und Lieb' und Treu."

Yet however charming Lotte might be as a baby play-fellow, and however intimate the tone which pervades Heine's later letters to her, with their characteristic mixture of tenderness and bantering irony, we must not think of her as one of those devoted sisters of great poets, of which German literature shows so many examples. Her life was not absorbed in that of her greater brother. She appears to have had little interest in or appreciation for his work, and what bound them together was chiefly the bond of common memories, and the usual Jewish family clannishness. She figures but little in his works, being mentioned only once more (in *Deutschland*—" Das Lottchen wohnt in der Nähe "), though to be sure the *Neuer Frühling* was dedicated to her.

The house where Heine was born was a small one-storied building which stood at the back of the present 53, Bolkerstrasse, and which has remained essentially unchanged, though the front-house was entirely rebuilt in 1821. Heine's parents lived there down to 1809, when they moved across the street to Number 42, which was their home till they left Düsseldorf for ever in 1819. Since 1867 the front-house has borne the inscription, " Geburtshaus von Heinrich Heine," together with a tablet containing a bronze relief after Ludwig Grimm's well-known Byronesque portrait of 1827, beneath which are the words from Chapter VI of the *Buch Le Grand* : " Die Stadt Düsseldorf ist sehr schön, und wenn man in der Ferne an sie denkt und zufällig dort geboren ist, wird einem wunderlich zu Mute. Ich bin dort geboren, und es ist mir, als müsste ich gleich nach Hause gehn. Und wenn ich sage, nach Hause gehn, so meine ich die Bolker-strasse und das Haus, worin ich geboren bin." There Samson Heine opened a business as draper and mercer, dealing among other things, as we have seen, in English velveteen. When he came to Düsseldorf in 1796 he was entirely without means, and probably it was the dowry of his wife which enabled him to start a business of his own. For a time things went well, especially while he could get contracts for the French army. However, with the down-fall of Napoleon his success left him, and in 1819 he went bankrupt, and added one more to the pensioners of his millionaire brother.

Düsseldorf, the capital of the Duchy of Jülich-Berg, was occupied from September 1795 till the Peace of Luné-ville in 1801 by the French, and after five years of German rule (1801-6) was ceded to France. Berg was then amal-gamated with other ceded Prussian territory to form a new Grand Duchy of Berg under Napoleon's brother-in-law Murat. At the Congress of Vienna in 1815 Berg fell to Prussia, and so Heine became a Prussian, though he him-self whimsically demonstrated that he was still a French subject. To many in the Rhineland this French rule ap-peared, not as an oppression, but as a liberation. The French were the champions of the new ideals ; their rally-ing cry of Liberty, Equality and Fraternity was to lead forth the oppressed peoples from the gloomy prison house

of an effete feudalism, with its serfdom, its intolerance, and
its class privileges. For the Jews in particular it meant the
attainment of civic equality, the removal of all humiliating
restrictions, and an immense increase in their confidence
and self-respect. The connexion with the larger, freer
economic life of France, in place of the cramping system of
customs barriers that prevailed in the petty German states,
brought, too, material prosperity in its train.

In a fairly prosperous Jewish home of this Franco-
German city, Heine spent his childhood's years. He had
only to go some four-hundred yards, down the Bolker-
strasse, across the market place under the colossal equestrian statue of the maker of Düsseldorf, and through the
short Zollstrasse, to reach the Rhine. How often the boy
must have traced that path ; how often played on the banks
of the great river, and seen the ships go by that carried his
thoughts far away into the wide world. It is quite a mistake to speak of Heine, as some writers do, as a town child.
That he was certainly not in the modern sense of being cut
off from access to nature. Düsseldorf was a small town
then, with the country on three sides ; quite beautiful
country, varied and hilly, and well-wooded, with rich fields
and orchards, and on the other side of the broad river the
lowlands stretching far as the eye could see. " The Rhine
from which you come," said Heine on his sick-bed to a
visitor, " is the river of remembrance to me. My whole
heart clings to it. I am not only by birth but also by nature
a Rhinelander." And if he owed much to the Rhine, he
well repaid the debt, for he has woven many threads into
its romance, and fixed one of its most famous legends for a
time.

The influence of the Rhine and the Rhenish population
of Düsseldorf is seen very clearly in the two works in

which he deals more fully with the events of his youth—the early *Buch Le Grand* and his last work, the *Memoirs*. As Moos points out, one needs only to remember the peculiar spirit of the race, with its romantic leanings, its light-hearted, pleasure-loving nature and its gifts of wit and satire, to find many points of contact which could not fail to wake an echo in the boy's sensitive nature, and early impress a definite stamp on his mind. Many biographers have made the mistake of underestimating the influence of his German home and compatriots when appraising the important influence of the French occupation on Heine's intellectual development. He had undoubtedly close intellectual affinities with the French, but emotionally he was and remained a German.

As the son of a small Jewish tradesman, who was a new-comer to Düsseldorf, and of no particular standing, the children Harry mixed with in his early years will not have been those of the wealthier classes, but of the humbler folk. With them he played in the streets and squares, in the *Hofgarten* and by the river, and picked up all the popular lore, all the local traditions and superstitions. There was some-one, however, who did not intend to let him settle down to this easy-going, lower-middle-class life. Betty Heine had great ambitions for her eldest boy. She wanted to make a great man of him—and a great man he became, whose name was to be known the world over in a degree she could hardly have imagined in her wildest dreams, though in a very different way and after travelling a very different road.

Heine's youth fell in the age of the intellectual emancipation of the Jews, of their first free full participation in European culture. That emancipation had begun with the philosopher Moses Mendelssohn (1729-1780), Lessing's friend, who first urged his co-religionists to shake off their prejudices, and take part in the work of modern European science and learning.

As the barriers of the ghetto fell, more and more Jews began to win distinction in Gentile society, and not least the women, who, freed from the traditional narrow home-life, made their salons vital centres of the intellectual life of their day. One has only to think of the romantic women in Berlin, one of whom, Rahel Varnhagen von Ense, later did so much for our poet.

However it was not such achievement as that which dazzled the mind of Betty Heine, but success in the world of affairs and finance, within the framework of official society. There the great star of Jewry was the mighty Rothschild—and the lesser star, her brother-in-law Solomon in Hamburg. The great Meyer Amschel, founder of the Rothschild dynasty, was still alive, and did not in fact die till 1812, when Harry was already almost fifteen, and his sons were all made barons of the Austrian Empire in 1822. He had been educated for a Rabbi, and the Church was one alternative career of Betty's for her own son, though he was destined to become neither millionaire nor pope.

It was not her eldest son who was to achieve the kind of success she desired, though other members of the family gained position and honours in plenty. They were a robust, long-lived family, with the exception of Samson, and even he reached the respectable age of sixty-four. Betty herself died in 1859 at the age of eighty-seven. Charlotte was ninety-one when she died, Gustav eighty-one, and Max seventy-two. And though he was only fifty-eight at his death, Heinrich's tenacity of life was as great as that of any of them, for a weaker man would have succumbed to his terrible sufferings years before.

Gustav, the second son, born in 1805, began as a farmer, became later an officer in the Austrian service, taking his mother's name of van Geldern, and ended as a journalist. He founded in Vienna a paper, the *Wiener Fremdenblatt*, which was a bulwark of constitutionalism and opponent of all liberal ideas, made a fortune, and was finally ennobled as Baron Gustav von Geldern. His daughter married a Graf Jizzo di Novis. Max, the youngest, became a military surgeon in Russia, took part in campaigns against Turkey and Poland, made a rich marriage, and was likewise ennobled, as Baron Maximilian von Heine-Geldern. Charlotte's son became Baron Ludwig von Embden, and her daughter the Principessa della Rocca, and all four of these titled people took a hand in their several ways in editing for the world at large an authorized version of the family history brought so prominently into the public eye by their uncomfortable relative. Even this by no means exhausts the list of noble names. The eldest brother of Samson went to Paris, where he founded the French line of the Heine family, as the Principessa says in her foolish book (*Erinnerungen an Heinrich Heine*), and his third son became Baron Gustav von Heine, while his granddaughter married the Duc de Richelieu.

No such success was to come Harry's way—neither wealth nor a fashionable wife nor a title. No one liked the material blessings of this world better than he, but he was a spendthrift and ne'er-do-well like his father, and, as far as outward success went, his own worst enemy his whole life through. There are many things in his life we shall never understand and appreciate properly unless we realize the glamour of emancipated Jewry that shone so freshly and strongly at this age, and which was so strikingly reflected in his own family. Great success and honour had come to them, and the Jewish clannishness regarded it as a common possession. One interesting thing in the Principessa's book is to see how clearly she thought it right and natural that Harry should insist on support from his rich uncle. And that very expectancy on the part of Heine himself was one of the greatest curses—perhaps the greatest curse—of his whole life, and one that more than anything else hampered his energies and soured his mind.

In the *Memoirs* Heine tells us at length of his mother's plans for the future, and of the spirit in which she guided his education :

" She had the greatest dread of my becoming a poet ; that, she always said, was the worst thing that could happen to me. She snatched away every novel which she found in my hands, did not allow me to visit the theatre, or to see any folk-plays, watched over my friendships, scolded the maids if they told ghost-stories in my presence, and, in short, did everything in her power to steer me clear of superstition and poetry.

" My mother had great ambitious plans for my future, and my whole education was planned to further them. She played the chief rôle in my development, she drew up the programme of all my studies, and her plans for my education began even before my birth. I obediently followed her express wishes, and yet I must confess that she was responsible for the failure of most of my attempts to establish myself in civil occupations, as they never accorded with my natural gifts. The latter, far more than the turn of historical events, determined my future.

In ourselves lie the stars of our fate."

His mother meant him to be a great man, as we have seen, but her ideas of the kind of greatness varied with the reigning constellations. At one time she was dazzled by the splendour of Imperial France, and since Marshall Soult's wife was a Düsseldorf friend of hers, and told her that her husband, who was already a duke, would soon become king, poor Harry had to devote himself to those military studies which were to bring him golden epaulettes and a high charge at the Emperor's court. With the fall of the Empire her views changed, and she set out to make him a Rothschild. Another plan was to make him a great prince of the church, and in the *Confessions*, and in a corresponding passage in the *Memoirs*, of which, thanks to the attentions of Max, only the last sentence remains, Heine, with fantastic irony, pictures himself as Pope, bestowing his blessing from the Lateran upon the kneeling multitude.

However, the greatest careers must have their modest beginnings, and little Harry was sent first of all at the age of four to an infant school kept by a Frau Hindermans, where he was the only boy among a dozen girls, and later to a Jewish private school. His real education began when he went, about the end of 1804, soon after passing his seventh birthday, to the lower school housed in the old Franciscan monastery. In 1811 he passed to the upper school in the same building, which was called under the French dispensation a Lyceum, but after the Prussian ' invasion,' as Heine puts it, received the name of Gymnasium. The teachers in Heine's time were mostly old Jesuit priests. The Rector Schallmeyer was an old friend of the family, a fellow-student in Bonn of one of his uncles, and consequently as a special favour Heine was allowed by him, even before he entered the Lyceum, to attend the lectures on philosophy which he delivered to the highest class.

The doctrines that Rector Schallmeyer taught to these

boys were inspired by the latest rationalistic French philosophy, which, as Heine says, were in crude contrast to
the orthodox dogmas of the religion, as whose priest he
sometimes officiated at the altar. He hopes this philosophic
teaching may on the day of reckoning be accounted to him
as an attenuating circumstance, and there is no doubt that
this crying contradiction of profession and real belief,
coupled with a similar contrast between external obser-
vance of Jewish rites and spiritual indifference which he
saw in his own home, early favoured the sceptical and
satirical bent of his mind.

All the same Heine always preserved a warm affection
and respect for his old teachers, and especially for Schallmeyer, and to the end of his life never lost his keen interest
and love for them and his old school.

In the early days, when things were going well with
Samson's business, Betty doubtless planned a university
career for her eldest son, in the tradition of her own family.
But with the waning fortunes of Napoleon, the prosperity
of the Heine family also declined, and Heine had to leave
school without completing his course, and turn to some
career in which he could earlier gain a living. So from the
autumn of 1814, when nearly seventeen, he attended the
Vahrenkampf Commercial School in preparation for a
business life. Of the year so spent before going to Frankfort we know very little, either from his own writings or
otherwise.

He was nearly eighteen years old when he left the last of
his five schools. In those formative years he had been subjected to very various and conflicting influences, but it
had been on the whole a not unhappy time. The iron had
not yet entered his soul ; he had not yet felt the relativity
of his freedom and social equality. All the same, the

world in which he lived had been far from an harmonious one, but had contained much of that dissonance which was later displayed in his life and writings. Orthodoxy and rationalism side by side, both at home and at school, patriotism and the actual benefits of foreign occupation, social complacence in face of social inferiority and even ostracism, had furnished material enough for a natural scepticism to work upon. He had no fixed social position himself, being uneasily balanced between various classes, while he fathomed some of the lowest depths, and made the acquaintance of characters who must have appealed unconsciously to his Ishmael-like nature.

To such belonged the world of "Red Sefchen", of whom he tells us the story in the *Memoirs*. Sefchen had lived up to her fourteenth year with her grandfather, the executioner ; her home was now with an old aunt who passed for a witch ; and her actual surroundings mingled in the boy's imagination with the gruesome folk-songs and stories she told him to form a very thrilling, uncanny, romantic world. How real the love of the sixteen-year-old boy for this red-haired pariah may have been, we cannot tell. The Sefchen episode is painted at great length and in very vivid colours by the reminiscent Heine of the *Memoirs*, but the whole story is undoubtedly very much worked up in order to fit symbolically into the framework of his life, and ends with one of the most melodramatic fanfaronnades that we find even with him :

" I kissed her not merely out of tender affection, but also in mockery of the old state of society and all its dark prejudices, and in that moment there flared up in me the first flames of those two passions, to which my later life remained devoted : the love for beautiful women and the love for the French Revolution, the modern *furor francese*,

by which I too was seized in the struggles with the myr-
midons of the Middle Ages."

There was a remarkable deal of symbolical content in
the kiss of that sixteen-year-old boy !

The other great experience of these Düsseldorf years,
along with this romantic adventure, and various literary
influences, *Don Quixote*, Sterne, *Gulliver*, Scott, Byron,
was the inspiration of the meteoric career of Napoleon.
Heine and his father were born to be his admirers ; he
just met the needs of their flamboyant natures. We
know what a liberation the French invasion was for the
Jews, and that it had brought to Heine's father in particular material prosperity as well. But if the reverse had
been the case, they would probably have admired him just
the same, for Heine's worship of Napoleon had an emotional rather than a rational basis, as had fundamentally all
his political and other views. This inspiration did not at
once bear poetical fruit, but it was stored up and burst forth
later, in his *Grenadiere* in 1820, and in the *Buch Le
Grand* in 1826, two of the most splendid pæans that all the
mighty epic of Napoleon has produced.

The long trumpet-roll, in which he describes the
greatest moment of his life till then, and, as he said later,
the only great man he had seen hitherto, may stand here as
a fitting climax to the story of his early years. The scene
described is from Napoleon's only visit to Düsseldorf, in
November, 1811, when Heine was a boy of thirteen, and
Monsieur Le Grand is the French drummer who was
quartered on his parents and who gave his name to the
book. The whole passage may well be taken as an example
of Heine's prose in its more passionate and rhetorical moods,
though it has more seriousness and less irony than we often
find. It shows us Heine as the rhapsodist. Yet here too

the search-lights flash backwards and forwards and the lightning plays, the commonplace is used to point by contrast the fire of the central theme, while even the very climax is prepared for by a cooling douche of bathos :

.   .   .   .

" When I think of the great Emperor, the world of my memory turns all summer green and golden, I see a long avenue of blossoming limes, on the leafy branches sit nightingales in song, the waterfall splashes, on the round beds the flowers wave their fair heads as in a dream—I am speaking of the *Hofgarten* at Düsseldorf, where I often lay on the turf and listened reverently, while Monsieur Le Grand told me of the military deeds of the great Emperor, beating the marches meanwhile that had sounded during those exploits.—What were my feelings when I saw him himself, with my own thrice-blessed eyes, him himself, hosanna ! the Emperor.

" It was in the avenue of the *Hofgarten* at Düsseldorf. When I forced my way through the gaping crowd, I thought of the deeds and the battles, which Monsieur Le Grand had drummed to me, and my heart beat to arms— and yet I thought at the same moment of the police regulation, forbidding anyone under pain of a fine of five Thaler to ride down the middle of the avenue. And the Emperor with his suite was riding down the middle of the avenue, the shivering trees bent forward as he passed, the sunbeams peeped shyly through the green leaves, and in the blue sky above swam visibly a golden star.

" The Emperor wore his plain green uniform and the little world-famed hat. He rode a white horse, and it stepped so calmly and proudly, so confidently and nobly— if I had been that day Crown Prince of Prussia I should have envied that horse. The Emperor sat carelessly, almost drooping, one hand held the rein, while the other good-naturedly patted the horse's neck——

" It was a sunny marble hand, a mighty hand, one of the two hands which had tamed the many-headed monster of anarchy and settled the quarrel of nations—and it was good-naturedly patting the horse's neck. The face, too, had that colour which we see in the marble heads of Greeks and Romans, its features were as nobly formed as those of the Ancients, and on this face were written the words : ' Thou shalt have none other Gods but me.' A smile that warmed and calmed every heart, played around his lips—and yet people knew that these lips had only to whistle—*et la Prusse n'existait plus*—these lips had only to whistle—and the whole priesthood had said its last Mass—these lips had only to whistle—and the whole Holy Roman Empire would totter. And these lips were smiling, and the eye was smiling too. It was an eye clear as the heavens, it could read in the hearts of men, it saw quickly and as one all the things of this world, whilst we see them only in succession and only their coloured shadows. The brow was not so clear ; there brooded on it the spirits of battles to come, and sometimes tremors passed over this brow, and those were the creative thoughts, the great Seven-League Thoughts, with which the spirit of the Emperor strode invisibly over the earth— and methinks each of those thoughts would have given a German author enough to write about for the span of his life.

" The Emperor rode calmly down the middle of the avenue, no constable opposed him ! behind him, proudly, on their champing steeds, loaded with gold and jewels, rode his suite ; the drums rolled, the trumpets blared ; by my side mad Aloysius turned and rumbled out the names of his generals, nearby drunken Gompertz was brawling, and the people with a thousand voices cried : ' Long live the Emperor ! ' "

Chapter Two

YOUTHFUL SORROWS

In the autumn of 1815, being then close on eighteen years of age, Heine left his native city and for the first time went out into the world. The attempt to make a Rothschild of him lasted nearly four years, and the length of the experiment shows his willingness to have his life planned for him by anyone who would take the trouble— in this case his compliance with the wishes of his strong-minded mother.

First of all his father took him off to Frankfort for the annual fair, and succeeded in placing him as a volunteer in a bank. In the birthplace of the Rothschilds he would see a larger world, and get his foot on the ladder. However, he kept his first post only a very short time, and a second, with a provision dealer, not much longer, and at the end of two months was already back in Düsseldorf.

Yet, if he did not make much progress on his path to riches, he gained some experience of life, and not only of its bright side, for he appears to have mixed in some very questionable society during these weeks. Frankfort had a great deal to show him in the way of historic buildings and associations. Yet even they failed to leave a favour-able picture of the place in his memory. Here his posi-tion as a Jew was brought home to him in a way that he had never experienced at Düsseldorf. The Frankfort Jews had already lost again the civic rights which, for a brief time, they had enjoyed under Napoleon, and were back in the ghetto, whose terribly narrow, sunless streets to-day make it possible for us to imagine their unsavoury condition a century ago. In that powerful fragment, *Der Rabbi von Bacharach*, Heine gave, nine years later, a vivid description of the "high, black houses, and the grinning, damp inhabitants," which clearly reveals the shock the sight gave him at the time.

He met, to be sure, one Jew, who in spite of his birth had won for himself a position in the world of letters, and who was to play a fateful rôle in his own life, Ludwig Börne, though he did not then come into closer personal touch with him. The Frankfort experiment was a failure, and he bestowed upon its "Krämervolk" the same contempt that he was later to feel for those of Hamburg and London.

Of the months passed in Düsseldorf between his return and his departure to Hamburg in the following summer, little is known, and so far as its external events are concerned, there is probably little to know. He did not spend too happy a time, and when at last arrangements were made for him to go to his uncle Solomon in Hamburg, he was doubtless ready enough to depart. He was to see the splendours of the house in Ottensen and its lavish hospitality, and to enter at last the charmed circle of which he had heard so much, and was to meet again "the golden star of the northern land," of which he had had a fleeting vision two years before in Düsseldorf. The three years in Hamburg were to see the end of Heine's more or less contented acceptance of life, the beginning of his youthful sorrows, and of his real work as a poet. The story of the business side of his life can be briefly told. After an unsatisfactory start, he appears for a time to have settled down to work, for at the end of two years Solomon established him in a business of his own, which at any rate would appear to show some belief in his capacity. Heine must have exerted himself in those opening years, whether inspired by the example of his uncle, for whom he had at bottom throughout his life, in spite of all disturbances, a great respect, or by the hope of winning the hand of his daughter, we cannot say.

However, the firm of " Harry Heine & Co." went into liquidation after a brief existence of less than a year, and the failure of his business career cannot really have touched him very deeply. From anecdotes told by those who saw him in action he appears to have treated his own company rather as a joke. He was too like his father to make a success in that career ; and it is surprising from what we know of his later life, and his irresponsibility in all matters of finance, that anyone would ever have expected him to settle down into a sober, hard-working business man. He could spend money, and he could even make money in his own profession, but he could never look after it properly. And in his Jewish clannishness he no doubt had the conviction, as we have seen his niece Maria had for him, that it was the duty of his rich uncle to provide for his material wants. Up to a point his uncle thought so too, and on the whole he treated his flippant nephew with very considerable toleration and generosity. Solomon had not amassed his great wealth for nothing, and he had all the pride, and rather more than the average arrogance, of the self-made man. Where he paid the piper he thought he had the right to call the tune. He was undoubtedly a big man, and very generous after his own fashion, to Gentiles as well as Jews, but he was a curmudgeon and a tyrant, and did not trouble much about the fine feelings and sensibility of his pensioners. Most people gave in to him, and he ruled his own household and his wider family like a despot. The only one who stood up to him was that failure Harry, the trifler and the dandy.

For his poetic gifts Solomon had not the smallest understanding or respect; the writing of poetry was in his eyes a mere waste of time, and unworthy to be regarded as the serious business of life. " Hät er was gelernt, so brauchte er nicht Verse zu schreiben," he once said of Harry. And the nephew later told his uncle that the best thing about him was that he bore his name. Two typical utterances ! The real trouble between them in Hamburg was that this fool of the family actually had the effrontery to want to marry his daughter !

In a later well-known poem Heine called Hamburg the " Schöne Wiege meiner Leiden." Here now he met the four people who were to bring him the great sorrows of his life—his uncle and three of his children, Amalie, Therese, and Karl. It was at Ottensen that Heine's real inner life was lived at this time, and it furnished the background and the scenery for much of his youthful poetry. Solomon had built himself there a fine country house, with grounds running down to the Elbe. There were fountains and marble figures, and nightingales sang in the trees—everything to appeal to the sentiment of an imaginative youth. There Solomon lived in great style and magnificence, and there the proudest of Hamburg's patricians were glad to be the guests of the powerful Jewish banker. Heine was even present once when " the homerically divine, glorious Blücher " was the guest of honour. And there was, as we know, beauty, too, to fire his inflammable heart. Solomon's wife had borne him six children—four girls and two boys. We have already quoted Heine's words that all these children were " without exception enchantingly beautiful."

The third, Amalie, was then a fair blue-eyed girl of sixteen, in the first bloom of her early Jewish maturity. When Heine arrived she was absent on a visit, and the impatience with which he awaited her return shews the impression she had made on him at their earlier meeting in Düsseldorf. To Sethe he writes on 6th July, 1816 : " Rejoice, rejoice ; in four weeks I shall see Molly. With her my Muse too will return. I have not seen her for two years ; old heart, how loud and joyously you beat ! " When she came she made him her captive at once, and his long years of trouble began. There is no reason to doubt the genuineness of Heine's feeling for her, as some have been inclined to do. His love may have been none the less sincere for not being eternal, and he was not the first to forget in the end an unreturned passion in a new attachment. For its expression he borrowed, it is true, some poetic requisites from the prevailing tone of the poetry of his day, but all great passions take on the mode of feeling of their age. Till 1823, when a new star dawned, his poetry is one great echo of this unrequited devotion.

At first Heine seems to have given himself up to vain illusions, and to have dreamt of the return of his love. He appears to have attached altogether too much importance to the gift of a lock of her hair made in these early days. He wore it next his heart in a sharp-edged black iron cross suspended from a black iron chain. Perhaps in his naivety he laid himself open to a rebuff. There is no evidence that Amalie ever gave him any serious encouragement, or fed him with vain hopes, though it looks as though she may have coquetted with him at first, till startled perhaps by his tragic intensity. The misunder-standing was probably all his own fault. The lock, and a kiss in the following summer, probably a quite indifferent embrace, after a longer absence, were, as far as we know, all that his hopes had to feed upon.

At any rate, Amalie must have made it quite plain to him that any serious wooing on his part was mere pre-sumption. Something definite must have happened before he wrote the long letter to Sethe on 27th October :

"She loves me *not !*—You must say this *last* word softly, very softly, dear Christian. In the first word lies eternal heaven, but in the last eternal hell. If you could but see the face of your poor friend, that looks so pale and distraught and demented, your just anger at my long silence would soon be appeased. . . . Although I have the most infallible, irrefutable proofs that she does not love me at all—yet my poor loving heart will still not be con-vinced, and says ever : what have I to do with your logic, I have a logic of my own. . . . To live far from her, to carry in one's heart a passionate longing through the years, is to suffer the pains of hell, and wrings from the breast cries like those of spirits in everlasting torment. But *to be near her*, and yet often to pine in vain through endless weeks for one redeeming glance, a—a—and—and—O !—O !—O Christian ! it is enough to make the purest and most pious heart flare up in wild, mad blas-phemy." All this is no doubt unbalanced and exaggerated, and more than a little self-conscious and theatrical, but it was the stuff of which that new poetry was being made, which was to differ so greatly from all he had written hitherto.

It is, after all, hardly to be wondered at that Amalie did not take his wooing very seriously. He did not cut a very imposing figure in the fashionable society of Ottensen, among the " diplomatic bigwigs, millionaires and senators," where he tells us he made many a social slip, and the prospects of his being able to keep Amalie in the manner of life to which she was accustomed were very remote. He was, it is true, a handsome boy, with a charm of his own, but short and slight, and looking even younger than his years. And as for his poetry, that appears to have counted for nothing with Amalie. She probably thought very much like her father, that if he was good for anything he wouldn't need to write verses. And so the tragic position developed. His poetry burst forth in new strains, in which the love for Amalie blends with motives learnt in the Sefchen milieu, with its gruesome legends and folksongs. Hitherto he had been the pious minstrel revelling in the sentiments of mediæval chivalry, and singing of blonde maidens and gentle knights. Now his poetry gets reality from his own sufferings, and unable to offer her wealth, he casts at her feet pearls of greater price. Heine was always conscious of his powers, and in this field he knew himself to be rich indeed, even though not the millionaire that he was shortly to become. She had, however, a different conception of the relative values. " It is heartrending to see her so bitterly and unworthily scorn my beautiful songs that I have written only for her." And he quotes lines from Goethe's *Tasso* :

" Und wenn der Mensch in seiner Qual verstummt,
    Gab mir ein Gott, zu sagen wie ich leide."

Heine's poetry now gains deeper notes in the presence of an overwhelming personal experience. All the verses that went before were little more than poetical exercises and mainly derivative—the *Wünnebergiade* of his last Düsseldorf year, and the other occasional pieces, and the patriotic poetry written under the inspiration of Fouqué and Schenkendorf. In that mediæval minstrelsy he uses all the apparatus and the stock phrases of the school. He was inspired, too, by the "heilige deutsche Sänger," Klopstock, by whose grave he stood with such emotion in his early Hamburg days.

Now he writes his *Traumbilder*—exactly how many it is impossible to say—and a few of the *Lieder*. It was earlier generally assumed that Sefchen was the subject of these dream pictures, but it now seems clear that the actual poetic impulse was given by his unhappy love for Amalie, though the background and the colouring were due to the Düsseldorf time, and to the love of the uncanny and mysterious which had early been fostered in him by his old nurse Zippel, by Sefchen and her aunt, by the Folk Songs, Hoffmann, and the general Romantic tradition.

All these various influences provided him with a medium for the expression of his present emotions, and not a very suitable medium either. Till Heine freed himself of that milieu, he never gave any distinctive expression to his love tragedy. There is nothing specially characteristic of him in these poems ; many other poets could have written them as well—his Westphalian contemporary, Annette, better. It was a fashion at the time, and much enjoyed ; now such an accumulation of graves and ghosts and church-yard horrors is found more than a little tedious, and it is doubtful whether any unprejudiced person would read these *Traumbilder* of Heine for themselves, apart from their literary interest, with any great pleasure. There is a redundancy, an accumulation of traits, which is in striking contrast to that great gift of the later Heine, pregnancy and economy and simplicity. Three of them, the third, fourth and fifth, have for their theme a betrothal, marriage and wedding feast, and they probably portray a later stage in his relation to Amalie, and are to be ascribed to the year 1821. The sonnet form of the first is further confirmation of this view.

The only one that is really interesting for itself is the eighth, in which, at the midnight hour, ghosts of those who have met their doom through love rise from their graves, and tell the story of their undoing. In it Heine weaves together skilfully into a vivid whole various traditional folk-song elements, and is inspired indirectly, too, in part by Burns' *Jolly Beggars*, though there we have living vagabonds, and not ghosts who must return to the tomb at the stroke of one.

There is more of Heine in the *Lieder* of that time, even in the first and second of the collection : " Morgens steh' ich auf und frage," and " Es treibt mich hin, es treibt mich her." They are—and we note a similar thing in countless poems now and later—poetic crystallizations of passages from a letter to Sethe, and express his impatient waiting for the coming of Amalie on his arrival in Hamburg in 1816. The third and fourth show clearly the influence of the " Volkslied," and Heine's still incomplete mastery of the form. But with the fifth what a difference ! " Schöne Wiege meiner Leiden." For the first time a poem here springs forth from the page to our eyes—beautiful in its simplicity, a perfect gem of expression, with all the virtues of the folk song, and no longer any artificial retention of its crudities. But that was not written till much later, at the end of the Hamburg time, in the summer of 1819, and under the emotional stress of parting, and when the influence of Byron, whose " Fare

thee well," among other poems, he had meantime translated, had been added to the other forces moulding his
poetic powers. It was the first of his poems that has
won universal fame. It was the first to be set to music
by Schumann, and it has been carried over the world by
the music of that greatest of all composers of Heine's
verse. If any one moment had to be chosen for the
emergence of the real Heine, I should be inclined to choose
the time in the summer of 1819 when he wrote those lines.

Some of his poems appeared at this time in the anti-
semitic " Hamburger Wächter " of all places, and under
the fanciful name of Sy Freudhold Riesenharf, an anagram
of Harry Heine Düsseldorf. But after the first few
months in Hamburg, extending possibly into the beginning
of 1817, Heine's productivity came to an end, and there
followed one of his periods of poetic stagnation. In spite
of the brave words he quotes from *Tasso* in his letter to
Sethe, poetry does not seem to have given Heine relief
from the repressed emotions from which he suffered.
He was not a Goethe in this respect. His poems were not,
as with Goethe, the clarification of an emotion, towards
which a certain poetic aloofness had already been gained,
but the immediate expression of the emotion itself. With
him the repression of his love found relief in other directions in this period—in ways hinted at in the often quoted
passage from a letter of 7th April, 1823, to Immanuel
Wohlwill :

" Perhaps I wrong the good city of Hamburg ; my
prevailing mood during the time I spent there was not
fitted to make me an impartial observer ; my inner life was
a brooding immersion in the gloomy chasm of a dream-
world, irradiated only by fantastic lights ; my outward
life was mad, dissolute, cynical, repulsive ; in a word, I

made it a glaring contrast to my inner life in order not to be utterly crushed beneath its weight."

The meaning of these words is quite plain, and accords with what we know from other sources. Here in Hamburg, as already in Frankfort, Heine plunged into those circles in which later in Paris he found his Diana, and Angelique and the "various" others. It was a matter which lay quite lightly on his conscience, and did not offend against his moral code. That he was not without scruples he most emphatically maintained, and in a well-known verse he declared later that he had never soiled purity or brought dishonour to a marriage bond, while elsewhere he said that he had never been any woman's first lover or her last.

That Heine was quite sincere in this attitude there is not the least reason to doubt. He regretted many things in his later days, and wished many of his deeds undone, and more than one of his writings unwritten, but there is no sign at all that he felt himself to have been a sinner in his relations with women. That the whole matter does not affect the question of his poetic powers is obvious, but we are concerned here also inevitably at the same time with Heine the man, and we must, therefore, study him or leave him as a whole. That great riddle, Heinrich Heine, is hard enough to read in any case, and certainly will not be read aright by those who consciously close their eyes to some of its aspects.

Chapter Three

STUDENT YEARS

In the May of 1819 Heine left the " the cradle of his sorrows," after a stay of nearly three years, and returned to his parents' home in Düsseldorf. He was a bankrupt in love, for Amalie had clearly given him no grounds for hope—indeed, if we may trust his poems, had driven him away in mockery. Yet he was to be kept still on the rack for two years before his fears became a certainty.

He was already more than twenty-one years of age, and he had outwardly not achieved much to justify those proud ambitions of his mother. The only field in which he had achieved any success at all was the very one from which she had tried so hard to ward him off. The unsuccessful attempt to make a Rothschild of him, in Frankfort and later in Hamburg, had lasted nearly four years, but it may have been a spark of comfort to her that the plan she had doubtless cherished in happier days of sending him to the university was now, somewhat belatedly, to be realized.

At home things had greatly changed during his three years in Hamburg. His father's business in the Bolker-strasse was tottering to its fall, for he went bankrupt in the following year, and the family left Düsseldorf for ever. They could doubtless do little to help him financially. The story he tells in the *Memoirs* of his mother's jewels being sold to keep him at the university during the first four years has probably as little relation to fact as the statement of the princess in her precious book that "his father sent him monthly a considerable sum while a student at Bonn to which Solomon added five hundred thalers." His dependence on his uncle was now, as throughout these six student years, undoubtedly fairly complete.

He stayed in Düsseldorf till October, when he entered the university of Bonn. It was only exchanging one Rhine town for another, though the neighbourhood of his new home had more striking features than the old, and the river, and the mountains, and the old castles fed his poetic imagination. Heine was older than most students, almost twenty-two, but in this Bonn year he gave himself up to the patriotic fervour of the student movement with the best of them. At school, in Frankfort, and in Hamburg he had been bound ; now he enjoyed to the full the freedom of academic life. It is true his professional studies did not go very far ; he only matriculated late in the first term, in December, and with a third class, and he made use of the "Lernfreiheit" of the German universities to neglect his legal studies pretty thoroughly, though he attended well in another faculty, that of Arts, the "philosophische Fakultät."

The University of Bonn, closed by Napoleon, had only been re-opened the previous year, but it had already attracted several very distinguished professors. The one who impressed Heine most was the elegant August Wilhelm von Schlegel, the "Great O.B." of Bonn. Heine attended his lectures on literature and prosody, and took advantage of his private advice and criticism, and was not chary in the expression of his debt, for all his later mockery of him. Under Schlegel's influence he wrote sonnets, including those addressed to the honoured master himself.

He translated Byron too. His interests at this time are well described in the letter to his friend Fritz von Beughem of 15th July, 1820:

"I could write many gratifying things about my relation to Schlegel. He was much pleased with my poems and almost agreeably surprised at their originality. . . . The more often I go to him, the more I feel what a great man he is. . . . His first question is about the publication of my poems, which he seems greatly to desire. Unfortunately, owing to the many changes which I have made on Schlegel's advice, I have to re-copy out many poems and metrical translations from the English. The latter are particularly successful, and will prove my poetical skill."

On the whole, this year in Bonn seems to have been a cheerful time. He had many friends, and entered fully into the spirit prevailing among the students there—the patriotic enthusiasm of the "Burschenschaften," inspired by opposition to the reactionary Metternich régime. Under these influences he becomes once more for a time the fervent German singer of the last Düsseldorf years. So we find him in the sonnet to his friend Jean Baptiste Rousseau speaking of the rulers trembling on their crumbling thrones while the crowns totter on their heads, and exhorting him, true to his name, to fight with German heart, with word and sword, for the threefold ideal of faith, freedom and love. He even took part in the torchlight celebration of the Battle of Leipzig on the Kreuzberg, though in his sonnet he transferred the scene to the more famous Drachenfels. When he left the university at the end of the summer term, he crossed the river to the village of Beuel, and there wrote the first two acts of his tragedy *Almansor*, with which he was entirely engrossed, and on which he placed the greatest hopes. The greatest

D

achievement of this year is seen, however, not in the field of translation, or even of the drama, but in the enhanced mastery of his own form, as shown especially in the two poems *Belsatzar* and *Die Grenadiere*.

Heine arrived in Göttingen about the middle of September, 1820, having made most of the journey on foot, with but one louis left in his pocket. The reason for the migration was perhaps in part that he hoped to find the new university cheaper, but mainly, no doubt, because he hoped there the better to be able to settle down to his legal studies. This at any rate, is the reason he gives in the letters to his friends. "Now I must grind terribly. And I am doing it, too. I came here indeed for this very purpose."

Göttingen appealed to him now as little as it did later, and the tone in which he speaks of it in his letters is very much the same as that which is so well known to us from his *Harzreise*. "You ought to have stayed in Bonn," he said to himself. "If I had not known from experience how long the way is, I would have run straight off back to Bonn." The time there appeared to him very happy in retrospect ; here everything seemed to him stiffer, drier and more formal than in the bright Rhine town. He speaks contemptuously of the students as elegant fops, and is indignant that Benecke's lectures on the older German language, which he attended with the greatest interest, attracted only nine out of the thirteen hundred students. "O Germany, land of oaks and apathy !" he exclaims. He also attended the lectures of the historian Sartorius, whom he greatly admired, and to whom he not only dedicated a sonnet at this time, but also paid later a glowing tribute in the *Harzreise*. Of attendance at lectures on law we have no record, in spite of his pious resolutions. The first fortnight he devoted entirely to the completion of the third act of his *Almansor*, " the most difficult and longest act," and hoped to add the two remaining acts in January, after the intended preliminary grind was over.   On 7th November he sent a collection of his poems to Brockhaus in Leipzig, pointing out that with the exception of six, which had appeared four years earlier in the Hamburg *Wächter*, none had yet been published.   They were, however, returned with the usual polite formula.

With the new year his Göttingen stay came to an end, for he was sent down from the university for six months for having challenged another student to a duel with pistols.   That was at the end of January, but his actual departure was delayed by illness for some weeks.   So once more his plans were upset, and however lightly he jokes about the matter, he cannot have been in any very happy frame of mind during those last days.   There was no great disgrace in his *consilium abeundi*, but he was anxious, all the same, that his " family " should not learn of it—which probably meant in effect Uncle Solomon. " Where am I to go now ? "   he says in a letter to his friend Steinmann.   " I shall not go back to Bonn under any circumstances.   I expect the new university will be deter- mined for me from home."   How the case was put to his uncle, and how his uncle took it, does not appear to be known.

He planned first of all a walking-tour to the Harz, but in the end he went to his parents at their new home at Oldesloe in Holstein.   The condition in which he. found things there was not such as to improve his spirits.   So he writes to Heinrich Straube : " I have found my family in a very bad state.   My father is still suffering from his mental trouble, my mother from headaches, my sister

41

from catarrh, and my two brothers are writing bad verses. This last rends my heart. I have not yet given up all hope of the younger. He doesn't like my poems at all. That is a good sign. My sister, however, passes a better judgment on my poetic merits. When I lately read to her one of my best works, she remarked, ' Oh, that isn't so bad.' "
That letter, with its typical laconic irony, is interesting as showing the degree of understanding and encouragement Heine, now as at all times, could expect from his own family, even including his favourite Charlotte. And though his love and admiration for his mother, to whom he addressed at this very time the two well-known sonnets, was as ever an important factor in his life, she had little sympathy with his literary ambitions.

From the same letter it appears that on the way from Göttingen he had paid a visit to Hamburg, and there, freezing at midnight in the cold of a damp winter's night beneath the windows of his " Dulcinea de Toboso," had brooded despairingly on the tragedy of his love. Any hopes he might ever have entertained of winning Amalie's hand must have vanished by now, and she was, in fact, soon afterwards engaged to an East Prussian landowner named John Friedländer, whom she married in the August of that year.

In March 1821 Heine arrived in Berlin, and he stayed there till May 1823. It was the longest of all his four university periods ; and the richest in intellectual experience and inspiration. On the other hand, it was the one in which he was least a student in the narrower sense of the term, and the one in which the university itself counted relatively for less than at any other time. He matriculated again to be sure, and did not entirely neglect student society—he even fought a harmless student's duel—but he was no longer a member of the "Burschenschaft," and his aims and ideals were not academic. He does not appear to have attended many lectures in the Faculty of Laws, though he was attracted by two famous professors in the faculty of Arts, Franz Bopp and Friedrich August Wolf. The teacher of the university who made the greatest and most lasting impression on him was Hegel.

Berlin was a very different town from any which he had seen hitherto. Here in the metropolis the university did not loom as large as in smaller university towns like Bonn and Göttingen, and the tone was not given by the world of big business and finance, as in Frankfort and Hamburg. At first he was interested and impressed, as he was later on in Paris, by the mere show and pageantry of this fuller life, by the doings of the court, the military display, and the various theatrical and artistic events. He recorded his impressions in the *Briefe aus Berlin*, which appeared in 1822, but which are little more than high-class journalism. In the absence of any participation in political life, Berlin society at that time was occupied with artistic interests, and poetry and the theatre stood prominently in the foreground. Women, and especially Jewish women, played a leading part ; literary lions were eagerly sought for their salons, and any promising young poet could hope for patronage and support. Heine got to know two of these women leaders, and each of them in her own way was important for his career.

The greater of the two, Rahel Varnhagen von Ense, he met soon after his arrival, and during the next few years she was the greatest and the most beneficial influence in his life. Rahel was one of the best types of the emancipated Jewess of the age, without the eccentricities and lack of balance which made some of the Romantic women

43

even more notorious than famous. She was already fifty when Heine first made her acquaintance, and if one almost inevitably thinks of the relation of Goethe to Frau von Stein, it is only to remember that the difference of age was here even far greater, and to discount some of the more fervent expressions that Heine employs in his letters to her. A few years before Rahel Levin had married the Westfalian, August Varnhagen von Ense, who was himself fourteen years her junior, and their joint means and connections made of their house one of the most hospitable homes, and one of the most important intellectual centres, of Berlin and of the whole country. It was a great thing for Heine to be adopted by this influential pair. Never before and never again did he stand in such close personal and spiritual relationship to a woman of her quality. Heine was unfortunate in his women friends and acquaintances ; only twice, now and later in the Princess Belgiojoso—perhaps also in the " Mouche " in his last days—did fate throw him in the way of women who could have given him that feminine counterpoise that he needed, and from none of them was he destined to receive the full and lasting benefit that they might have bestowed.

Perhaps no one ever understood Heine so well as Rahel ; to no one probably did he so unreservedly lay bare his soul, and he maintained for her the most sincere respect and affection till her death in 1833. His consciousness of what he owed to her speaks from the letter he wrote at the end of this Berlin time, on 12th April, 1823: " I am going away soon, and I beg you not to cast my image into the lumber-room of oblivion. I could forsooth not make any reprisals, for if I said to myself a hundred times a day, ' You must forget Frau von Varnhagen,' I could

not do it.　Do not forget me !　You cannot excuse yourself with a bad memory, for your mind has made a bargain
with time ; and if perchance after some centuries I have
the pleasure of seeing you again as the fairest and most
splendid of all flowers in the fairest and most splendid of
all celestial dales, then be so kind as to greet me poor holly
(or shall I be something worse ?) with your friendly radi-
ance and sweet exhalation as an old acquaintance.　You
will do it for sure ; for you did the like in 1822 and 1823,
when you treated me, a sick, bitter, morose, poetic and
intolerable being, with a kindness and courtesy that I have
certainly never deserved in this life, and can only owe to
the benevolent memories of an earlier acquaintance."

That letter was written in a copy of the " Tragedies ",
which like all his writings of this time he sent to her with
a personal message.　One of the sections of the *Buch der
Lieder, Die Heimkehr*, was indeed dedicated to her, though
without her consent, and not to her liking.　In her salon
he met many of the literary celebrities of the day, Fouqué,
Chamisso, Michael Beer, Willebald Alexis and others.
There he found himself for the first time in a world in
which an unbounded admiration for Goethe was taken as
the first article of belief.　Rahel herself had been all her
life his enthusiastic disciple, had herself written about him,
and had gathered around her a company of the faithful.
Heine's admiration for Goethe was, now as always, not
without reservations; but at this time, doubtless, was
strengthened in him that underlying conviction of his
greatness, which went deeper than all hostile criticism of
certain aspects of his nature.

We hear an echo of these influences in the letter with
which Heine, on 29th December, 1821, sent a copy of his
Gedichte to Goethe:

"I might give a hundred reasons for sending my 'Poems' to Your Excellency. I will mention only one : I love you. That seems to me a sufficient reason. My versifyings have, I know, as yet little value : only here and there perhaps something might be found to show what I could do. I was for a long time uncertain as to the very nature of poetry. People said to me, ' Ask Schlegel.' Another said ' Read Goethe.' I have honestly done so, and if ever I do any good work I know to whom I shall owe it.

" I kiss the sacred hand, which has shewn me and the whole German people the way to heaven."

The tone of reverent enthusiasm in that letter is no doubt to be ascribed to the spirit of Rahel's " Goethe congregation," and one has to compare with it a letter written the next day for a similar purpose to Müllner, in which he says that if he is a poet at all he owes it to his *Schuld*—" War Ew. Wohlgeboren *Schuld* schuld dran." But there is, at any rate, no reason to doubt that Heine did study Goethe seriously at this time.

The other literary lady who played an important part in his life at this time was of more doubtful benefit. This was the poetess Elise von Hohenhausen, whose own verses are now forgotten, but who is still known as a translator of Byron. Heine had met her in Hamburg, and she gladly welcomed him in her salon, which had become an important literary meeting-place of Berlin, where every Tuesday evening the Varnhagens and their friends and other celebrities assembled. She proclaimed Heine as the " German Byron ", and Heine was greatly flattered by this highest praise from her lips, and gladly assumed the rôle, calling himself Byron's cousin.

He copied even the mannerisms of the Byron legend, the ironic smile telling of titanic woes, and all the rest of it, while this Byron-pose is reflected in the portraits of him at the period. Fundamentally, however, the two poets had very little in common, either in their life or their works, and as far as Byron influenced Heine at all, it was more to his disadvantage than his gain. That the influence, such as it was, decreased with the years is evident from the letter he wrote to Moser on 25th June, 1824, though he still liked to flatter himself with the delusion of a similarity between their fate and character: "Byron's death has moved me deeply. He was the only being with whom I felt an affinity, and we probably resembled one another in many respects, laugh at the idea as you will. I have read him but little for some years ; we prefer to consort with people whose character is different from our own. But with Byron I always get on as comfortably as with a perfect equal and comrade." Strange words when one reflects on the career of the Düsseldorf Jew and the English lord, their outlook on life, and the essential difference of their work as a whole. The one important trait they had in common was hostility to a somewhat vaguely conceived Philistine element in their respective countries, and their delight to "épater le bourgeois."

Another side of Heine's character, which found no satisfaction in the fashionable salons, drew him to the famous wine-shop of Lutter and Wegener in the Gendarmenmarkt, where one can still see the vaulted cellar in which he often sat. There in noisy, free and easy Bohemian style, some of the wittiest and most original of Berlin's artistic sons met, and indulged their bent for boisterous conviviality and irresponsible wit and satire. E. T. A.

Hoffmann, the founder and leading spirit of the circle, was no longer to be seen, for illness chained him to his bed, but Heine met there many well known men, such as the actor Devrient and the dramatist Grabbe. Not that he shared in their excesses, for he could not endure tobacco, and he was never a great drinker. Moreover, his health was even now not of the best, and he suffered a good deal in Berlin from the headaches which were one of the trials of his life.

Far different interests from any of those already spoken of are represented by Heine's participation in the work of the " Verein für Kultur und Wissenschaft der Juden," which he joined towards the end of his Berlin time, in August, 1822. The association had only been founded in 1819, and it was a part of the movement, of which Moses Mendelssohn was the pioneer, for breaking down the intellectual barriers which separated the Jews from their Christian fellow-countrymen, and making them participators in modern European culture. The most important members were Ludwig Marcus, on whom Heine, in 1844, wrote a brief memoir, Eduard Gans, later a distinguished Professor of Laws, and the great authority on Jewish antiquities, Leopold Zunz. The one who fired Heine's enthusiasm for the cause was a young banker, of wide intellectual and artistic interests— Moses Moser. He became an intimate and confidant of Heine, who played an important part in his life in the following years, and to him some of Heine's most interesting letters are addressed. An Academy was founded, in which the leaders delivered learned addresses on historical and scientific subjects, and a *Zeitschrift für die Wissenschaft des Judentums*. There were also educational courses, and Heine himself gave instruction in history.

At first Heine threw himself with enthusiasm into the

movement, and was full of zeal for the plan of raising the status and illuminating the history of the Jews. It was at this time that he began his *Rabbi von Bacharach*. But the association never made much progress ; it never had as many as a hundred members in all, and it lived only four years. With Heine the disillusionment soon set in, and the disappointment of his hopes for the Jewish cause expressed itself in bitterness against Christianity. So he writes to his brother-in-law, Embden, on 3rd May, 1823, that his attachment to Judaism has its roots in a deep antipathy against Christianity, while in an earlier letter to Wohlwill in the same year he speaks with a ferocity (which he himself later admits goes too far) of the " firm of *Gott, Christus und Co.*, which fortunately cannot long survive, since its drafts on philosophy are returned dishonoured and it is going bankrupt in Europe, even if the branches its missionaries have established in Africa and Asia may last some centuries longer."

In this mood he even thought the state of the Polish Jews, whom he had seen on his visit to Poland in the autumn of 1822 with his young Polish friend Graf von Breza, for all their ignorance and superstition, preferable to that of many in Germany. His essay, *Über Polen*, which was the product of that experience, was, when it appeared in the *Gesellschafter* in Berlin in January, 1823, his first publication on a political theme.

Meantime, amid all these conflicting interests, Heine's real work was making progress. Separate poems of his had already appeared in the Hamburg *Wächter* and in the Berlin *Gesellschafter* and elsewhere, and at last, after several fruitless efforts, he found a publisher for his poems in Maurer of Berlin. They appeared at the end of 1821, with the date of 1822, under the simple title *Gedichte*.

The collection corresponds generally to the *Junge Leiden* of the *Buch der Lieder*, and will be discussed in that connection, so far as the separate poems have not been already dealt with. The little volume was well received, and definitely established Heine's standing in the literary circles of Berlin. That he himself was active in bringing his poems to the notice of distinguished contemporaries we know from his letters, of which the one to Goethe has been already quoted.

While the *Gedichte* were mainly the product of the earlier periods, the next and far more important collection contained the poems written during these Berlin years. It appeared in April, 1823, with Dümmler in Berlin, under the title of *Lyrisches Intermezzo*, as a poetic interlude between his two plays, *Almansor* and *Ratcliff*, and was dedicated to his uncle Solomon. The significance of the *Intermezzo* can best be appreciated when considered in the place later allotted to it by Heine in the *Buch der Lieder*. The full title of the volume was *Tragödien nebst einem lyrischen Intermezzo*.

We have already spoken of the beginnings of his prose tragedy, *Almansor* ; how he worked at it with fervent enthusiasm at the end of his Bonn year, and devoted entirely his first fortnight in Göttingen to the addition of the third act. It was finished in 1821; while in contrast to this slow growth and completion, the second tragedy, *Ratcliff*, was dashed off in three days in 1822. Heine was woefully disappointed in the hopes he placed upon them, especially *Almansor*. The two plays form dull reading for us to-day, and the words that he wrote to Steinmann on 10th April, 1823, seem to us very strange : " My ' Tragedies ' have just left the press. I know that they will be roughly handled. But I will confess to you

in confidence ; they are very good, better than my collection of poems, which is not worth a shot of powder."
Heine's genius was anything but dramatic ; he has created
few living characters, and he did not naturally incline
towards works demanding sustained effort. Moreover,
the concentration of theme required of the drama was
uncongenial to his roving creative instinct.

In both works we recognise clearly the influence of
literary forerunners, and at the same time find the embodi-
ment of Heine's own feelings and experiences. In both
we have a story of unhappy love, and a hero who is the
victim of bitter wrongs. The action of *Almansor* takes
place in the period after the conquest of Grenada in 1492,
and the expulsion of the Moors, which was made possible
by the marriage of Ferdinand of Aragon and Isabella of
Castile, and the union of their two kingdoms. Many of
the Moslems have proved false to their faith, and adopted
Christianity, and with it Spanish names. The hero
Almansor, who had fled the country rather than become
an apostate, and has been reported as dead, returns to
Grenada to find his beloved Zuleima as Donna Clara and
the bride of a Christian. On her wedding-day he carries
her off, after a bloody fight, and flies to the hills, but, surrounded by pursuers, plunges with her to death from the
summit of the highest rock.

This matter of apostasy is the central theme. Christianity is shown in a very unfavourable light, and Heine,
the future apostate, took to himself no little credit for the
boldness with which, under the mask of Moors and
Spaniards, he treated the relationship of Jews and Christians of his own day. He writes to Moser on 21st January, 1824, that he wishes Michael Beer would " speak
out straight, in true Almansor-fashion, in the matter of

Christianity." He felt himself a champion of Judaism,
and it was a grievance with him that others did not recognise the position he had taken up, and the risks he had run
in throwing down the gauntlet thus openly.

Any virtues the work possesses are certainly not dramatic.
His deliberate purpose of combining romantic contents
with classical plasticity of form was not achieved. The
fine passages and the poetic images and the originality
cannot avail against its one fault of lacking the true drastic
spirit of tragedy. It was performed once only, at Bruns-
wick, in August of the same year; and was hooted down.
Various explanations have been given for this, but though the
hissing at the end may have been due to personal hostility
arising from a misunderstanding, the failure of the work
as a stage play was obvious, and not only was the performance never repeated, but the intention of producing Heine's
second tragedy was abandoned in consequence.

William Ratcliff was, as we have seen, not like *Almansor*
the fruit of long and earnest toil, but a brilliant impromptu,
thrown off without preliminaries in the space of three days.
It is hardly more than half the length of *Almansor*, and has
in fact about the dimensions of two of the best-known
representatives of the type to which above all it owes its
inspiration, *Der Vierundzwanzigste Februar* of Werner,
and *Der neunundzwanzigste Februar* of Müllner. The
popularity of " Fate Tragedies " still survived, and the
indebtedness of Heine's play to well-known examples of
the species, to those mentioned above in points of detail,
and to Grillparzer's *Ahnfrau* for the central theme, are
palpable. The ghosts of the older lovers, Edward and
Schön-Betty, which hover constantly around the younger
pair, his son William and her daughter Maria, to whom

they have bequeathed a mystical and fateful passion, can, like Grillparzer's heroine, only find rest with the death of their unhappy descendants. The influence of Scott, whose novels Heine read at the time, is also clear. The scene is laid in Scotland, and the misty landscape, MacGregor's castle, and the thieves' meeting-place in the lonely forest form an effective setting for this typical product of Romanticism.

This time Heine was firmly convinced that he had written a real tragedy, whatever his doubts about *Almansor* might be. So we find him writing to Immermann on 10th May : " I am convinced of the value of this poem (hark ! hark !), for it is true, or I myself am a lie ; everything else that I have written, and shall still write, may perish and will perish." And in dedicating it to his friend Christiani he expressed the same thought in the lines :

" Ich und mein Name werden untergehn,
    Doch dieses Lied wird ewiglich bestehn."

In May, 1823, Heine left Berlin and spent the rest of the year with his parents, who had meantime moved to Lüneburg. In two separate letters he speaks of the town as the " Residenz der Langeweile"—a typical instance of self-repetition on the part of this great phrase-maker. Apart from the intercourse with Christiani he found little intellectual sympathy or stimulation there. He knew his family well enough not to expect from them much interest in his latest publication, and so would at any rate be saved disappointment on that score. " My mother has read the 'Tragedies' and ' Poems ' to be sure," he writes to Moser soon after his arrival, " but not enjoyed them particularly, my sister merely tolerates them, and my father has not read them at all."

Dull his life no doubt was in many ways in those eight months, but it was a period significant for his life and poetry in two respects. He spent six weeks of the summer at Cuxhaven—the first of many visits to the sea, which soon came to exercise an irresistible fascination for him. Ever, as occasion offered, he returned— to Norderney in 1825 and 1826, to Ramsgate during his English visit, to Norderney and Wangeroog in the same year, while later in France he visited the watering places of the northern coast over and over again.

The other event was a visit paid after four years' absence to Hamburg, "at once my Elysium and my Tartarus", as he writes to Moser. "The old passion breaks forth again with might. I ought not to have come to Hamburg; at any rate, I must see that I get away again as quickly as possible." It was not to see Amalie that he came—she had been married two years and was now away—but to discuss with his uncle his future plans and prospects. Above all he was doubtless anxious to get support for the new project of going to Paris in the autumn, and, after further study there, of embarking on a diplomatic career. Though Solomon was not to be won over to that fantastic change of front, he did consent to continue the allowance for the completion of his nephew's university studies, and for all Heine's complaints in his letters to his friends about his uncle's meanness, and his threats to make himself independent of his uncle's charity—than which nothing could have been better for his soul now or later—we cannot but be surprised at the tolerance and long-suffering of the self-made banker.

Heine came to Hamburg dreading to re-open the

wounds of an old love, and to spend an unpleasant time in financial discussions, and lo! a wonder happened! Out of the grave of the old sprang forth a new love! The younger sister, Therese, had been a child when he saw her last; now, though not yet sixteen, she had grown into a beautiful girl, who had a resemblance to Amalie, but joined to her beauty more temperament and heart. And so his heart was caught on the rebound, or, to quote his own striking phrase, "die neue Thorheit auf der alten gepfropft"—the new folly engrafted on the old.

The poems written in this period appeared in May, 1826, in the first volume of the *Reisebilder*, and in the following year in the *Buch der Lieder*, under the title *Die Heimkehr*—that is, the return from Berlin to the house of his parents. The two best-known of them all, *Die Lorelei* and *Du bist wie eine Blume*, reflect the mood in which Heine at the beginning of these months in Lüneburg thought first of the "siren" Amalie, and then of the awakening love for her gentler sister.

In January, 1824, he set out for the university once more, and for the last time. Göttingen was once again his choice, being preferred to Berlin probably for the same reasons that it had previously been preferred to Bonn, namely, that it was cheaper and offered fewer distractions. It was serious business this time. He was already turned twenty-seven, and now or never his legal studies must be brought to a conclusion. He was a student there for a year and a half, and he must have forced himself to grips with his books at last. How little taste he had for it can be judged from the wry jibes of the *Harzreise* and from his letters. "I am working hard at my law," he writes to Christiani at the beginning of March, "but curse it, I can't get on with it. I still know the titles of Scott's novels, or the stories of Boccaccio or Tieck, much better than the chapters and sections in the Corpus juris. Oh, holy Justinian, have pity on me ! So many an old sheep has understood thee, and I am filled with despair ! "

At first he felt very uncomfortable, and addressed his letters from " O weh ! Göttingen ", or " Verfluchtes Nest-Göttingen." He complains, too, of his ill-health and continuous headaches. However, it was not all hard work and melancholy. He took more share in the student life than in his first Göttingen time, and his real knowledge of the place is mainly due to this second visit. He attended pretty regularly at the students' duels. " I am mixed up with a lot of students' affairs," he writes. " I am present at most duels as second, or witness, or umpire, or at least as spectator." He himself challenged another student, though there is no record of the duel actually taking place. When in the mood he could shine, as he ever could in any society, by his high spirits, his witty conversation, and power of repartee. Some interesting peeps of him are given in the diary of a Göttingen student of the time, recently edited by H. H. Houben.[1]

He was not tied down to Göttingen either. In the Easter vacation of his first year he paid a visit to Berlin, calling at Magdeburg on the way to make the personal acquaintance of Immermann, whom he esteemed very highly, both as man and as writer, and with whom he was to be brought a few years later into so disastrous a connection. In Berlin he found the Varnhagens and many other of his old friends again, and was received with the consideration of one whose poetic fame had recently been

[1] Eduard Wedekind : *Studentenleben in der Biedermeierzeit.* Göttingen, 1927.

so greatly enhanced. He had, moreover, prepared for his arrival by sending a cycle of his latest poems to Gubitz for the *Gesellschafter,* where they duly appeared in March, these *Dreiunddreissig Gedichte* being the most important publication of the *Heimkehr* poems before the appearance of the collection in 1826. He had a very lively and even riotous time there, to judge by his own account, and it must have been a great contrast to his recent life in Göttingen. The object of his journey was not however mere pleasure, or even the not unwelcome "incense" which he breathed. "Ich habe in Berlin viel antichambriert," he writes, and the attempt to establish a footing in Berlin for his future life was the serious purpose he had in view. He even had thoughts of becoming, in spite of his law degree, a lecturer in the Philosophical Faculty of Berlin.

Another of his trips has been immortalised—that to the Harz in the autumn of the same year. In the *Harzreise* he speaks of his wanderings in the mountains, but ignores the detour which he made on the return by way of Eisleben, Halle and Jena to Weimar, and the interview with Goethe, as it would not have fitted into the artistic scheme, nor harmonised with the tone of that work.

He had already sent Goethe his *Gedichte* and *Tragödien nebst einem lyrischen Intermezzo,* accompanied by words of homage, but without receiving the desired recognition from him. He now wished to see face to face the master, for whose works and personality his interest had been aroused by the Goethe enthusiasts with whom he had lived, Rahel and her circle in Berlin, and Christiani in Lüneburg. Arrived in Weimar, he addressed to Goethe on 1st October a letter, in which there is no trace of presumption on his own performances, and only a very discreet reminder of the previous despatch of his works :

" I beg your Excellency to grant me the happiness of standing for a few moments in your presence. I will not make myself troublesome to you, but desire only to kiss your hand and depart again. My name is H. Heine ; I am a Rhinelander, have been for a short time in Göttingen, and lived previously for some years in Berlin, where I met several of your old acquaintances and admirers (the late Wolf, Varnhagens, etc.) and daily learnt to love you more. I am also a poet, and took the liberty of sending you three years ago my ' Poems,' and a year and a half ago my ' Tragedies with a Lyrical Intermezzo ' (*Ratcliff* and *Almansor*). I am, moreover, ill, and therefore set out three weeks ago on a journey to the Harz for the sake of my health, and on the Brocken I was seized with the longing to make a pilgrimage to Weimar to pay my homage to Goethe. In the true sense of the word I have now come here as a pilgrim, namely, on foot and in weather-worn dress, and in expectation of the granting of my request remain,

" Your enthusiastic and devoted,

" H. HEINE."

Yet, in spite of the modesty of this approach, he did not succeed in breaking through Goethe's guard, but found him as Olympian and inaccessible as did Kleist and Grillparzer and other young poets of the time. His disappointment is obvious. The first mention is in a long letter to Moser of 25th October, in which he speaks at some length of his journey, while all he has to say of Weimar is: " I was also in Weimar ; one gets very good roast goose there. . . . The beer in Weimar is really good ; more about it when we meet."

To judge by a letter to Christiani of 26th May of the same year, the only thing about Heine that interested Goethe was his health, concerning which he showed a touching human sympathy. He gives there a very drastic picture of Goethe's physical decline, which forms a striking contrast to the best-known description of his visit—that written some years after in the *Romantische Schule*. That famous passage may stand here as an illustration of the way in which Heine was carried away by the demands of an artistic setting. It is nothing but a set-piece, with Goethe serving as a typical figure, as Napoleon did elsewhere :

" His form was harmonious, clear, joyous, of noble proportions, and one could study Greek art in him as in an antique statue. . . . Goethe's eye remained in age as divine as in his youth. (The clear radiant eye is mentioned in the letter, as the only thing that had escaped the general decrepitude !) Time has indeed covered his head with snow, but has not been able to bend it. . . . Around his lips a cold expression of egoism is said to play ; but this trait belongs to the immortal gods, and above all to the father of the gods, the great Jupiter, with whom I have already compared Goethe. Indeed, when I visited him in Weimar, and stood before him, I involuntarily glanced aside to see the eagle with the lightnings in his beak. I was near addressing him in Greek, but when I saw that he understood German, I told him in German that the plums along the road between Jena and Weimar were very good. In so many long winter nights I had pondered on the many sublime and profound things I would say to Goethe when I saw him. And when I did see him at last I told him that the Saxon plums were very good. And Goethe smiled. He smiled with the same lips, with which once he had kissed fair Leda, Europa, Danae, Semele and so many other princesses and ordinary nymphs. . ."

Most significant of all were the words he wrote to Moser on July 1st, 1825 :

"At bottom I and Goethe are two natures, which through their heterogeneity cannot but repel one another. He is fundamentally a light epicurean, ("ein leichter Lebe-mensch "), for whom enjoyment of life is the highest good ; who indeed sometimes feels and has a presentiment of the life for and in the idea, and expresses it in his poems, but has never deeply comprehended it, and still less lived it. I, on the other hand, am fundamentally a visionary, that is, inspired for the idea to the point of sacrifice, and ever urged to sink myself in it. Yet at the same time I have realised the life of enjoyment and found pleasure in it, and now the great fight with me is between my clear reason, which approves of the life of enjoyment, and rejects all self-sacrificing enthusiasm as folly, and my visionary tendency, which often shoots up unexpectedly, and takes me by force, and will one day per-haps draw me down again into its immemorial realm, or as we should perhaps better say, up into it ; for it is a very great question, whether the visionary, who sacrifices his life for the idea, does not live in one moment more and more happily than Herr von Goethe during all the seventy-six years of his egoistic and comfortable life."

This passage gives, as it were, the programme for the whole of Heine's future life. The meeting with Goethe, inconclusive and trivial as it was on the surface, was of the greatest importance for him, for it led him, in the search for self-justification, to crystallize his own conception of him-self.

Schiller did something of the same kind in presence of

the phenomenon of Goethe, and came to the conclusion that there was room for him, by the side of Goethe's naive, spontaneous genius, as a sentimental and reflective poet. Heine never questioned the greatness of Goethe's poetry. " To my credit I must say," he writes in the *Romantische Schule*, " I have never attacked Goethe the poet, but only the man. I have never found fault with his works." Where he felt he differed from Goethe, or had the ambition to differ from Goethe, was in the moral field, and there, as a self-sacrificing enthusiast, he claimed to be Goethe's superior.

From this time on this conception constantly recurs, and the claim to be the champion of the " idea " is ever repeated in varying forms. The " Kunstperiode," of which Goethe was the great representative, was over, and poetry must now be placed at the service of humanity, and he, Heine, was " the sword and flame " that should show the way to a new world of ideals. The " idea " for him meant the devotion to a cause, a central enthusiasm which could knit up the diverse and tangled threads of his being, and throughout his life there undoubtedly was some such fire of unselfish devotion, though it was far from burning with a steady flame, and was often obscured by the other instinctive side of his nature. The words he uses in the above letter of the " great fight " within him are a striking self-revelation, and one almost uncannily prophetic of his future development.

When he got back to Göttingen he began the writing of his *Harzreise*, and it was completed in November. A mutilated version of it appeared somewhat later, in Gubitz ' *Gesellschafter*, but its real publication did not take place till May, 1826, when it appeared with the *Heimkehr* poems and the first part of the *Nordsee* as the first volume of the *Reise-*

bilder. A discussion of it will be reserved for the next chapter.

Another prose work which he began and nearly finished in Göttingen was *Der Rabbi von Bacharach*. Unfortunately only three chapters have been preserved, the bulk of the manuscript having been destroyed by a fire in the house of his mother. Even the third chapter is probably not preserved in its original form, but was added at the time of the publication of the fragment in the fourth volume of the *Salon* in 1840. The loss is greatly to be regretted, for the *Rabbi* would have been Heine's greatest epic achievement.

The origins of the work go back to the time of his interest in the "Verein für Kultur und Wissenschaft der Juden," and his association with Gans, Zunz and Moser, and the other leaders of their movement. He wished to write a book on the historic past and the tribulations of his co-religionists, that should stand as a monument for the generations to come. He studied zealously sources and authorities on Jewish history, and took advantage of the greater knowledge of his learned fellow-workers. The hero of the story, which is laid in the fifteenth century, is the Rabbi Abraham von Bacharach, a cultured Jew, who returns from Spain to his native land to aid and uplift his oppressed compatriots He is celebrating the Passover in the hall of his dwelling, when he sees two strangers, who have entered and joined them, throw the body of a child beneath the table. Realising at once that these were Gentiles, who were planning to incite the rabble to plunder and murder, under the pretext that the Jews had killed a Christian child for their festival, hurriedly, at the first possible moment, he dragged his beautiful young wife Sara from the house, and fled with her up the Rhine to take refuge in the Judengasse in Frankfort. Very fine are the descriptions of the Feast of the Passover, of the river in the spring moon-light, and of the Frankfort ghetto. Nowhere is Heine so simple, direct and sincere ; the events and characters are left to speak for themselves, without that obtrusion of the author's personality, the irony and subjectivity, that he otherwise so rarely laid aside. Heine was never to complete a rounded work of sustained power. Here for once he was on the way to creating a work dealing seriously with a big and profound theme—the place of Judaism in the western world—and to refuting his own doubts as to his possession of the true epic faculty.

Meantime his legal studies had been progressing, and at long last, after six years, and many vicissitudes, he faced the examiners, and on 25th July, 1825, was awarded his degree, even if it was only with a " Zeugnis III."

Heine was now a Doctor of Laws, and so far qualified for the official career, with a view to which all this distasteful labour had been undertaken. And he had already taken another step which was a necessary qualification for state or official service, since only the medical profession was open to Jews ; on 28th June he had been baptised in the little town of Heiligenstadt near Göttingen, taking advantage of the occasion to change the English form of his name, Harry, for that of Heinrich.

This was one of the things, along with the book on Börne, and the pension from the French government, for which Heine has been most bitterly criticised. It was, too, one of the things which he most bitterly regretted in later years. He was attacked on both sides—by the Jews as a renegade Jew, and by the Christians as a mere opportunist Christian. It is, however, unfair to blame him severely for the step. To begin with, if blame there was to be, he committed himself when he accepted his uncle's money to fit himself for a legal career, for the baptism was a part of the undertaking he then entered into. Moreover, formal religion, whether Jewish or Christian, was to him a matter of indifference, his attitude being an almost inevitable result of those influences in his home life and at school on which stress has already been laid.

And so a fresh dissonance was brought into his life, while the step did not even bring him the material advancement for which it was the necessary preliminary. His uncle's good money had been thrown away, except in so far as these six university years furnished him with a greater amount of leisure than he could then possibly have secured otherwise. His mother's plans for him were never to be realised—he was never to settle down, but to remain outside the pale of official society, homeless and a wanderer, for the rest of his life.

Chapter Four

HEINE ON THE HEIGHTS

The two years which followed the completion of his university studies, and his departure from Göttingen, were for Heine, in spite of the fits of depression and changes of mood inevitable with a temperament such as his, on the whole a time of high achievement and rising confidence. His fame had been steadily growing, and now with rapid strides he emerged as a poet of wide renown and great notoriety. In those years appeared the two works which for England represent Heine to some extent to the exclusion of all others, the *Harzreise* and the *Buch der Lieder*; and another which runs them a close third, the *Buch le Grand*.

This period of his life was spent mostly in Hamburg, or with his parents in Lüneburg, though with some notable exceptions. After staying on in Göttingen for a short time after his " Promotion ", he went for a really long visit to the sea, spending the months of August and September in Norderney. The necessary funds were provided by a present of fifty louis d'or from his uncle, but already before August is out we find him very urgently asking Sethe for a loan of six louis, while in July he had already borrowed six from Moser. This is typical of Heine's recklessness in money matters. He had his distasteful legal studies behind him, his spirits rose, with the sea and the bathing his health improved, and he spent a lively and expensive time in aristocratic company on the island. He got on well with the Hanoverian officers, and enjoyed their stories of the many lands they had visited in the course of their service. He saw much of an elderly friend of the Varnhagens, the witty Princess Solms, and probably still more of a younger "schöne Dame aus Celle", whose name we are not told. "Ich habe hier wunderschöne Tage gelebt", he writes. The visitors on the island led the simple life, dwelling in the cottages of the fishermen, and coming into the closest and most intimate relations with them. This was "Nature" in the romantic sense, and Heine entered fully into this primitive existence, and in the sea above all saw the "element that was his elective affinity." And so in this and the following year were written the two cycles of *Die Nordsee*, in which he has given such grandiose expression to the thoughts and phantasies inspired by that ever-changeful ocean, in which he beheld an image of his own turbulent and restless spirit.

The first cycle appeared in May of the following year, along with the *Heimkehr* poems and *Die Harzreise*, as the first volume of the *Reisebilder*—with a publisher who was to play a very important part in his future life, Julius Campe of Hamburg. The appearance of this book was a notable event in Heine's life, for it was the first instance of that association of prose and verse, which is one of his out-standing characteristics as an author. He had already repeatedly appeared before the public as a poet ; after the modest beginnings of his *Brief aus Berlin* in 1822, and the essay *Über Polen* in 1823, he now presented for the first time a considerable work in prose, and one that was to win a great and enduring popularity.

In England, at any rate, *Die Harzreise* has always been Heine's favourite prose work. Why has it occupied this

very special position with us ?   Why does it always seize
and hold the imagination of everyone who reads it for the
first time, and remain a possession for ever ?   There are
probably two chief reasons for this.   It is in the first place
less specialised than most of Heine's other prose works.
It depends less on an appreciation of his attitude to the
political and social questions of the day ; though satiric
enough in parts, it is less concerned with " ideas," which
are proclaimed, for instance, in the very title of the second
volume of the *Reisebilder*.   And so it has a more general
appeal to a foreign and to a modern public not greatly concerned in these problems.   But the chief reason is its
joyousness and its fun.   It is bubbling over with the spirit
of springtime and youth ; it remains for many of us the
classic expression of the delight in wandering among rush-
ing streams and rustling woods and pine-clad hills.

Heine's Travel Pictures are not, in the main, accounts
of travel in the ordinary sense.   But here we have for
once a real journey with a real route ; a break-away from
the prison house of a town, such as all town-dwellers dream
of, and one carried through with all the high spirits of
irresponsible youth.   Nowhere is Heine so " burschikos,"
so much the " ragging " student, ready to take his fun
where he finds it, and respecting nothing and nobody under
God's high heaven.   And this freedom is emphasised in
the humorous parodies of the ordinary guide-books—a
device of which Heine, here as elsewhere, was fond.

It owes, of course, something to literary forerunners.
It is of the family of Sterne's *Sentimental Journey*, in which
mere objective description is the least important element,
and wit and fancy are allowed to range freely over all the
subjects, for which the actual journey and the actual
localities furnish only the occasion and the starting-point.

The essentials are " the bright threads that are so prettily woven in." But if a Sterne, he is a Romantic Sterne, related to Jean Paul and Brentano and Hoffmann. The Romantic contrast of bourgeois and poet, of the philistine herd and the soul-free artist, runs through the whole. The *Harzreise* looks down with the same Romantic contempt on all settled professions as Eichendorff's *Taugenichts*, which appeared in the same year, 1826. The artist alone is free, and hence all these Romantic " Künstlerromane". Heine himself was to have this freedom, for what it was worth, his whole life long.

What the Romantic misses in the citizens of the town, he finds, like Rousseau, with the simple folk, and in the *Harzreise* the evocation of this spirit of the life of the humble is one of the finest things. Very beautiful is the passage in which he speaks of the " Unmittelbarkeit ", the directness of association, which binds all thought and feeling of these simple folk, in their supposedly narrow lives, to the things around them ; and how with them, as in the childhood of each one of us, all familiar objects have a personal character of their own, and the world of fairy-tale takes shape. The poems in which he describes the idyll of the night spent in the miner's cottage, and his talk with the miner's little daughter, are, apart perhaps from the Faust-like confession of creed, which is there somewhat out of place, among the most sincerely simple he ever wrote. And in the *Harzreise*, as everywhere, Heine is great in the use of contrast, of the high tones and the low tones, employing bathos to prepare for an effect, or ironically to relieve tension from becoming overstrained. So from the bathos of a quotation from Gottschalk's *Taschenbuch für Harzreisende* he leads up to the poem, " Steiget auf, ihr alten Träume," while from its heights he descends again to the comic episode of the journeyman tailor, with his cheap sentimentality and mock pathos. Similarly the lyrical description of the sunset is followed by the inimitable outburst of the young merchant : " Wie ist die Natur doch im allgemeinen so schön ! " (" How beautiful Nature is when you come to think of it ! ") They are the means which he employed for similar effects in the poems, too.

The second half of the year was a very fruitful time. He visited Norderney again in July and stayed there till the middle of September. Again he seems to have spent a very lively time, mostly in aristocratic company, and again we find him writing to a friend for a loan for his travelling expenses—he has enough to live comfortably for eight or twelve days, but without his help will not be able to get away! For the last fortnight he was the only visitor left on the island. " I hired a boat and two sailors," he writes, " and sailed about the whole day long on the North Sea. The sea was my only company and I have never had better. Nights by the sea ; glorious, great." There, and after his return, he wrote the second cycle of the *Nordsee*.

The time from September to January he spent with his parents in Lüneburg. His mood during this time does not appear to have been a very cheerful one, and he is considering seriously the plan of leaving Germany for a new home. Already from Norderney we find him writing to Moser that he is fervently longing to say farewell to his German fatherland, though it is less the love of travel than the trouble of personal circumstances (i.e., the ineffaceable Jew—" der nie abzuwaschende Jude ") that is driving him away. Now in October he writes to Immermann, that after spending some time during the winter in Hamburg for the printing of the second part of the *Reisebilder*, he will leave Germany for ever. The Varnhagens know of his intentions—others are to be left in the belief that he is going to Berlin.

Yet in spite of this depression and unsettled feeling, he worked away during that summer and autumn at his next big undertaking, the second volume of the *Reisebilder*. Its most important part, *Das Buch Le Grand*, was written in the summer and autumn, and the third part of the *Nordsee*, which had been begun in 1824, completed in the latter part of the year. He expressed the greatest confidence concerning this new venture. "This part will be an extraordinary book and make a great stir"—"the most wonderful and interesting book these days have seen." It appeared in May, 1826, and consisted of the second and third parts of *Die Nordsee*, *Das Buch le Grand* and the *Briefe aus Berlin*. The later final edition retained only the two middle works.

The third, prose, section of *Die Nordsee*, after beginning with a description of the inhabitants of Norderney, and recording many of the impressions which received their final form in the poems, soon wanders away from the original subject. From the Hanoverian aristocracy, and their charge of irreligiosity against Goethe, he passes on, by way of the lady's question : " Doktor, was halten Sie von Goethe ? " to speak of the master's universality and greatness. Especially striking is his enthusiastic appreciation of the *Italienische Reise*, which he praises for those very qualities in which it most differs from his own works of the kind. " We all know Italy from our own observation, or from the description of others, and can thus easily perceive how each views it with subjective eyes, one with the ill-humoured eyes of an Archenholz, which see only the bad side, another with the enthusiastic eyes of a Corinna, which see nothing but what is glorious ; whilst Goethe with his clear Grecian eye sees everything, the dark and the bright, nowhere colours things with his own subjective feeling, and describes the land and its people in the very outlines and colours in which God has clothed them."

He finds his way also to his favourite theme, for the desolate island makes him think of Napoleon on St. Helena. Scott is writing the life of " the new man, the man of the new age ", and he fears that it may well prove " the Russian campaign of his fame." On the completed book he had more to say later in his *Englische Fragmente*, and of its subject in the other part of his present volume. At the end he gave to his friend Immermann the hospitality which he had offered him in the preceding October, with an assurance of " the best place ", and printed those *Xenien* which were to lead to the disastrous quarrel with Platen.

Of the larger and far more important prose work contained in this second volume of the *Reisebilder, Ideen: Das Buch Le Grand*, something has already been said. The book, which is in the unusual form of a monologue, addressed to a " Madame," whose prototype Elster suggests may well have been the beautiful Frau Robert whom Heine knew in Berlin, has a three-fold description. To the first title, that of a " Travel Picture ", it has little formal right—far less even than the *Harzreise*. The only justification, one that it shares with his other works, is that it is a poetic description of his journey through life, of his joys and sorrows on that passage. The *Ideen* are the liberal ideas of the French Revolution. Napoleon was for Heine the appointed champion of those ideas ; a symbol rather than a man. Heine only saw Napoleon once, as a boy of thirteen, when he visited Düsseldorf in November, 1811, but in Monsieur Le Grand, the French drummer who was quartered on his parents, he had a visible representative and spokesman of his idol, and from him the book gets its final title. But beyond all that, the book is a most important fragment of Heine's scattered autobiography. Here the fragrant memories of his childhood are recorded, and here we find the well-known tribute to the beauty of his native city which has already been quoted.

And yet another element enters into its composition—one which we should not expect to find lacking in a work of his—for the whole is set in a frame-work of his own unhappy love for the " fair flowers of the Brenta ", the daughters of his uncle Solomon in Hamburg. From the opening chapters there still speaks the grief for the loss of Amalie. Yet in spite of the tragedy, he " is still alive ", and " though only the shadow of a dream, even that is better than the cold, black, empty nothingness of death." The great pulse of nature beats in his breast, too, spring has sent a thousand nightingales, and he presses forward to new life and new hopes. And at the end is pictured the dawning of the new love for Therese. Elster suggests that Therese is also the Eveline to whom the whole work is dedicated.

The book met with an immediate and well-deserved success, for it possesses in a high degree the most effective qualities of Heine's prose style, and, in his childhood memories and the cult of his almost legendary Emperor, two themes in which his pathos and his brilliance could unfold their powers to the full. And so he was borne along on the flowing tide in this, his *annus mirabilis*. His confidence in his own powers grew, and dreams of future influence and success rose before his eyes. He felt himself a champion of liberty of speech. " The book had to be written. In this shallow, servile time something had to be done. I have played my part and shamed those hard-hearted friends who were once going to do such great deeds and now hold their peace." So to Varnhagen ; and to his confidant Moser he writes: " I have won an enormous following and popularity in Germany through this book. If I get my health, I can now do a great deal. I have now a far-reaching voice. You shall often hear it yet, thundering against all enslavers of thought and all oppressors of sacred rights. I shall get a very Extraordinary Professorship in the University of great minds."

This letter of 7th June, 1827, was written from London, for on the very day the volume was published Heine had set out on the longest journey he ever made, that to England. The English visit was only an incident, and not a supremely important one in his life. The reason for the journey which he suggests in a letter to Varnhagen, namely, that he had gone to England, not from fear but from prudence, was probably not a serious one, for it is not likely that he thought himself to be in actual danger on account of his latest work. He tells Moser that his chief object was to leave Hamburg. His real object, apart from the desire for change, was probably to see something of English liberalism with his own eyes. In this he was to some extent successful, and he, at any rate, learnt something of the working of a responsible parliamentary system. What he saw of English life itself was mainly from the outside and on the surface, for he does not appear to have got into touch with English people either at their work or in their homes. Apart from the short stay at Ramsgate, he saw nothing of the country outside London, and so made the mistake of many foreigners, who confine themselves to the largely cosmopolitan life of the metropolis. It is true he was well supplied with money, and so was free to enjoy everything that the public life of London offered. Apart from the fees for his books, he brought from his uncle a letter of credit for four hundred pounds on the Rothschild house in London, which was to be used only in case of emergency, and was really intended to make an impression, and serve as an introduction to the influential bankers. Heine, however, looked at the matter differently, and cashed the amount at once. A part of the sum he used to pay off all his debts, and it has to be set down to his credit that he rakes his memory to recall and settle even the smallest sums, while with a prudence unusual with him, he entrusted eight hundred thalers to Varnhagen to be kept as a reserve fund in case of emergency. Needless to say his uncle was furious, but Heine met him as usual very coolly, and merely replied that he had only done what his uncle would himself have done in the like case.

He took up his quarters in a house at 32, Craven Street, near Charing Cross, on which is a stone tablet, affixed by the London County Council, bearing the inscription : " Heinrich Heine, German Poet and Essayist (1799-1856), lived here 1827." He originally planned to stay in London only till the middle of June, and then to spend three months for the sake of his health near the sea. At first he was greatly impressed by all that he saw. " London has surpassed all my expectations by its vastness." " I am seeing much and learning much here." " There is much that is attractive here—Parliament, Westminster Abbey, English tragedy, beautiful women." He appears to have gone a great deal to the theatre, and to the debates in the Commons, where Canning made a great impression on him. From his letters at the time one would not indeed expect the harsh criticism found in his later writings and sayings. Even in the *Englische Fragmente* there is some attempt at an objective appreciation ; it is only later in Paris that England and Englishmen were reduced to something like a caricature.

The fact is that Heine came to England, as so many foreigners go to a strange country, with preconceived ideas, and saw above all the things that fitted in with those ideas. He had already drawn a picture of England in his *Ratcliff*, and he declared later in the Preface to the *Englische Fragmente* that just as Willibald Alexis, who had never been in England, had painted it most faithfully, thanks to that strange intuition which makes direct observation of the reality superfluous for a poet, so he himself had not only given there a faithful description of England, but the germ of all his later reflections were there contained. It is, in fact, rather the work of an imaginative artist than mere prose. He had come to England, he said, to get away from Hamburg, and probably he found in England, and especially in the financial circles, to which alone his uncle's introduction gave him the entry, too many types that reminded him of those men of Hamburg for whom he had so little liking. Moreover, the English writer with whom he was most familiar was Byron, and he had got used to seeing England through his glasses. And above all, it was the land that had brought about the downfall of his hero Napoleon, and that harboured Napoleon's enemy Wellington, and his views were largely coloured by that fact. Scott had now finished the

life of Napoleon, on which Heine had given an antici-
patory verdict in his *Nordsee*. So in the *Englische Fragmente*, which were written after his return, though they
only appeared in the fourth volume of his *Reisebilder*, in
1831, one of the longest chapters is that devoted to " The
Life of Napoleon Buonaparte by Walter Scott." If Heine
had divined that the book would prove to be Scott's
" Russian campaign ", he now judges that " Britain's
greatest poet has lost his laurels." If in his tolerance he
can forgive him all the great failings of his book, he can
never forgive " its purport, which is nothing less than the
exculpation of the English ministry for the crime of St.
Helena." He is indignant that the " Ex-poet" should dare
to speak of the " Ex-Kaiser ". What more characteristic
than the opening of the chapter on Wellington :

" The fellow has the misfortune everywhere to be
successful, where the greatest men of the world met with
misfortune, and that revolts us and makes us hate him.
We see in him only the triumph of stupidity over genius—
Arthur Wellington triumphs where Napoleon Buonaparte
falls ! " " There are no two greater contrasts than these
two, even in their outward appearance. Wellington, the
dull ghost, with an ashen-grey soul in his starched body, a
wooden smile on his frozen face—beside that, think of
the image of Napoleon, every inch a god !

" Never will the picture pass from my memory. I
still see him astride his charger, with the eternal eyes in his
marble emperor's face, looking down with the calmness of
destiny as his guards defile before him—he was sending
them then to Russia, and the old grenadiers looked up at
him, in such sacred devotion, and solemn understanding,
such proud defiance of death—

" *Te, Cæsar, morituri salutant !* "

That is the vision of a poet, antithesis *in excelsis*, not the calm judgment of a historian, and no sensible person dreams of taking it as the basis of a discussion on the relative merits of the two men. It would be just as foolish to consider the other things in the volume detached from their artistic value. No one reads it because he expects to find there a mirror held up to the English soul, so we can appreciate it for such insight as he shows, and for the wit without which it would not be a work of Heine. One of the things most frequently quoted occurs in the opening chapter : " the Englishman loves freedom like his lawful wife, the Frenchman like his chosen bride—the German like his old grandmother." The real, unprejudiced opinions of Heine on English life and character, based on adequate knowledge, would have been something to be thankful for. One thing can be said with confidence, that none of his criticisms, and England gets some pretty shrewd blows, have anywhere created any English prejudice against him. All the same, if we did not know the author so well, we might be somewhat surprised to find a Jew treating so harshly that country which has afforded such a measure of equality and protection to his race.

" Send a philosopher to London but for heaven's sake not a poet ! " he says, and the poet had indeed not been too fortunate in his experiences. The weather seems to have done its worst ; his health was not good, and he suffered much from depression. He appears to have enjoyed himself better at Ramsgate, where he spent a fortnight— all that came of the proposed three months. " I am now on the east cliff at Ramsgate, sitting on a high balcony, and as I write, I look down on the beautiful wide sea, whose waves climb up the cliff, and whose roar is the most joyful music in my ears." He " was much in the company of Irishmen," and especially of the " belle Irlandaise ", who reappears in the Italian travels. From Ramsgate he returned for a few days to London. The last comment on the English visit at the time is found in the letter written from Hamburg to Varnhagen on 19th October : " On the eighth of August, the day of Canning's death, I left London ; great intellectual profit. The life there is too big and too dear. I had plunged up to the neck in adventures, and through bad luck and folly had lost over three hundred guineas, and am glad to be out of the country again. The women there are beautiful and the men great and large-minded."

He went first of all to Holland, but the only thing we know of his time there is his own statement that he had " a lot of fun ". Then for the third time to Norderney. It was rather like a piece of bravado to go to the island after the things that had appeared about the Hanoverian nobility in his recent work, and he said himself that it " required some courage ", and that he had this time some right to boast, and " had shown himself a hero." However, nothing happened, beyond that he was given the cold shoulder ; he went on to the quieter island of Wangeroog, and by the end of September was again in Hamburg.

Chapter Five

BUCH DER LIEDER

On his return to Hamburg Heine's first care was to see through the press his *Buch der Lieder*, which appeared in the month of October. The idea was not new. In the previous November he had written to Merckel :

" Some friends are urging me to bring out a selection of my poems, in chronological order, and carefully chosen, and believe that it would become as popular as those of Bürger, Goethe, Uhland, etc. Sound Campe whether he would be in favour of such a plan." Campe was not enthusiastic, and Heine may have been affected by his indifference when he described it as " a harmless merchant-vessel that, under the protection of the second volume of the *Reisebilder*, will sail peacefully down into the sea of oblivion." However, in the end, Campe agreed to pay fifty louis, (forty pounds) for all rights in the volume. At first it looked as though Campe's estimate was going to prove right, for it was ten years before the first edition of five thousand copies was sold out, but after that its popularity called for such frequent editions that it did as much to establish Campe's prosperity as its author's fame.

None of the poems in it were new—they had all appeared in the collections which we have noted, from the *Gedichte* of 1821 onwards—though many were left out which, for one reason or another, might have stood in the way of its popularity with the general public. He described it as nothing but " a virtuous edition of his poems." Yet when the *Buch der Lieder* appeared, it was not merely the sum of those previous publications, but, as a work of art, a new creation. Heine was a great master of arrangement, and the *Buch der Lieder* owes its fame, not to the individual poems alone, but also to the work as a whole, the inter-relation of the various parts, the transitions and contrasts, the changes of mood and key between poem and poem, and the heightening of effect which they thus mutually conferred. One of its parts, the *Lyrisches Intermezzo*, shows this " composition " in an even more definite sense.

This Heine, who now presented to the world his poetic achievement, had entered, it is true, into the Romantic inheritance, but he added to that inheritance property of his own. The " Blaue Blume " still had its appeal for him ; but he has little of the mystical vagueness in which the older Romantics sought their ideal world. He has on the contrary a clearness of definition and outline, a plasticity and sureness, which are the very antithesis of their art. Their Orientalism no doubt influenced him, combined with that of his blood, but it did not lead him to seek to transplant to German poetry the externals of Oriental art, as other Romanticists had done. But if Heine was, as he said, the last of the Romantics, he was also the defrocked priest of Romanticism. The " Kunstperiode " was over ; and that Modernism, of which he was the representative, was no longer content to limit poetry to the seeking of " beautiful " themes in a " beautiful " world, and the clothing of them in " beautiful " language.

The old canons of an eclectic art should no longer run ;

no longer would the poet select from out the whole wealth of creation certain themes only as worthy of treatment, and certain words only as worthy to treat them in. All the world should lie open to him, and beauty be sought, not in the subject itself, but in the expression of the artist. And so we find with Heine those common words and common things, which are used so largely by him to point the ever-present and tragic contrast between the world of the poet's dream and harsh reality. He employs to the full this power of antithesis, and it is one of his distinguishing features. He is a master of dissonance ; nor does he always trouble to resolve that dissonance in a final harmony.

His irony is well-known, and it is no doubt a part of his Romantic inheritance—of that emphasis of the sovereign rights of personality, which must stand aloof and apart even from the artist's own work. Irony is dissimulation ; the statement of the opposite of that which is actually meant. If Heine dissimulates and indulges in this self-mockery, it is often a form of self-defence, since tragic emotion cannot be sustained indefinitely at the same height. If he ends a sublime passage or a lovely poem with a strident note, some common word or commonplace, with some glaring bathos, it is not necessarily that the former vision of beauty is for him untrue, but that he feels the sorrow that lies in the fate of all things beautiful in this imperfect world.

This irony takes with Heine various forms. The sudden drop from the height of the emotion at the close of the poem is well-known, though it is not shown in so many of his poems as is often assumed ; is not mere common form with him. He frequently used foreign words for

this purpose, as in the famous " Madame, ich liebe Sie "
at the end of one poem, or the close of another with :

> " Das kömmt, weil man Madame tituliert
> Mein süsses Liebchen, so süss und aimabel."

In one of his best known and most effective, the studied
familiarity of the expression heightens the intensity of the
repressed emotion ; the sadness of the tragedy lies in the
very commonness of its experience :

> " Ein Jüngling liebt ein Mädchen,
> Die hat einen andern erwählt ;
> Der andre liebt eine andre,
> Und hat sich mit dieser vermählt.

> " Das Mädchen heiratet aus Ärger
> Den ersten besten Mann,
> Der ihr in den Weg gelaufen
> Der Jüngling ist übel dran.

> " Es ist eine alte Geschichte,
> Doch bleibt sie immer neu ;
> Und wem sie just passieret,
> Dem bricht das Herz entzwei."

We have with Heine a restless, never-ending play of
fancy and imagination, so piquant and arresting as with
few poets of the world's literature. In epigrammatic
brevity and simplicity he is unsurpassed ; he never uses the
flat, stale and unprofitable word, but prunes the thought to
the starkest minimum of its expression. No one understands better than he that the poet works in the memory

and imagination of his hearers ; that his words will get their effect, not by their painting of concrete detail and their enumeration of individual traits, but by their suggestiveness and their power of evoking images in the hearer's mind. Words for him are not mere counters, each with its own connotation, but symbols.

And finally he possessed in the highest degree that supreme gift of the pure lyrical poet, the gift of music and song, the melody of speech. His poems seem almost to sing themselves and have suggested countless settings to great composers, whose tunes have become wedded with them to form one indissoluble whole. One need only mention Schumann, the greatest of his composers, Schubert, Mendelssohn, Franz, Liszt, Wagner. Not even Goethe's lyrics have been so frequently set to music. Goethe's " Kennst du das Land " has been set more than sixty times, the most frequently of all his songs ; but Heine's *Fichtenbaum* more than seventy times, " Leise zieht durch mein Gemüt " about ninety, and " Du bist wie eine Blume" about one hundred and seventy times !

To turn now to the *Book of Songs* in detail. In this chronological arrangement the individual parts show Heine's development and the amazing growth of his maturity. The *Junge Leiden*, which corresponds generally to the *Gedichte* of 1821, comprises the four sections *Traumbilder*, *Lieder*, *Romanzen* and *Sonette*. The *Traumbilder* are not among his greater works—others could do that kind of thing as well. Some of the *Lieder* show the emergence of the real Heine, and one, *Schöne Wiege meiner Leiden*, is worthy to rank with those jewels, perfect in their simplicity, which we come later to identify with his name.

Among the *Romanzen* are three which Heine never later surpassed, *Der Arme Peter*, *Die Grenadiere* and *Belsatzar*. The second and third are universally known, but the first is a no less perfect work of art. It is especially interesting as an early example of that constructional feature which Heine later developed in so characteristic a way, the tripartite form. Here we have a three-fold tripartism—three linked poems, each of three stanzas.

The restraint and economy of means are in the very best tradition of the Folk Song. In the first poem the situation is given ; in the second we have a monologue of " der arme Peter," who, on the lonely mountain top, pours out the full bitterness of his grief. In the third the maidens, who see poor Peter stagger by, whisper that he is like a ghost that has left his grave. But no, he is going now to his grave, for he has lost his love, and for him the grave is best, where he may lie and sleep till the judgment day.

The occasion that gave rise to *Die Grenadiere* is described in the tenth chapter of the *Buch Le Grand*. Heine had decided to exchange Bonn for Göttingen, and on the way, in September, 1820, he went back to Düsseldorf for one day, and for the last time in his life, and there, sitting on a bench in the Hofgarten, he saw ragged French soldiers returning from long years of captivity, among them his old friend, the Tambour Monsieur Le Grand. The poem was probably written immediately afterwards, in that same month :

> " Nach Frankreich zogen zwei Grenadier',
> Die waren in Russland gefangen.
> Und als sie kamen ins deutsche Quartier,
> Sie liessen die Köpfe hangen.

" Da hörten sie beide die traurige Mär' :
Dass Frankreich verloren gegangen,
Besiegt und zerschlagen das grosse Heer—
Und der Kaiser, der Kaiser gefangen.

" Da weinten zusammen die Grenadier'
Wohl ob der kläglichen Kunde.
Der eine sprach : ' Wie weh wird mir,
Wie brennt meine alte Wunde ! '

" Der andre sprach : ' Das Lied ist aus,
Auch ich möcht' mit dir sterben,
Doch hab' ich Weib und Kind zu Haus,
Die ohne mich verderben.'

" ' Was schert mich Weib, was schert mich Kind !
Ich trage weit bessres Verlangen ;
Lass sie betteln gehn, wenn sie hungrig sind—
Mein Kaiser, mein Kaiser gefangen !

" ' Gewähr' mir, Bruder, eine Bitt' :
Wenn ich jetzt sterben werde,
So nimm meine Leiche nach Frankreich mit,
Begrab mich in Frankreichs Erde.

" 'Das Ehrenkreuz am roten Band
Sollst du aufs Herz mir legen ;
Die Flinte gib mir in die Hand,
Und gürt' mir um den Degen.

" ' So will ich liegen und horchen still,
Wie eine Schildwach' im Grabe,
Bis einst ich höre Kanonengebrüll
Und wiehernder Rosse Getrabe.

85

> " 'Dann reitet mein Kaiser wohl über mein Grab,
> Viel Schwerter klirren und blitzen ;
> Dann steig' ich gewaffnet hervor aus dem Grab—
> Den Kaiser, den Kaiser zu schützen ! ' "

Heine wrote other poems later, and different poems, and longer poems, but never a greater, for it is perfect of its kind and unsurpassable.   It is the epilogue to all the great drama of his hero Napoleon. *Sic transit gloria mundi !* Yet it does not end on the note of vanity and human frailty ; the spirit of man can triumph over defeat, and loyalty defy the grave !

The third, *Belsatzar*, was probably written in the same year, 1820. The Bible story found in Daniel Heine treats with great freedom of omission and addition, while he owed to Byron's tame and mediocre *Vision of Belshazzar* in his *Hebrew Melodies* nothing beyond perhaps the realisation of the possibilities of the theme. It is especially interesting as showing the youthful poet's command of a metrical form, differing so greatly from that of the rest of the *Buch der Lieder*, and which he later employed with such good effect in the final poem of *Der Dichter Firdusi*.

> " Die Mitternacht zog näher schon ;
> In stummer Ruh' lag Babylon.

> " Nur oben in des Königs Schloss,
> Da flackert's, da lärmt des Königs Tross.

> " Dort oben in dem Königssaal
> Belsatzar hielt sein Königsmahl.

" Die Knechte sassen in schimmernden Reihn
  Und leerten die Becher mit funkelndem Wein.

" Es klirrten die Becher, es jauchzten die Knecht' ;
  So klang es dem störrigen Könige recht.

" Des Königs Wangen leuchten Glut ;
  Im Wein erwuchs ihm kecker Mut.

" Und blindlings reisst der Mut ihn fort ;
  Und er lästert die Gottheit mit sündigem Wort.

" Und er brüstet sich frech und lästert wild ;
  Die Knechtenschar ihm Beifall brüllt.

" Der König rief mit stolzem Blick ;
  Der Diener eilt und kehrt zurück.

" Er trug viel gülden Gerät auf dem Haupt ;
  Das war aus dem Tempel Jehovas geraubt.

" Und der König ergriff mit frevler Hand
  Einen heiligen Becher, gefüllt bis am Rand.

" Und er leert ihn hastig bis auf den Grund
  Und rufet laut mit schäumendem Mund :

" ' Jehova ! dir künd' ich auf ewig Hohn—
  Ich bin der König von Babylon ! '

" Doch kaum das grause Wort verklang,
  Dem König ward's heimlich im Busen bang.

G

" Das gellende Lachen verstummte zumal ;
   Es wurde leichenstill im Saal.

" Und sieh ! und sieh ! an weisser Wand,
   Da kam's hervor wie Menschenhand ;

"Und schrieb, und schrieb an weisser Wand
   Buchstaben von Feuer und schrieb und schwand.

" Der König stieren Blicks da sass,
   Mit schlotternden Knien und totenblass.

" Die Knechtenschar sass kalt durchgraut,
   Und sass gar still, gab keinen Laut.

" Die Magier kamen, doch keiner verstand
   Zu deuten die Flammenschrift an der Wand.

" Belsatzar ward aber in selbiger Nacht
   Von seinen Knechten umgebracht."

Of the Sonnets the best known are those to his mother
and to August Wilhelm von Schlegel, but they are not
among Heine's outstanding successes, were due to a
temporary stimulus only, and he never again bound himself to such a set and rigid form.

The *Lyrisches Intermezzo,* which appeared in 1823,
had shown Heine in complete command of his powers,
for whatever tones might be sounded in the graver poems
of his later years, he never surpassed in light and graceful
beauty this cycle of songs.   They shew Heine, moreover,
as a master of composition on the larger scale ; for the

several poems are welded into one great love-poem, moulded in a general way on his own fate with Amalie. The story moves forward from a bright opening, in which it is so unlike his own, to its gloomy close, when he buries in one great coffin his songs and his dreams, his love and his grief.

It is almost invidious to single out any poems in particular in this collection of gems, containing as it does favourites like "Im wunderschönen Monat Mai", "Auf Flügeln des Gesanges", "Die Lotosblume ängstigt", "Ein Fichtenbaum steht einsam", "Vergiftet sind meine Lieder", which have been borne round the world on the wings of the melodies which they themselves evoked.

Many of them are in that strophe which in this country is best known through its use by Heine, and which is sometimes, indeed, spoken of as his "Intermezzo-strophe", because it was here first freely employed by him—the strophe of his "Fichtenbaum".

> "Ein Fichtenbaum steht einsam
> Im Norden auf kahler Höh'.
> Ihn schläfert ; mit weisser Decke
> Umhüllen ihn Eis und Schnee."

> "Er träumt von einer Palme,
> Die fern im Morgenland
> Einsam und schweigend trauert
> Auf brennender Felsenwand."

That strophe had, however, already been used by famous poets before him, e.g., by Goethe in his *König in Thule* (1774), by Uhland, and by Wilhelm Müller, by the last of whom Heine was most directly influenced. It receives its characteristic lilt through the use of additional unaccented syllables at will in one or more of the lines of the strophe, a freedom natural to German poetry, and one which the Volkslied had never surrendered.

No less than ten of the 65 poems of the *Intermezzo* are in three strophes, an instance of that tripartition of which Heine was so fond. Such poems, with the free and delicate structure of their verse, and the development of one emotional theme in three brief bursts of song, are unsurpassed for airy lightness and grace, and it is no wonder that later poets have ever and again been attracted to the form.

The third part, *Die Heimkehr*, has not the same unity of the whole as the *Intermezzo*. Heine did not attempt to repeat that success by a repetition of its form. All the same, it shows the usual artistic feeling for arrangement in the succession and variation of the poems, and in the grouping of its parts. There is a wider range of tones ; there is an increase in the note of bitterness and satire. Here, too, the old love and the new furnish the background for many of the poems ; the *Lorelei* probably echoes his own fatal love for Amalie, while " Du bist wie eine Blume " was inspired by the new love for her gentler sister.

There are many favourites among its eighty-eight poems—" Was will die einsame Träne ", "Mein Kind, wir waren Kinder ", " Du hast Diamanten und Perlen ", and the fisher songs, of which the following is the best known and most characteristic.

> " Du schönes Fischermädchen,
>   Treibe den Kahn ans Land ;
>   Komm zu mir und setze dich nieder,
>   Wir kosen Hand in Hand.

" Leg' an mein Herz dein Köpfchen,
Und fürchte dich nicht zu sehr ;
Vertraust du dich doch sorglos
Täglich dem wilden Meer !

" Mein Herz gleicht ganz dem Meere,
Hat Sturm und Ebb' und Flut,
Und manche schöne Perle
In seiner Tiefe ruht."

The fourth section consists of the poems from the *Harzreise*, of whose naive, idyllic beauty we have already spoken, while the fifth comprises the two cycles of the poems of the *Nordsee*. Here Heine throws off all restraint of metrical structure, lightly as he had worn its fetters before, and uses those free rhythms, in which Klopstock and Goethe had been his greatest forerunners.

In these sea pictures we have a weight and majesty, which is in striking contrast to the airy grace of his songs. Heine reveals himself here as a mighty lord of language, who can coin great words to his need, and make a couple of them stalk at will through a whole long line. He himself described them as " colossal epigrams." The sea in all its moods sweeps through these surging periods ; it becomes for him a symbol of human destiny, reflecting its changes of fortune and its insoluble mysteries. And that sea is alive ; peopled with the beings of a mythology partly his own, partly borrowed from Greek and Northern saga.

This Heine of the *Buch der Lieder* is in the main the English Heine. If Heine's poems are studied in schools and universities, it is chiefly the *Buch der Lieder*, and this is reflected in the English editions, which, too, mainly

choose that collection of his songs. Of the many translations of Heine's poems into English also, probably something like four-fifths are from the same source. And
this is true of the five books of translation that have
appeared during or since the War.

The Heine of the *Buch der Lieder* was, to be sure, a
great poet, but this English attitude is all the same regret-
tably one-sided. Heine is not only the poet of beautiful
songs, tinged with some sentimentality and not a little
irony and malice. The reason why Heine has attracted
such an amazing amount of interest, was that he represented certain tendencies in the evolution of human sus-
ceptibility in a degree rarely, if ever, embodied before in a
single individual. And for an appreciation of Heine's
poetic achievement, we must not only know the poetry of
his youth and earlier years, but must realise the greatness
of that later tragic poet, who fathomed the depths of
human experience, as he touched the heights of courage
in the calm acceptance of fate, and who, for years, with
death at his elbow, interpreted life from an angle of vision
which it has mercifully been given to few poets to hold.
Who knows Heine who has not read, for example, his
Bimini, one of the most profound, and beautiful, and saddest
things he ever wrote, and one that expresses most truly that
tragic fate of youth and beauty which ever provoked
his not unpitiful smile.

Heine's *Buch der Lieder* has lived already a hundred
years, and though his poetry is too musical for some exigent
modern tastes, it is likely to live for many years to come.
Who can say that it will not be as popular a century
hence as it is to-day, a hundred years after it was first given
to the world ?

Chapter Six

LAST YEARS IN GERMANY

The few years which Heine spent in Germany after the publication of the *Buch der Lieder* were the time in which the whole course of his future life was to be decided. What was to become of him ?   Some sort of decision had to be made ; he was thirty, and his student years had already lasted long enough. Would he marry Therese and settle down in some fixed occupation, as journalist, or professor ?   He was still quite prepared to make his peace with the existing order and accept its service.   Or would he leave his fatherland, and try his fortunes abroad ?

There were many waverings and indecisions and changes of plan ; alternations of boundless self-confidence and bottomless dejection.   His last two books had made him very famous, and at first the triumphant mood prevails on the whole, and even rises to a climax in Italy.   It speaks from the defiant tone of the two letters addressed on the same day, October 30th, to Moser and Varnhagen, and caused by some adverse criticism of Goethe.   " That I do not find favour with the henchman of the aristocracy, Goethe, is only natural.   His blame is an honour, since he praises everything that is feeble.   He fears the rising Titans.   He is now an impotent worn-out god, who is vexed that he can no longer create." So to Moser, and   to   Varnhagen   he   writes : " They   tell   me from   there   (Berlin)   that   Wolfgang   Goethe   is   speaking unfavourably of me. . . . . I shall fall out with the aristocrat still worse. Wolfgang Goethe may forsooth violate the spiritual Law of Nations, but nothing he can do will prevent his great name being one day often coupled with that of H. Heine."

If he had great fame, he had at the same time many enemies. It was his nature to write his books with no respect of causes or persons, and afterwards to be surprised that they should be taken amiss. The real reason no doubt is that he rarely meant his strictures to be taken quite literally, inspired as they were by the mood of the moment and their artistic setting, and did not realise that other people could not see the back of his mind, but only the printed word. A good instance is the remarkable passage in a letter from London to Varnhagen: " If I had had a chance of a good appointment in Berlin, I should have returned there direct, regardless of the contents of my book (*Reisebilder II*). Since our ministry is sensible, I think I have more chance now than ever, and shall in the end probably come back to you in Berlin."

In these years, and especially towards the end, he often suffered from something approaching persecution mania. It was in that mood that he had deposited a fund with Varnhagen. " The persecutions to which I am subjected are serious, and it is necessary for me to be at all times provided with travelling funds," he writes to him.

The end of all the many projects—of going to Paris, or to Berlin, or of settling in Hamburg—was that he accepted, though not without many hesitations, the invitation of Cotta to become joint-editor in Munich of the *Neue Politische Annalen*, the negotiations concerning which had been begun from London through Varnhagen. One of the last events before his departure from Hamburg was a meeting with Amalie, which he announces in a strange ironical mood :

" I am about to visit this morning a lady whom I have not seen for eleven years, and with whom it is reported that I was once in love. Her name is Mad. Friedländer of Königsberg, so to speak, a cousin of mine. I saw the husband of her choice yesterday, as a foretaste. The good lady has been in a great hurry, and arrived yesterday, on the very day when the new edition of my *Junge Leiden* was published by Hoffmann and Campe. The world is dull and stale and unprofitable and smells of dried violets."

He travelled by way of Lüneburg and Göttingen to Cassel. Here he spent a week, visiting Jacob and Wilhelm Grimm, and here their brother Ludwig made a characteristic Byronesque portrait of him. Then he went to Frankfort, where he spent three days with Börne, and where in spite of a difference of their temperaments, which made the future clash inevitable, they appear to have found enough common ground to be very friendly, and indeed "inseparable " down to the last moment. After visiting his brother Max, who was a student in Heidelberg, he came to Stuttgart, with recommendations from Börne to the other and even fiercer leader of the anti-Goethe crusade, Wolfgang Menzel. With this future enemy, too, he managed now to put himself on a friendly footing. He has some praise for his *Deutsche Literatur*, which had appeared the year before, but his real feeling about Goethe is revealed by his reaction to Menzel's attacks on him. " I could not read without pain the passages about Goethe. I would not have written them at any price. How can you imagine, dear Varnhagen, that I, I should write against Goethe ! If the stars in heaven turn against me, can I on that account declare them to be mere will-o'-the-wisps ?

It is altogether foolish to speak against men who are *really great*, even if one could say things which were true."

The protest was probably called forth by some comment of Varnhagen on the letter of Heine quoted above, and was in so far justified as Heine, however much he might be irritated by Goethe's coolness and indifference, never in his serious moments questioned his greatness as a poet, whatever he might think of him politically.

Heine arrived in Munich towards the end of November, and stayed there till the following July. He was well received by Cotta, who had delayed his departure in order to meet him. Heine found him an " edlen Menschen " and very different from Campe, and Cotta's wife liked both his poetry and his person. He had no special experience or qualifications for his post ; it was as a famous poet that Cotta had secured him. Nor were his duties onerous ; he could apparently write as much or as little as he chose, and left most of the serious work to his fellow-editor, Lindner. To Campe he wrote expressing great satisfaction with his colleagues, saying that everything had been arranged to his satisfaction, and that, whether he took an office or not, his living was secured.

Yet when Cotta wished him to take charge of another paper, the *Ausland*, founded at the wish of the King to attract scholars to Munich, he declined, and refused to bind himself. He is restless and unsettled ; talks of packing his bag and going off to Italy. He finds the climate very trying ; his first letters are full of pitiful complaints about his wretched health. In spite of this he did think seriously of establishing himself in Munich—and of all things as a Professor of the University ! King Ludwig I. was a liberal ruler and a patron of the arts, and Heine soon made friends with one of his ministers, the dramatist von

Schenk, whom he described in a letter to Varnhagen as "the greatest poet of the world."

In such conditions he was full of hope, and in the *Annalen*, which enjoyed the royal favour, he "aimed at a praiseworthy moderation of expression," as he wrote to Cotta. His spirits improved; "the life here is very pleasant for anyone who has a good chest and can stand the climate." He again found much congenial company in aristocratic circles, where he met the "wunderschöne Gräfin Bothmer," who was the inspiration of many of the poems of the *Neuer Frühling*, and with artists, to one of whom, Ludwig Gassen, we owe the well-known portrait. In June he begged Cotta to present personally to the King his *Reisebilder* and *Buch der Lieder*. "It would also benefit me greatly if you could indicate to him that the author is now quite a different person from the writer of his earlier works. I think the King is wise enough to judge the blade by its edge, and not by any good or bad use that has already been made of it," he wrote.

He was, indeed, ready for large concessions, and to make his peace with official society when encountered in this benevolent, liberal form. Everything looked favourable, Schenk was confident, and nothing was lacking but the royal signature to his appointment, when he gave up his post and started for Italy on July 1st. It was the nearest he ever got to a settled existence, but he was doomed to disappointment once more. He would have been all the more ready to settle in the south at this time, for the last hope of winning Therese had vanished with her engagement to a Dr. Halle. He wrote to Varnhagen on February 12th: "I shall never return in this life to Hamburg. My uncle there, the millionaire, has acted like the commonest scoundrel towards me. Things of the utmost bitterness have befallen me there ; they would not be endurable but for the fact that I alone know of them ". The whole relationship to Therese, including their later meetings, is recapitulated in the poems to *Clarisse*, which are found—a strange setting—in the section entitled *Verschiedene* in the *Neue Gedichte*.

Meantime, amidst his other occupations, his own work was not standing still. Nearly the whole of the *Englische Fragmente* appeared in Cotta's journals, mostly in the *Politische Annalen*, and probably some parts of the *Reise von München nach Genua*, dealing with Munich, were already written when he left for Italy. His muse was not idle either, and a number of the poems of the *Neuer Frühling* are to be ascribed to these Munich months.

He stayed in Italy till the end of November, using for the purpose the 800 thalers which he had deposited with Varnhagen. He probably regarded the journey as a real holiday for the benefit of his health, which he could well afford himself on the strength of his approaching appointment. Looking back on his Munich time, he wrote from Lucca that he had had a grand time there, and would joyfully return and stay there for good. His brother Max, who had now moved from Heidelberg to Munich, accompanied him as far as Kreuth on the Bavarian frontier, and he then went on through the Tyrol, over the Brenner to Trent, saw Verona, Milan and Genoa, and thence crossed by ship to Leghorn. After a stay in the Baths of Lucca, he went to Florence, where he spent some six weeks. That was the farthest point ; and he never saw Rome.

Apart from his ignorance of the language, he had prepared himself well, and in the sixteenth chapter of the *Reise* he gives a long list of the books on Italy which he had read, placing first and foremost, along with Goethe's work, Lady Morgan's " Italy " and Madame de Staël's " Corinne." He repeats the judgment he had already given on Goethe's *Italienische Reise*, finding his anticipation only confirmed now that he himself knows its subject : " Goethe holds up the mirror to Nature, or rather he is himself the mirror of Nature. Nature wished to know how she looked, and she created Goethe." The complete difference of his own subjective, romantic approach to the classical land of art is seen very plainly from the letter which he wrote to Edward von Schenk from Leghorn in August; he could have turned round his expression concerning Goethe, and said that Nature holds up the mirror to Heine:

" The lack of knowledge of Italian troubles me greatly. I cannot understand the people and cannot talk with them. I see Italy, but do not hear it. Yet I am often not entirely without converse. Here the stones speak, and I hear their dumb language. They, too, seem to feel deeply what I am thinking. This broken column from the Roman days, this crumbling Gothic pillar understand me very well. I am, forsooth, myself a ruin walking among ruins. Like and like understand each other well. Often indeed the old palaces would whisper some secret to me, but I cannot hear them for the rumbling noises of the day ; then I return at night, and the moon is a good interpreter, who understands the lapidary style, and can translate into the dialect of my heart. . . .

"Meantime, there is a language with which one can make oneself understood from Lapland to Japan with half the human race. And it is the fairer half, what one calls the fairer sex *par excellence*. This speech flourishes very specially in Italy. Why words, when such eyes shine with so deep an eloquence into the heart of a poor Tedesco. . . ."

In the Baths of Lucca his health and spirits revived, and his dionysian exuberance reached its very summit. He describes it as a " most divine time ", and later from Potsdam as " the most brilliant time of my life, a time when, drunk with the pride of life, I roamed in transports on the peaks of the Apennines, and dreamt of great wild deeds, which should spread my fame over the whole earth to the farthest island."

Though he may turn again to the God of his Fathers in his tribulation, there is nothing of the Jew in him now at the height ; he is the Hellene and not the Nazarene of his own antithesis. Now the senses triumph, and he boldly proclaims that emancipation, which was to be elevated to a doctrine in the Paris time:

"I have indeed got on in the world ! Of that be my witnesses ye Tuscan nights, thou light-blue heaven with the great silver stars, ye wild laurel-bushes and secret myrtles, and ye, O nymphs of the Apennines, who hovered around us with bridal dances, and dreamed yourselves back to those better days when the old Gods reigned ; when there was no Gothic lie, which suffers only blind groping enjoyment in secret, and cloaks all free emotion with its hypocritical fig-leaf."

That passage is found at the end of the sixth chapter of the *Bäder von Lucca*. There, and in the next chapter, with its declaration that to be in love on the Apennines is to feel that he is Adam, the first of men, in the morning-dawn of creation, there speaks no doubt, for all its fantastic expression, something of the well-nigh titanic sense of fullness of life which Heine experienced in these weeks.

From Lucca he went on to Florence. The first thing he did on arriving was to hasten to the post, but the hoped-for letter from Schenk was not there. He began to get anxious, and wrote asking Schenk to inform him as soon as possible of the confirmation of his appointment. He stayed on for six weeks, waiting for Schenk's reply, and then was seized with a strange uneasiness concerning his father's health, and a desire to see him again. In the middle of November he hurriedly left for home, heard in Venice that his father was dangerously ill, and in Würzburg that he had died on December 2nd. In Munich he had learnt that the King had finally refused to ratify his appointment.

So the high hopes of this year ended in grievous loss and bitter disappointment. He returned first of all to Hamburg to console his mother, and it was there that he spent most of his time in the two remaining years in Germany, though he never settled down, and was frequently on the move. In January he went to Berlin, and saw all his old friends again. Yet his moods were so trying, and his arrogance at times so great, that he even for a time quarrelled with Rahel, the best friend he ever had. From April to June he was in Potsdam. There he lived in retreat, " seeing nothing but sky and soldiers," and "ill and miserable, as though in self-mockery, described the most glorious time of his life." Parts of the *Reise* were already written ; he wrote to Schenk from Florence that in the Baths of Lucca he had already written half a book " a kind of sentimental journey ", and in November he sent to Cotta the manuscript of the first seventeen chapters, which were printed in the *Morgenblatt* in December. Now, working with great concentration, he not only finished the *Reise*, but also wrote the two following parts, *Die Bäder von Lucca* and *Die Stadt Lucca*.

The months of August and September he spent on the island of Heligoland. Once more the sea exercised its beneficent influence on him. He is very well and cheerful on the red rock, he writes to Moser: " the sea is my natural element, and the very sight of it is salutary for me. Only now do I feel how unutterably wretched I was in Berlin. . . . I wish you could see the sea ; perhaps you would understand the rapture with which every wave inspires me." But it was an unpoetic period, and no more odes were written.

When he got back to Hamburg he was at once occupied with the printing of the third volume of the *Reisebilder*, which appeared in December, the last chapters of the *Bäder* being hurriedly added, to complete the necessary number of sheets, while the printing was actually in progress.

The year 1830 was spent mainly in Hamburg with his mother, in the Neuer Wall. His mood at its beginning is shown in the letter to Varnhagen of January 3rd : " With a heavy head and a breast full of horrible pain, surrounded by a thousand vexations, I write you this letter. How sadly, how disquietingly this year begins—if only one could escape from time as one does from a place ! Alas ! I have to last out this whole year, before I get to 1831 ! " He is anxious about his attack on Platen—as usual only after it is launched. Even Cotta is being led by his wife to act dishonourably towards him, while Campe is a regular scoundrel. He is troubled about his personal safety, and asks whether there is any chance for him in Berlin, since he has spoiled everything in the south. Altogether the most lugubrious of moods and gloomiest of letters !

In Hamburg he had little society, apart from the various members of his own family. He was equally suspect to Christians and Jews for the things he had said about their respective religions ; the new Christian was no better liked than the late Jew. At the end of March he went to Wandsbeck, drawn by the need of solitude which spring commonly engendered in him. He spent there a quiet three months, occupying himself much with the reading of books on the French Revolution ; thence again to Heligoland, where his health and spirits once more improved, and where he enjoyed the social life after the seclusion of Wandsbeck, though again without receiving any poetic inspiration from his beloved sea. It was altogether an unpoetical period of his life, the only poems written in these years being all, or nearly all, of the 45 poems of the *Neuer Frühling*, and even of those more than half were written in the autumn of 1830. Political questions and ideas had gained the upper hand, and when he received on the island the news of the July Revolution in Paris, he thought his dreams had come true, and his eyes were turned more than ever to the "New Jerusalem." When he returned to Hamburg he busied himself with the preparations for the publication of the *Nachträge zu den Reisebildern*, as the fourth volume was originally called. The manuscript of the *Englische Fragmente* was completed in January, 1831.

The third and fourth volumes of the *Reisebilder* each contained two sections, though the division was a purely formal one, since the three Italian parts really form a connected whole, while the fourth section, the *Englische Fragmente*, belongs in the main to an earlier period. Heine's "Italian Journey", like his other "Travel Pictures", is far from being in the first place, or pre-eminently, a description of peoples and places. There is in fact a certain similarity of movement in each of the three parts. The description, and the story such as it is, lead up in each case to the serious topic, to Napoleon and the political "ideas" in the *Reise*, to the Platen feud in the *Bäder*, and to the disquisition on religion in the *Stadt Lucca*.

The first part, the *Reise von München nach Genua*, has of all the travel pictures most right to the title. The earlier chapters actually do give, in an unusually sober tone for Heine, an account of his Munich impressions, and his experiences on the way. But in Milan he sees the cathedral, " whose completion was one of Napoleon's favourite plans ", and he is off at once on a subject that has little to do with Italy. " The great Emperor has left behind a monument that is much better and more enduring than marble." But now his admiration is qualified, and a new symbolical champion of freedom will have to be found. " Pray, dear Reader, do not take me for an unqualified Bonapartist ; my homage extends, not to the actions, but only to the genius of the man. I love him unconditionally only till the eighteenth day of Brumaire—then he betrayed freedom. And he did it not from necessity, but from a secret love for aristocracy. Napoleon Buonaparte was an aristocrat, a noble enemy of civic equality, and it was a colossal blunder that the European aristocracy, represented by England, waged war to the death against him ; for even though he intended to make some changes in the personnel of this aristocracy, he would have preserved the greater part of it and its vital principle; he would have regenerated this aristocracy, which now lies prostrate from senile decay, loss of blood and the weariness due to its last, assuredly its very last victory."

We see Heine's real belief and real hopes—the optimism of many liberal thinkers at this period, who believed that a new era of liberty was about to dawn in a new cosmopolitan world :

" It often seems to us as though military fame were an

antiquated pleasure, and wars would get a nobler meaning, and Napoleon be perhaps the last conqueror. It really looks as though the fight will be now more for spiritual than material interests, and as though world history will be no longer a history of brigandage, but of the spirit. The chief lever which ambitious and grasping princes used formerly to set so effectively in motion for their own private purposes, namely nationality, with its vanity and its hatred, is now rotten and worn out ; daily the stupid national prejudices vanish more and more, all harsh idiosyncrasies are submerged in the universality of European civilisation, there are in Europe no longer any nations, but only parties. . . . Time presses with its great task.

But what is this great task of our time ?

It is emancipation. Not only that of the Irish, Greeks, Frankfort Jews, West Indian blacks, and such oppressed races, but the emancipation of the whole world, especially of Europe, that has come of age, and is now wresting itself free from the leading-strings of the privileged classes, the aristocracy——"

One of his enemies of freedom is arraigned there. The other is the church, and the greatest thing of all is " liberation from the survivals of feudalism and clericalism." Those are the foes against which Heine raises the standard, and calls to arms again and again in this and the following years. And who, we may well ask, is to be the standard bearer ? The answer is surprising ! " The most fervent friend of the revolution sees the salvation of the world only in the victory of Russia, and looks on Emperor Nicholas as the *gonfaliere* of freedom. Strange turn of fortune ! But two years ago we endowed with this office an English minister; the howl of Tory hatred against George Canning then guided our choice. . . . But we took the flag from

Downing Street and planted it in Petersburg, and chose for its bearer the Emperor Nicholas, the Knight of Europe."

And before leaving this visionary inset, to close the chapter, as it had begun, with more sober narrative, Heine makes the bold and often-quoted proclamation of his mission, which doubtless, he seriously believed in in this more unpoetic period. In the *Harzreise*, and also in one of his letters, he had already called himself a " Ritter von dem heil'gen Geist ", probably without attaching any very definite idea to the words, beyond a somewhat general championship of "liberalism "; now he "sees his two foes clearly before him " :

" I do not indeed know whether I deserve that my coffin should one day be adorned with a laurel wreath. Poetry, much as I loved it, was for me never more than a sacred toy, or a consecrated weapon to be used for divine ends. I have never attached great value to poetic fame, and it troubles me little whether my songs are praised or blamed. But on my coffin you must lay a sword; for I was a good soldier in the Wars of Liberation of mankind."

With the beginning of the second part, *Die Bäder von Lucca*, we are transported at once from such high and serious themes into a company where the spirit of high comedy holds revel. Heine had been reading Sterne again, and it was to be a humorous " sentimental journey " on the English model, with many of its cranks and oddities, and not a little of its drastic expression. The maddest mood prevails ; the tone is one of irrepressible fun and laughing raillery. The poet, " maddest of mortals," meets again Lady Mathilde, a friend of the Ramsgate time, and with her a fine set of originals. They are grouped around Signora Lätitia, " a quinquagenarian rosebud ", with her two antique seladons, a professor and a poet, whose devotion has lost nothing of its sentimentality after twenty-five years of service, and the beautiful dancer, Signora Franscheska, in whose love the poet finds the supreme rapture of these Tuscan days.

But the greatest figures of them all are the Markese Christophoro de Gumpelino, and his squire, Hirsch Hyazinth. It has been said of Heine that he has created few characters, and there is some truth in the statement. But here, at any rate, he has drawn two real beings, full and round and alive. He said himself that he had tried here for the first time to make a character live and speak, and that Hyazinth was the first full-fledged, life-size character that he had ever created. The man who could put such characters on the stage would have done something in the theatre if he had tried his hand at comedy instead of tragedy. He indeed thought of doing so, for in the letter to Varnhagen from which the last words are quoted, he says that he shall attempt to create other such characters as Hyazinth, both in comedy and in the novel.

For both of the pair Heine appears to have had living models. When he first meets the Markese in the house of Lady Mathilde, he recognises to his astonishment " his old friend, the banker Christian Gumpel." His real name was Lazarus Gumpel, and he was an acquaintance of his Uncle Solomon, and well known on the Hamburg Exchange, while the model of Hirsch Hyazinth was a lottery agent, whose real name, Isaak Roccamora, at once captured Heine's imagination when first he heard it. Whether Heine actually met either of them in Italy, and whether the two of them ever met in actual life, is not known. The characters are Heine's own artistic progeny, suggested no doubt by the two immortal figures of Don Quixote and Sancho Panza, but independent creations all the same.

The more lovable of the two is Hyazinth, who follows Gumpelino in his romantic pursuit of culture as blindly and uncomprehendingly as Sancho followed his master on his chivalric quest. Yet for all the humour in which they are steeped, they are caricatures of some of the most unpleasing traits of the Jewish character, and it is no wonder that he aroused hostility in Jewish circles through this part of the book, as he did in Gentile circles through the other. Very bitter are the words he puts in the mouth of Hyazinth, in a comparison of the Catholic, Protestant and Jewish religions : " Doctor, don't talk to me of the Jewish religion ; I wouldn't wish it my worst enemy. One gets nothing but shame and disgrace from it. I tell you, it is not a religion at all, but a misfortune." This first part of the book is a satire on Jewish characteristics by a Jew who renounces kinship with his race, and it is a tragic irony that the fateful second part was called forth by Platen's attacks on this superior young man on the very grounds of his Jewish birth.

Die Bäder von Lucca falls, indeed, into two quite distinct parts, for with the ninth chapter we are introduced to very serious matters. Mathilde and Franscheska are dropped, and Gumpelino and Hyazinth only serve to lead with their " Bildung " to the disastrous attack on Platen. Anyone reading the work for the first time feels that these Platen chapters, which form nearly half the book, are deliberately dragged in, without any artistic necessity, and with a transition that is somewhat artificially effected. As a matter of fact they were only added when the book was already being printed.

The theme has been slightly prepared by references to Platen in earlier chapters ; poor Hirsch-Hyazinthos suffers the worst pains of his whole martyrdom for culture's sake in his struggles with the feet of Platen's poems. But with Chapter XI, which opens with the words, " Wer ist denn der Graf Platen ? " , all poetic fiction is laid aside, all pretence of impersonality is dropped, and Heine demolishes his opponent with ruthless murderous thrusts. " You, Immermann, have played the judge, I will play the part of executioner," he wrote.

What, then, was the origin of this greatest of all German literary scandals ? Platen was really the aggressor, since Heine's only offence was the indirect one of giving hospitality, at the end of the second volume of the *Reisebilder*, to some epigrams of his friend Immermann, directed against the imitators of Goethe in the field of Oriental poetry, and obviously intended for Rückert and Platen. Platen was already at work on *Der romantische Ödipus*, in which Immermann was held up to ridicule as Nimmermann, when he heard of this satire, and he resolved to put the poetaster and his Jewish associate in their proper place. Platen had an overweening sense of his own importance, and probably but little doubt that his heavy artillery would utterly demolish this small fry. And so we have the arrogant, tasteless attack in the fifth act of his *Ödipus*. He knew little of Heine except by hearsay, and so, any genuine destructive criticism or satire being impossible, he fell back on the crude shift of mocking at his Jewish descent and his change of faith. It was pointless and stupid, and he did not know his man. Heine was himself fully conscious of the vulnerabilities of his Jewish compatriots, and was, as we have seen, at the very time occupied with a book in which he ridiculed some of the very traits which rendered them obnoxious to their Gentile critics, implicitly claiming for himself a standing as a cultured European independent of his race.　And now to be thrust back into the ghetto, as it were, and that by a man whom he had otherwise little reason to love !　For he suspected, not perhaps unreasonably, but probably without cause, that this very Platen had, in league with the clerical party, taken a hand in bringing about his Munich discomfiture.　Hence, Platen became for him the representative of the two elements which he now hated most of all, the priest and the aristocrat, and when there is added to that the personal grudge, we are in a position to understand, if not to excuse, the extreme virulence of his attack.

That attack was, forsooth, a much more subtle thing than the one to which it replied.　If Platen dealt in commonplaces of insult, Heine studied his victim's armour, and found the joints through which to fire his poisoned shafts. Platen was pompous and olympic ; Heine, in a diabolically skilful fashion, made him a figure of fun before he flayed him alive.　This Goliath indeed met his David !　It is true that, even on the literary side, Platen offered abundant openings for attack.　As a poet he was, of course, much more than the metrical equilibrist that Heine makes of him, but on the other hand, he was far from being the giant of his own imaginings.　Heine could legitimately jeer at his boastings of the " great deed in words " that he was going to perform, the Odysseys and Iliads and other *Unsterblichkeitskolossalgedichte* that he was going to write, and all his other drafts on the bank of posterity.　An even more unpleasant trait was his envy and depreciation of all his fellow poets, referred to by Goethe in the often-quoted passage, which, oddly enough, has frequently been cited as applying to Heine : " It is not to be denied that he possesses many brilliant qualities, but he is wanting in—love." As Heine puts it, " he pours whole flower-pots of abuse on the heads of the German poets," and those who get the worst abuse of all are " the baptised Heine ", and his friend Immermann.

Where Heine went wrong was in repaying personalities with personalities, and coarseness with coarseness, and above all in bringing against Platen, publicly and with every circumstance and elaboration, the charge of sexual perversion, which was, it is true, common talk at the time, and apparently not without foundation. If Heine had even done it in genuine moral indignation, there would have been some justification for this public pillory of an opponent, but to use this knowledge as he did was hypocritical and mean, and is one of the most unworthy actions he ever committed.

The result of the duel was a victory for Heine, but that victory was more costly than a defeat. He felt some satisfaction over the destruction of his assailant, and the revenge for the attack on himself and his friend, but this was outweighed by the consciousness of the injury he had inflicted on himself. This Platen affair was one of the three things—the others being his conversion and the book on Börne—which he most regretted in his life. The letters of 1830 are full of the subject. In the long letter to Varnhagen of 4th February, he says that no one is better aware than himself that he has done himself unspeakable injury through the Platen chapter, that he ought to have gone about the business differently, and that he has offended the better part of the public. He feels the need of support, and begs Varnhagen to urge Gans to take the field on his behalf, and in a later letter of 7th March, he asks Immermann to get Beer to stand up for him in Munich in the Platen affair. And in the spiritual discomfort caused him by the book, he had recourse, as he told Varnhagen, to his usual remedy, and plunged into all the dissipations of Hamburg life.

Nothing came of the expected challenge to a duel, nor of the threatened legal action, which Heine was prepared to meet by the *exceptio veritatis,* but the injury sat deep, and could not have been cured even by the surgical method of cutting out the offending parts of the book, which he contemplated, but never carried out. The surprising thing is that the full realisation of the blunder he had committed did not save him from a similar exhibition of bad taste and bad tact a few years later, in the other fatal book on Börne.

The fourth and last part of the *Reisebilder* contained the *Stadt Lucca* and the *Englische Fragmente. Die Stadt Lucca* carries on the thread of the story, such as it is, and we hear again of Lady Mathilde and Franscheska, whom he goes to meet by appointment in the town. This setting is, however, even more incidental to the chief interest than in the preceding portion, and the book is devoted in the main to a disquisition on that other evil of which for him the time lay sick, namely, "dogmatic religion with its diplomatic corps of priests, rabbis, muftis, dominicans, consistorial councillors, popes and bonzes."

He arrived at night to find the town astir with a Catholic procession, and seeing the priests moving along so sadly and woefully, flanked by their military escort, he imagined he saw the Saviour Himself being led to the place of execution. Life itself is a sickness, the whole world a hospital, and death the only physician. And from this mood is born his famous picture of the dethronement of the Hellenic gods by the Nazarene. The old gods are enthroned on high Olympus, and all day long, till the setting of the sun, they hold revelry, to the sound of Apollo's lyre, and the song of the Muses. "Then suddenly there approached, panting, a pale Jew dripping with blood, with a crown of thorns on His head, and a great wooden cross on His shoulder ; and He threw the cross on the high table of the gods, so that the golden goblets trembled, and the gods were struck dumb, and grew pale and ever paler, till at last they dissolved utterly in mist.

"Then came a mournful time and the world grew grey and dark. The joyous gods were no more ; Olympus became a lazar-house, where flayed, burnt, and spear-pierced gods crept gloomily around, and bound up their wounds and sang mournful songs. Religion no longer afforded joy, but only consolation ; it was a melancholy, blood-stained, malefactors' creed."

Religion here is not the Roman Catholic faith in particular, for if it fares badly, Protestantism fares little better, and Judaism worst of all. If in the *Bäder* the Jewish religion is described as not a religion but a calamity, here the Jewish people is represented as the source of all the evils that have befallen mankind in the name of established religion :

"There came a people out of Egypt, the home of crocodiles and priestcraft, and along with its skin-diseases and its stolen vessels of gold and silver, it brought with it, too, a so-called positive religion, a so-called church, an edifice of dogmas in which one had to believe, and of sacred ceremonies which one had to observe, a prototype of the later state-religions.

"Now began the jobbing in souls, the proselytising and persecution, and all those sacred horrors which have cost the human race so much blood and so many tears.

"Goddam ! this people ! This fount of all evil ! ' O Mathilde, it has long been damned, and has dragged the pains of its damnation through the ages.' "

At the same time he protests that he is no enemy of the throne and of the altar, as has been falsely alleged. It is not the religions themselves which he hates, for he honours the inner sanctity of every religion, but only the priest-craft that entrenches itself behind every state religion; just as he does not hate the throne, but only the aristocratic vermin that nests in the crannies of the ancient thrones. And what is his remedy for this twofold evil of aristocracy and priestcraft—doubly fatal in alliance ? On the one hand the abolition of all state religions, of all privilege of any one dogma and any one cult, free rivalry among the various religions, or, as he sums it up in one pregnant phrase, " free trade among the gods "; and on the other the liberation of the kings from their self-seeking aristo-cratic parasites, so that they may become free like other men, and walk freely amongst them, and feel freely, and marry freely, and express their true opinions freely—in other words " the emancipation of the kings."

The whole book then closes with the praise of Quixotism as the most precious thing in life. Throughout the whole of this Italian part the inspiration of the Don is present with him, and it is interesting to find him in a letter to Merckel, of 9th October, 1829, asking him for the loan, among other books, of the second part of Cervantes' great work. He is himself a Don Quixote, and the reader who has followed the crazy poet through all the mazes of this book is, without knowing it, his Sancho Panza. Yet he is an inverted Quixote, for while his great prototype aimed to restore the vanishing world of chivalry, he would destroy once for all every remaining trace of that age. And in the sixteenth chapter, which, eight years later, he repeated as the opening of his "Introduction to Don Quixote", he describes how, as a child, he read Cervantes' book for the first time, on a beautiful May morning in the *Hofgarten* at Düsseldorf. Then he took everything in childish earnest, for he did not yet know irony. Now the famous knight is for him the symbol of all youthful, disinterested enthusiasm and idealism, that mocks the selfishness of calculating age, and represents the triumph of cosmic humour over stolid reason and comfortable self-satisfied worldly prosperity.

The second part of this final volume, the *Englische Fragmente*, had been written two years earlier, and has already been discussed. When that fourth volume of the *Reisebilder* went out into the world in the January of 1831, it seemed to Heine that many of the aspirations which it expressed were on the point of fulfilment, for the July Revolution in Paris appeared to him as the dawn of a new era. In the full enthusiasm inspired by that event he added in November, 1830, a Preface and a Postscript to the *Stadt Lucca*, and an Epilogue to the *Reisebilder* as a whole. In the first of the three he says that he presents the book, not as an independent picture, but as the end of a period in his life, which coincides at the same time with the end of a period of the world's history. In the postscript he points out that the book had been written almost a year before "the third Bourbon Hegira—at a time when it looked as though the triumph of liberty might be postponed for another century." Now he is seized with a great joy ;

as he writes he hears music under his window, and recognises the Marseillaise. "What a song! It thrills me with fire and joy, and kindles in me the glowing stars of enthusiasm and the rockets of scorn." And he ends the whole with the refrain : "*Aux armes, citoyens !* "

The last of them all, the Epilogue, written on 29th November, speaks not only of his joy and exultation, but also of his triumphant pride in his championship of the right cause. He had suffered for the boldness of his writings, and he looks back over the years, and thinks how bold were some of the speakers in the gatherings of the *Burschenschaft* in his Bonn and Göttingen days, and how little they have performed. "How they reviled the French and the modern Babylon, and the un-German, impious traitor who spoke in praise of France. That praise has come true in the Great Week." He compares himself in his fiery enthusiasm with Goethe in his cool objectivity, who lived for his eighty years and became a minister and wealthy—"poor German nation ! that is your greatest man ! " And the note he chooses on which to end the *Reisebilder*, the long four-volume allegory of this whole phase of his life's journey, is given by the story of the Emperor Charles V, who, when solitary and abandoned by all those who had flattered him in the days of his prosperity, saw his prison doors open and recognised in the man who entered disguised his court fool, Kunz von der Rosen. He is himself Kunz von der Rosen, and the German fatherland is his Emperor. Under his mantle he brings sceptre and crown, for the people is the true Emperor, its will is sovereign, and the only legitimate source of power. The day of liberation approaches, the new age is beginning ; the night is over, and yonder glows the dawn.

Such was the mood conjured up in Heine by the events

in Paris. He received the news, as we have seen, during a stay on the island of Heligoland. The plan to go to Paris was an old one, taken up again and again in times of discouragement, and postponed when things were going better with him. We already see him writing to Moser on 8th July, 1826, that he is urgently longing to say farewell to his German fatherland, it being less the desire of travel than the distress of personal circumstances (*e.g.*, the ineffaceable Jew) that is driving him away. A year later we find him writing to Moser with the confidence in a brilliant future in Germany inspired by the success of the *Buch Le Grand* and his journey to England.

But now all his hopes in Germany were shattered and he heard a clear call to France. In Germany he had made himself enemies indifferently in Jewish and Gentile circles, though actual fears for his personal safety had probably not much to do with his decision. His latest political work, the brief Introduction to *Kahldorf über den Adel* by Robert Wesselhöft, written in March 1831, with its further bitter and one-sided attacks, was not calculated to improve his position. Moreover all chance of an appointment in Berlin or Munich or elsewhere had completely faded away. It is true that as late as the January of 1831 he was still prepared to settle in Hamburg as an official, and urged Varnhagen to further his candidature for the vacant office of Syndic, though he will doubtless have been little surprised that nothing came of it. On the other hand Paris was now something more than a refuge from his German troubles ; Paris was the " New Jerusalem ", and the Rhine the " Jordan " by crossing which he could enter this new " Promised Land of Freedom." And in Saint-Simonism, his " New Gospel," he saw a positive creed, which was going to build up a new world on a ground rid of the old encumbrances, and in whose establishment he wished to take an active part.

So at last he did actually take the step, which was to be of decisive importance for his whole future. He no more thought of spending there the rest of his days than did Goethe when he went to Weimar. He left Hamburg towards the end of April, and after staying a week in Frankfort, crossed the Rhine on the first of May, and two days later was in Paris.

Chapter Seven

FIRST YEARS IN PARIS

With the migration to Paris, Heine turned his back on one whole phase of his life and acknowledged the bankruptcy of his hopes of official success, and the waste of those six years of University study spent in fitting him for a legal career. He had failed in business and in the law. What was he going to do now? It is true that his uncle, even after this two-fold disappointment, still continued his allowance, with a tolerance for which he got little thanks. But that yearly grant of 4,000 francs, even with the income from his books, was not going to meet his expensive tastes. The rest had to be furnished by his own pen, and the importance of his decision was that he now deliberately launched himself upon the profession of journalism. He was one of a band of German writers, the most gifted it is true, who had flocked to Paris after the events of the "great week", in order to spread from there the news of those stirring events upon which the eyes of the whole world were turned.

However, such considerations, serious though they might be, weighed very lightly upon him at the start. Paris in early May was as delightful then as ever, and he plunged with fervour into its many-sided life. Novelty and change were always the breath of his being. Here new experiences crowded on him in full flood, and at the outset, and

119   I

indeed for the first few years, he was enthusiastic for his
new home. In the *Geständnisse* he describes, with a good
deal of poetic liberty no doubt, but probably with poetic
truth, his arrival in Paris and his first impressions. Everything enchanted him : " The men were all so polite, and
the beautiful women all so smiling. If anyone bumped
into me by accident without at once begging my pardon, I
could wager that it was a fellow-countryman ; and if a fair
one looked too sour, she had either eaten sauerkraut, or
could read Klopstock in the original. I found everything
so entertaining, and the sky was so blue, and the air so kind
and generous, and moreover the lights of the 'sun of
July' were still shimmering here and there ; the cheeks
of fair Lutetia were still red from the fiery kisses of that
sun, and the bridal wreath was not yet quite faded on her
breast. At the street corners to be sure the *liberté, égalité,
fraternité* were here and there already effaced again. . . .
In the manners and even in the speech of the French there
is so much charming flattery, which costs so little, and is yet
so beneficial and refreshing. My soul, that poor sensitive
plant, which had contracted so for fear of the native rude-
ness, opened again to the flattering tones of French urban-
ity. God has given us our tongue in order that we may say
pleasant things to our fellow men."

He troubled himself little about his political mission,
but gave himself up to a study of the external aspect of
this new life. Paris was then the acknowledged centre of
culture and of frivolity. He visited the picture-galleries
and museums, the theatres and concerts and libraries. He
made acquaintance with the literary, social, and political
circles, and also acquaintances of a more questionable kind,
to which his poems bear witness. He dined in expensive
restaurants, and took part in that gaiety to which no other

city could then offer a parallel. It was a free, cosmopolitan world, which appealed to him greatly after the narrower life and more conventional ideals of Hamburg and Berlin, a world in which he was no longer conscious of any handicap of birth.

The rush and excitement of his early days in Paris are graphically described in the first letter which he wrote to Varnhagen on 27th June : " I am drowning here in the maelstrom of events, the daily flood-tide, the roaring revolution." More than a year later, too, we find in a letter to Hiller of 24th October, 1832, the often-quoted words : " If anyone asks you how I am here, say : ' Like a fish in the water,' or rather, tell the people that if one fish in the sea asks another how he feels, he replies : ' Like Heine in Paris '. " And in November of the same year he speaks of " the grandiose city where every day an act of world history is staged."

Yet, nice and enjoyable as all this was, and much as it appealed to Heine, who above all things liked a good time, and an open-handed and spacious mode of life, it all cost a great deal of money, and he was now, as ever, in financial straits. And though he never succeeded in balancing his expenses and receipts, he had to keep them in some sort of relationship to one another. There is a very interesting letter of 24th August, 1832 to Friedrich Merckel, which accounts concisely for the general character of his literary production in these years, and shows the influence of his financial irresponsibility upon his work :

" I am living through many great experiences in Paris, watch with my own eyes world history in the making, am on a friendly footing with the greatest heroes, and shall one day, if I live, be a great historian. In writing of a belletristic nature I have lately had little success. The

whirlpool in which I was swimming was too strong for me
to be able to do any free poetic work. . . . I have written
few poems—otherwise I am more industrious than usual,
for the simple reason that I need six times as much money
in Paris as in Germany."

What then was the work which his present position pre-
eminently fitted him to do ? He was obviously most
favourably placed for enlightening his fellow-countrymen
on the turn of events in Paris ; that work lay immediately
to his hand. At the same time he could re-interpret his
fellow-countrymen to the French, for the presentation by
Madame de Staël stood badly in need of revision. Here
perhaps his very exile might be an advantage, and enable
him at a distance to see German affairs in a truer perspective. To some extent he did gain that broader outlook, and
for a time profited from his aloofness, though as years
went on he lost touch with the currents of German development, and fell more and more into that *a priori* general-
ising on political matters to which he was always inclined.

His immediate work was done for Cotta, for whose
Augsburger Allgemeine Zeitung he wrote from December,
1831 to June, 1832, a series of articles, which at the end of
the latter year appeared in book form under the title of
Französische Zustände. The constitutional monarchy of
Louis Philippe, the citizen-king " Egalité ", appealed to
him in principle, and he defended it against the various
attacks from the Carlists, the Bonapartists and the Republicans. He is indignant at the shameless treatment of the
king in the Carlist papers. Being a royalist by natural
inclination, he is becoming one in Paris from conviction.
He thinks that Louis Philippe might do a great work :
" He ought to place himself at the head of European liberty,
merge its interests in his own, identify himself and liberty,

and whereas one of his predecessors boldly said, ' *L'Etat c'est moi* ', he ought to proclaim with still greater self-confidence, ' *La liberté c'est moi !* ' "

However, he has not assumed this mission, and Heine criticises him freely ; he doubts his genuineness, and how far he is serious with his " citizen-kingship " :

" Louis Philippe has forgotten that he owes his throne to the principle of the sovereignty of the people, and now in his miserable infatuation he would like to maintain it by a quasi-legitimacy, by alliance with absolute princes, and by a continuation of the Restoration period." The king was cutting off a part of the Tuileries gardens for his private use by the much-discussed *fossés des Tuileries*, and Heine takes this as a symbol of the moat which the king is digging between himself and his people. His similarity to the absolute kings grows daily greater, he says.

Heine's criticism of the July monarchy, of the régime of the *juste-milieu*, strikes one as on the whole fairly mild, especially for him, but once again he did not succeed in pleasing either party. It was held to be more damaging to the French Government than all the attacks of the opposition papers, and through Metternich's influence Cotta was induced to stop its further publication. In another quarter it was liked even less, namely, in the camp of the German republicans in Paris. Heine had not been the first of the German liberal leaders to be attracted to Paris by the revolution ; others had hastened thither forthwith in the first flush of the enthusiasm which it evoked. When Heine came, the German colony took it for granted that this bold and outspoken champion of liberty would join them in their work of uniting all the republican elements of Europe in the great work of " liberation " ! Their leader was Börne, a doctrinaire and fanatic, but single-minded in his devotion to the cause of liberty. Their organ was the "Tribune", whose violent irresponsible propaganda was rather a nuisance than a real danger to the French or any other government. They all took themselves very seriously, and lacked Heine's many-sided interests. He was a man-of-the-world, who mixed in fashionable circles, and this was in itself enough to make him suspect to moralists of the type of Börne. A clash was inevitable, and between these two it came before many years were over.

Moreover, their instinct was not so entirely wrong; Heine was not in fact with his whole heart in the " cause ". He believed in "emancipation" as strongly as any of them, but it was an emancipation from the class privilege of the Metternich régime, from the aristocrats and priests around the throne, and no doctrinaire objection to the throne itself, for which he fought. It is to Heine's credit that he was clear-sighted enough to see that monarchy might give as great liberty as any other form of government, and that the mere presence of a king at the head of a constitutional government would not necessarily make it any less essentially democratic. Added to this was probably the personal equation; his vanity could not be offended by a single ruler, whose social position was so unquestionably above his own, and allegiance to whom carried with it no feeling of personal inferiority, whereas the arrogation of social superiority on the part of the aristocrats galled his sensitive pride, and the Jew in him resented the power and influence of the representatives of the established church. We are so used to a certain measure of democratic equality to-day that it is not easy for us to realise what social prejudice still meant in the first half of the nineteenth century for a highly-gifted, sensitive, proud member of the middle-class, let alone a Jew.

However, all this was too mild meat for the fiery German republicans ; the air of philosophic detachment of Heine's articles filled them with suspicion ; there seemed little left of the " flame and sword " in this Paris Heine, who could contemplate entrusting the honour of the " cause " to the hands of an Orleanist king. Heine himself was well aware of the suspicions which he had aroused. He was, it is true, getting rather tired of politics, and would have been glad to devote himself to poetry and fiction. All the same he could not make up his mind to resign the leadership which he had won ; vanity and interest probably combined to hold him back from such a course. If he lost the " far-resounding voice ", he would have been as a journalist of no more value than the rest of them, and for all the excellent work seen in some parts of the *Zustände*, such as the striking description of the cholera days in Paris, and the piquant things which he again wrote about his bugbears, the English, there was in them little of the sensationalism which had come to be associated with his name.

And so he resolved to show these critics of his that the old fire was still there. He wrote to Immermann on 22nd May, 1832 : " I am now on a peace-footing with the existing order, and even if I do not yet disarm, it is only on account of the demagogues, with whom I have had and still have a lot of trouble. When I would not share their crazy folly, these people, the enemies of all moderation, were determined to force me to resign as a tribune. But that I had no desire to do."

The Preface to the *Zustände*, which was to give the party of the left proof of his orthodoxy, contains some of Heine's most bitter attacks, especially against Prussia. Apart from any motives of expediency suggested above, it was inspired, too, by a perfectly genuine indignation against the atrocious *Bundestagsbeschlüsse* of 28th June, 1832, one of the most crudely reactionary of all the measures originated by the Metternich régime. Heine begins by declaring that his life is devoted to the work of emancipation, which is his office, and that he will not return home as long as one of the noble fugitives, whose enthusiasm has drowned perhaps the voice of their reason, remains in exile. Austria is acknowledged as an open, honest foe, who has never denied her fight against Liberalism ; Metternich has never ogled with the Goddess of Freedom. But upon Prussia are poured out all the vials of his wrath ; words of such concentrated bitterness as even Heine has hardly excelled on any other occasion, except perhaps in the unpardonable poem, *Der Wechselbalg*, which is almost hysterical in its hatred. Here again we have to allow for the personal equation. Prussia was a land which treated Jews with scant consideration, and had failed to find place for him in its service ; Prussians were, along with Hamburgers and Englishmen, his own very special antipathy :

" I never trusted this Prussia, this long, canting martinet, with the capacious stomach and the big mouth and the corporal's stick, which it dips in holy water before it strikes. I could never stand this philosophical Christian militarism, this mixture of white beer, lies and sand. I have always felt a repulsion, a deep repulsion for this Prussia, this stiff, hypocritical, sanctimonious Prussia, this Tartuffe among the nations."

He makes another protestation of his monarchistic bias, and a show of impartiality, and of praising the many virtues of Frederick William III., but it only leads up to a thing which he could not expect any monarch to forgive, and which many Germans have still not forgotten or forgiven, his picture of the king as " the Prussian ass ", which, when all the kings of Europe are banded together against Napoleon, gives the dying lion the last kick.

Heine, indeed, professed surprise that this Preface was considered in Germany to be too bitter, and in a Preface to the Preface, which he wrote a month afterwards, protested against the attempts to discredit the principles he championed in the public estimation by representing them as " French revolutionary doctrines ", and their spokesman as the " French party in Germany ". " Germany can be no longer deceived by the old tricks ; even the Germans have seen that national hatred is only a means for enslaving one nation through another, and there are no longer any nations at all in Europe (almost these identical words had already been used by him in the *Reise von München nach Genua*), but only two parties, of which the one, called Aristocracy, considers itself privileged by birth, and usurps all the splendours of civic society, whilst the other, called Democracy, vindicates its inalienable human rights, and wants to see all privilege of birth abolished in the name of reason. In truth, you ought to call us the heavenly party, not the French ; for that Declaration of the Rights of Man, upon which our whole political philosophy is based, does not come from France, where to be sure it has been most gloriously proclaimed, not even from America, whence Lafayette imported it, but it comes from Heaven, the eternal home of Reason."

In these words speaks the complete cosmopolitanism of these thinkers of the nineteenth century, which had had its counterpart in the eighteenth, and was to have a startling revival in the twentieth. If Heine had been suspected by the German colony of anti-liberal tendencies, and of being a renegade to the cause of freedom, he must have convinced them at any rate that the old fire was still there to be kindled, and there is no doubt that he did work himself into a genuine enthusiasm in this glowing Preface. Nor was he in fact so surprised at the feeling it caused in Germany, as, by an artistic fiction, he pretended to be. He writes to Varnhagen in the July of the following year : " This passionate product of my anger at the resolutions of the Federal Diet will perhaps for ever prevent my return to Germany ; but it will perhaps save me from being strung up on a lamp-post at the next insurrection, since my dear countrymen cannot now accuse me any longer of an understanding with Prussia. Rascals like Börne and Co. have had their fangs drawn by it, as far as I am concerned at any rate."

It was a decisive step, and he went through a series of hesitancies before deciding upon publication. He had been virtually driven by circumstances into a position which forced from him this manifesto, and that at a time when he would gladly have left politics alone. He was not a single-minded, whole-hearted fanatic like Börne, though his whole soul could flare up into a geniune passion when he was confronted with any glaring act of injustice or oppression. Nor, on the other hand, had he the strength of mind, or, as he saw it, the coldness, of his great counterpart Goethe, to renounce crusades and attend to his own poetic business. Hence all his political work brought him little of the joy of the true crusader, and at the same time the suspicions of less complex characters, who knew nothing of the inner conflict from which he suffered.

Meanwhile he had begun another work, which was to be the main undertaking of his first Paris decade, and which was to occupy in it very much the same position that the *Reisebilder* did in the twenties. This was *Der Salon*. It consisted likewise of four volumes, which appeared from 1834 to 1840, and was even more heterogeneous than the earlier production. The loose framework suited Heine's nature, since he was essentially a fragmentist. His imagination was too active, and his wit too lively, for a long work of sustained power, and show at their best where the form laid the lightest of fetters upon him. This " picture-gallery " of his opens, it is true, with an account of the *Salon* of 1831, but that would be but a poor justification for the title of the whole work. The name is used, just as *silvae* was in Latin, and *Wäldchen* in German, to describe writings which, while grouped together, each retain their own independence.

The first instalment of the *Salon, Französische Maler,* was one of the earliest things Heine wrote in Paris, and was indeed prior to the *Zustände,* which we have already discussed. It deals with the exhibition of paintings in the *Salon* of 1831, which, according to Heine, was by general consent the most remarkable that France had ever seen. It is not the technical aspect of the paintings that interests him, but rather their subject-matter. The pictures he discusses are mainly historical works, of Vernet, Delacroix, Delaroche and others, and they furnish him with abundant material for his favourite themes, while he even dramatises the galleries themselves through the spectators he places before the paintings, and the dialogue he puts in their mouths. Louis Philippe, " le roi des barricades, le roi par la grâce du peuple souverain," gets his due share of not too friendly comment, and he does not omit to mention the famous caricatures in the papers and on the walls of the houses, showing the king's head in the shape of a pear.

Above all he is interested in the new school of painting in France as a manifestation of the new age. " My old prophecy[1] of the end of the *Kunstperiode*, which began at Goethe's cradle and will end at his coffin, appears to be near its fulfilment. The present art must perish, because its principle is rooted in the outworn old régime, in the past of the Holy Roman Empire. Therefore, like all the faded relics of that past, it stands in most unedifying conflict with the present. This conflict, and not the trend of the age itself, is inimical to art ; on the contrary, this trend of the age ought to be beneficial to it, as once in Athens and Florence, where art unfolded its most glorious flowers in the midst of the fiercest storms of war and party conflicts. Those Greek and Florentine artists led, to be sure, no isolated life of art, working at leisure with their souls hermetically closed against the griefs and joys of the age ; on the contrary, their works were only the dreaming mirror of their age, and they themselves were real men, whose personality was as great as their creative power. The new age will give birth to a new art, which will be in an inspired harmony with it, which will not need to borrow its symbols from the faded past, and which cannot fail indeed to produce a new technique, different from that of the past. Till then, in colours and in sounds, may the most ecstatic subjectivity, unfettered individualism, the divine gift of free personality in the full joy of life, have play, for that is after all more salutary than the dead, phantom life of the old art."

Here again, as once before in the already quoted letter to Moser of 1st July, 1825, Heine joins issue with Goethe, and claims a place, not as his like nor his equal, but as his successor. This doctrine of the re-union of life and art was the programme of the new school of " Young German " writers, and if Heine did not actually formulate

[1] In his article on *Die deutsche Literatur* by Menzel in 1828.

that programme, and coin its title and battle-cry—Ludolf Wienbarg in his *Ästhetische Feldzüge* in 1834 first used the term " Junges Deutschland " in relation to literature— he was the greatest purely literary representative of the new tendency, and the one who did in effect become for the world at large Goethe's successor in the field of German poetry.

The other chief parts of the first volume of the *Salon* were a collection of poems, later embodied in the *Neue Gedichte* in 1844, and *Aus den Memoiren des Herrn von Schnabelewopski*. The latter is one of the maddest mixtures that Heine ever wrote : the nearest analogy to it being the *Bäder von Lucca* of his Italian journey. Here as there Heine shows his great comic power, and makes us feel what a writer of comedies was lost in him. We have such a gallery of characters, indeed, as he nowhere else presented. It is one of the liveliest of his writings, and the most full of movement. It is as a whole one of the most frivolous and the most coarsely sensuous ; and yet there are serious tones all the same. The brief character- isation of the father of the hero is obviously reminiscent of Heine's own father, and is one of the touching tributes which he paid to that well-loved parent. The description of Hamburg is of the type known from the earlier days of the *Harzreise*, a parody of the usual guide-book style, while its tone is no more flattering than his other references to the stolidly-prosperous city of his own mercantile failure and his unhappy love.

One of the best-known and finest things it contains is Heine's version of the story of the *Flying Dutchman*, which by a poetic fiction he describes as seen by him in a theatre in Amsterdam, and upon which Wagner based his famous opera. Very characteristic is the mixture of burlesque, wit, and seriousness in the disputations on the existence of

God by Schnabelewopski and his six table companions. The faithful champion of Deism is Simson, the little Frankfort Jew, and he is made the occasion of one of Heine's wittiest sallies, which at the same time conceals a deep and tragic satire on the contempt for Jews in Christian lands. The Jews are always the most obedient deists and subservient henchmen of their Jehovah, the old fetish, who will no longer have anything to do with their whole race, and has been transformed into a God who is Pure Spirit :

" Methinks this God–Pure Spirit, this parvenu of heaven, who is now so moral, so cosmopolitan and universal, bears a secret grudge against the poor Jews, who knew Him in His first crude form, and daily in their synagogues remind him of his former obscure circumstances. Perhaps he no longer wants to know that he is of Palestinian origin, and was once the God of Abraham, Isaac and Jacob, and was then called Jehovah."

The completed first volume of the *Salon*, when it appeared in 1834, was accompanied by a Preface written in the October of the preceding year. There Heine repeats what he had already said more than once ; that he would gladly give up his political office to live his own life and write poems, comedies and novels. The ways of some of the demagogues so disgust him, that he hates everything that bears the name of patriotism. To Immermann on 19th December, 1832, he wrote: " For Heaven's sake do not take me for a Saviour of my Country." And to his mother now, in announcing to her the appearance of the volume on 4th March, 1834, he used the very same expression : " I have received the *Salon* at last ; there are some horrible misprints in it. Many ribald stories. The latter was political intention. I wanted to give a certain turn to public opinion. I would rather be called a guttersnipe than a serious Saviour of my Country. The latter is at this moment no desirable reputation. The demagogues are furious with me ; they say I shall soon appear publicly as an aristocrat. I think they are wrong. I am withdrawing from politics. The fatherland may look for another fool."

What Heine always dreaded above all was banality. The over-statements of the demagogues drive him to ribaldry by the same impulse that made him add the ironic reaction at the end of many of his own most soaring lyrical outbursts. However, his personal inclinations must be set aside, for " all my words and songs blossom forth from a great divinely-joyous springtime idea, which, if not better, is at least as respectable as that gloomy, mouldy, Ash-Wednesday idea, which has mournfully deflowered our beautiful Europe, and peopled it with ghosts and Tartuffes. . . . We do not seize an idea, but the idea seizes us, and enslaves us and drives us into the arena to fight for it like conscript gladiators. We are indeed not the masters, but the servants of the word." This new joyous springtime idea was the Saint-Simonian doctrine, and the poems in the volume that would " call forth the sighs of the sanctimonious of all colours " were those in which some phases of that doctrine found expression, and especially those contained in the group " *Verschiedene*."

It is not necessary here to give an exposition of the Saint-Simonian doctrines, the more so as we possess in Miss Butler's recent volume[1] such an excellent account of the movement, more particularly in its relations to Germany. The first mention of Saint-Simonism in Heine's letters is found at the beginning of 1831, before he had left Ger-

[1] E. M. Butler, *The Saint-Simonian Religion in Germany*, Cambridge, 1926.

many, and the new doctrine may probably be counted as one of the factors that brought about his final decision to go to Paris. On 10th February, 1831, he wrote to Hartwig Hesse, a wealthy Hamburg patron of letters, giving an extract from his new gospel, and asking for his support, whether for the cause directly, or for himself as its priest, is not quite clear. In any case he feels himself upheld by an " extraordinary self-confidence that is akin to religious pride." The other letter of the Hamburg time is addressed to Varnhagen on 1st April, 1831: " I dream every night that I am packing my traps and going to Paris, to breathe fresh air and devote myself entirely to the sacred emotions of my new religion, and perhaps to be consecrated as its priest."

What the Saint-Simonian doctrines seemed to offer to Heine was not so much new ideas, as a resolution of the conflict of his own, and a positive, constructive philosophy of life. Heine's whole life was a struggle, a more or less conscious struggle, between the two sides of his nature, between the spiritual and the sensual side, the Nazarene and the Hellenic conception. Hitherto one or the other principle had fought for mastery and attained it for a time ; we have seen him swinging between the one extreme and the other. We have seen him in a fervour of self-devotion consecrating himself to the service of the " idea " as a " Ritter von dem heil'gen Geist." In that mood he saw himself as the antithesis of Goethe ; the visionary inspired by the idea to the point of sacrifice, opposed to the epicurean, for whom enjoyment of life is the highest good, as he wrote to Moser already in 1825. In the *Reise von München nach Genua* he declares that his poetry was for him never more than a consecrated toy to be used for divine ends, and that on his coffin must be laid the sword of a good soldier in the Wars of Liberation of mankind.

Yet in the *Bäder von Lucca* we see him swept away by the fullness of life, and, like some ancient pagan, revelling through Tuscan nights on the heights of the Apennines. And that polarity is seen from these early years right through his life, and accounts for the many dissonances and palpable contradictions which form the great difficulty of any true appreciation of him.

In these circumstances it is not surprising that Heine saw in the "new gospel" his own personal salvation. Tossed to and fro on the stormy sea of his own conflicting inclinations, he saw in Saint-Simonism a philosophy which could reconcile those antitheses, and instead of demanding the renunciation of one or the other side of his nature, harmonise them in a higher synthesis. He, too, believed, as they did, that the age of gold was not in the past but before us, that an earthly paradise was to be preferred to one in the hereafter ; that mankind was in a state of progress, and life not an expiation for a primal fall from grace. He, too, rejected the gloomy doctrine of the mortification of the flesh.

This new gospel of Heine the thinker, Heine the poet crystallised in a brief poem, which is among other things an example of his wonderful gift of concise and witty expression :

> " Auf diesem Felsen bauen wir
> Die Kirche von dem dritten,
> Dem dritten neuen Testament ;
> Das Leid ist ausgelitten.

> " Vernichtet ist das Zweierlei,
> Das uns so lang betöret ;
> Die dumme Leiberquälerei
> Hat endlich aufgehöret.

" Hörst du den Gott im finstern Meer ?
Mit tausend Stimmen spricht er.
Und siehst du über unserm Haupt
Die tausend Gotteslichter ?

" Der heil'ge Gott der ist im Licht
Wie in den Finsternissen ;
Und Gott ist alles, was da ist ;
Er ist in unsern Küssen ".

It may at first sight seem strange to find this poem
among the *Verschiedene*. It is certainly bold, especially
as the opening is an obvious echo of the words in St.
Matthew xvi, 18 : " Auf diesen Felsen will ich bauen
meine Gemeine." But Heine, in the first flush of his new-
found solution to the riddle of life, was nothing if not filled
with exuberant confidence, and the challenge here to " the
sanctimonious of all colours " is in keeping with his mood.
The surprising thing is to find it among the poems to Seraphine, since they have none of the coarse sensuousness
found in some of the other groups, in which Heine flaunted
the new " emancipation of the flesh ".

One is indeed inclined to think, in spite of Elster, that
there is something in the allegation that these poems, apart
from the one in question, were actually written earlier,
in 1827, and that by some strange whim Heine afterwards
placed this poem where it now stands. It certainly is
very effective among these sea lyrics, with its setting of
rock and wave, and has all the element of surprise which
Heine so dearly loved. It belongs in subject to the
Zeitgedichte, but placed in isolation amongst them the
effectiveness of the imagery would have been lost.

If Heine's interest in Saint-Simonism had been awakened

even before he left Germany, he lost no time on arriving in Paris in gaining first-hand knowledge of the movement, and getting into touch with its representatives. It is somewhat remarkable that the first works in Paris show little traces of the new influence ; it is hardly mentioned in the *Französische Zustände*, or in the first volume of the *Salon*. He was collecting the material and, as so often with him, it did not immediately take literary shape. Only with the second volume of the *Salon* and the *Romantische Schule* is it seen how deeply the new religion had engaged his thoughts.

The famous Père Enfantin, the propounder of the doctrine of the " emancipation of the flesh ", appears to have attracted him especially, and he attended the meetings in the Salle Taitbout. He was, in fact, present on 22nd January, 1832, when the government descended upon it and closed it, as we know from his letter of three days later to Cotta. There appears to have been a mutual sympathy between the two men, though there is little direct information as to their personal relationship. Heine dedicated *De l'Allemagne* to him, and was rewarded by some fatherly advice on the avoidance of profane pleasantries in his next work.

Yet Heine did not surrender himself blindly to the famous fascination, or become a confessing member of the church. That religion, which at a distance had seemed to offer such a simple and satisfying creed, was seen at close quarters to contain endless complexities and seeds of dissension among its members. Even when Enfantin retired on 12th April, 1832, with his forty apostles, to the monastic life of Menilmontant, Heine was still studying and learning. This crisis in the church, and the celibate life which was the later phase, were little calculated to induce Heine to throw in his lot whole-heartedly with them. His attitude is clear from the letter to Varnhagen of 22nd May, 1832, which is his first clear and explicit statement on the whole matter : " I am now much occupied with the history of the French (July) Revolution and with Saint-Simonism. I am going to write books about both. But I have still many studies to make. However, I have come to understand a lot of things this last year by watching the party manoeuvres and the Saint-Simonian developments. . . . The retreat of the Saint-Simonians will perhaps prove very useful to the doctrine ; it will pass into wiser hands. Especially the political part, the theory of property will be better worked out. For my part I am really interested only in the religious ideas, which only needed to be propounded to come to life, sooner or later. Germany will fight longest for its spiritualism, ' mais l'avenir est à nous.' "

Heine, after all, was too independent a thinker ever to adopt any creed ready-made, and much less one of the various versions of Saint-Simonism. What he did produce was not the projected book on the doctrine, of which he speaks above, but his own reaction to the stimulations of St. Simon, Bazard and Enfantin and the other leaders of the school. This is seen in the two works which are the chief product of those first Paris years, *Die Romantische Schule* and *Zur Geschichte der Religion und Philosophie in Deutschland*. They are really parts of one work, as Heine himself pointed out—a survey of the whole of German intellectual life. Heine wrote them both originally in German, but had them translated for publication in French journals. The literary part was begun first, probably at the end of 1832, and appeared in *L'Europe Littéraire*, and at the same time in Paris under the title

*Zur Geschichte der neueren schönen Litteratur in Deutsch-
land,* later changed to the well known form, *Die Romantische Schule.* The other work, *Zur Geschichte der
Religion und Philosophie in Deutschland,* probably begun in
1833, appeared in 1834, in the *Revue des deux Mondes,*
while in the German edition it forms the second volume
of the *Salon.* A French edition of 1835, under the title
De l'Allemagne, contained both works, as well as the first
part of the *Elementargeister.*

The relation to the Saint-Simonian doctrine is even
more explicit in the second of the two, and it will be well
for that reason to consider it first. Moreover, Heine
himself tells us that it was originally intended as a general
introduction to the literature of Germany. Heine begins
by saying that he is not going to employ the technical
jargon of German philosophers, but show in plain language
the social importance of German theology and philosophy.
The fundamental idea of Christianity he sees in the
doctrine of the two principles of good and evil—the world
of the spirit represented by Christ, the world of matter by
Satan. To the former belongs our soul, to the latter our
body. The whole visible world, Nature, is accordingly
the original evil, and Satan, the Friend of Darkness, lures
us therewith to our destruction. We must renounce all
sensuous joys of life, mortifying our body, the fief of Satan,
in order that our soul may the more gloriously soar to the
bright heaven, the radiant realm of Christ. This is the
" catching disease " that has lasted throughout the whole
of the Middle Ages.

To that conception he opposes his new Saint-Simonian
gospel. " One day, when mankind wins back to perfect
health, when peace is restored between body and soul, and
they merge again in primal harmony, then men will

scarce be able to understand the artificial feud that Christianity created between them. Happier and more beautiful generations, who, begotten in free elective union, blossom forth in a religion of joy, will smile mournfully at their poor forefathers, who gloomily renounced all pleasures of this beautiful earth, and well-nigh faded away to pale spectres through the mortification of all warm, bright sensuousness! Yes, I assert confidently, our descendants will be more beautiful and happier than we. For I believe in progress. I believe that mankind is destined for happiness, and I hold therefore a higher opinion of the Deity than those pious people, who believe that He created man only for suffering. Already here on earth I should like to see, through the blessings of free political and industrial institutions, that happiness established, which, in the opinion of the pious, will be found only on the Last Day in heaven."

That was the nearest Heine ever got to a categorical statement of his new faith, of his hopes for a regeneration of mankind through the combined religious and industrial programme of the Saint-Simonians—a joyous worldliness, as opposed to the " other-worldliness " of the Christian dualism.

In the second book he still further elaborates the social and material aspect of the creed. " The great pronouncement of the Revolution, uttered by Saint-Just : ' le pain est le droit du peuple ', runs with us : ' le pain est le droit divin du peuple '. We fight, not for the human rights of man, but for the divine rights of man. In this and in many other things besides, we differ from the men of the Revolution. We want to be no Sansculottes, no frugal citizens, no cheap presidents : we are founding a democracy of equally glorious, equally holy, equally blessed Gods. You demand simple dress, frugal habits and unspiced dishes; we on the other hand demand nectar and ambrosia, purple mantles, precious perfumes, revelry, and splendour, dance of laughing nymphs, music and plays."

The main thesis of the work is the conflict between the two principles of spiritualism and sensualism. The final fate of Christianity will depend on whether we still have need of it. It was during eighteen centuries a blessing for suffering humanity, providential, holy, divine ; above all a great consolation. The national religion of Europe, however, is pantheism. In the Germanic north Christianity did not reject the old national gods as mere fiction, but gave them a real existence as evil spirits that tempted men to sin. This daemonology is developed in the earlier part of the work, and it was to be further expounded in the *Elementargeister* in 1835, and in his *Götter im Exil* in 1853. Even Luther believed in all kinds of dæmoniac beings, and his *Tischreden* are full of stories of goblins and witches.

The whole exposition pivots, as it were, on Spinoza, " the providential man ", who, long regarded with scorn and hatred, yet in our present day is attaining to an undisputed supremacy in the world of thought. Goethe, " the great heathen ", is acclaimed as the " Spinoza of poetry ", while the older Romantic poets were moved by a pantheistic instinct which they did not themselves understand. " The feeling which they took for a nostalgia for the Catholic mother-church was of deeper origin than they themselves realised, and their respect and love for the traditions of the Middle Ages, for its popular beliefs, daemonology, magic, witchcraft—it was all nothing more than a suddenly awakened but unconscious longing for the pantheism of the old Germanic world."

The way in which the Saint-Simonian doctrine appeared to him against the background of a deeper philosophic system is well brought out in the pages on Spinoza :

"God, who is called by Spinoza the one substance, and by the German philosophers the Absolute, is everything that is (the " Gott ist alles was da ist " of his poem). He is both matter and spirit ; both are equally divine, and whoever offends against divine matter is just as sinful as he who sins against the Holy Ghost. The Deists differ among themselves only in relation to the nature of this government. The Hebrews think of God as a fulminating tyrant, the Christians as a loving Father, the disciples of Rousseau, the whole Genevan school, think of him as a wise artist, who has constructed the world just as their father made his watches, and as connoisseurs they admire the work and praise the Master above. The first object of all our institutions is, therefore, the rehabilitation of mankind, the re-establishment of its dignity, its moral recognition, its religious consecration, its reconciliation with the spirit."

Such was Heine's reaction to a study of the Saint-Simonian doctrine at close quarters ; and far from bringing him into their camp, or making him a mere exponent of their views, it made him an independent critic, as appears plainly from the oft-quoted passage, which gives the central theme of the whole book :

"The Saint-Simonians have understood and aimed at something of the above sort. But they found themselves on unfavourable ground, and the materialism by which they were surrounded has overwhelmed them, at any rate for some time. In Germany they have been better appreciated. For Germany is the most favourable soil of pantheism ; it is the religion of our great thinkers, our best artists, and deism . . . in theory has there long been over-thrown. It survives only among the unthinking mass, without rational justification, like so much else. Nobody says so, but everybody knows it ; pantheism is the open secret in Germany. In fact we have outgrown deism. We are free, and want no fulminating tyrant. We are come of age and need no paternal tutelage. We are not the products of a great mechanic. Deism is a religion for serfs, for children, for Genevans, for watchmakers. Pantheism is the secret religion of Germany."

This was the conclusion that Heine in the last phase of his life, when in 1852 he wrote the preface to the second edition of the book, expressly recanted, declaring that " deism was still alive, and living its most living life."

The general survey of German philosophy which forms the body of the book need not here be reviewed, since, whatever its value as an introduction for his French public, it has no special objective value to-day. The interest now lies above all in the fine and spirited character-isations of some of the great personalities among the German thinkers, above all of two of his heroes, Luther, " not only the greatest, but also the most German man of our history ", and Lessing, " that wittiest man in Germany, who was at the same time the most honest." There is a tragic irony in the words he writes concerning the con-version to Catholicism of Fichte, " the man who once pronounced in Germany most boldly of all the religion of pantheism, who proclaimed most loudly of all the consecra-tion of Nature and the restoration of man to his divine rights. So many free-thinkers have been converted on their death-bed—but do not make too much to-do about it. These stories of conversion are at most a question of pathology."

At the end Heine assumes the mantle of the prophet, and warns his French readers of the horrible things that may be expected when the sleeping German giant—in whose latent might and fury he at all times firmly believed—should awaken. "The philosophic revolution is ended, the political revolution may soon begin. Then a play will be staged in Germany that will make the French Revolution look like a simple idyll. The nations will group themselves around Germany as on the steps of an amphitheatre to watch the mighty combats."

It is a warning that Heine often gave, but the kind of German Revolution he foresaw has still to make its appearance. Certainly those we have known since his day have not shown much of the "Berserkerwut." One might on the contrary say that there never were such idyllic revolutionaries as the Germans. As an example one might recount the fate of Frederick II, Grand Duke of Baden, who died in August 1928. When he abdicated after the Revolution of 22nd November, 1918, the Socialists passed a resolution expressing recognition of his services to the State, and on his seventieth birthday the Government conveyed to him its congratulations, and an expression of the affection and esteem in which he had always been held by the people.

Die Romantische Schule, too, has a certain Saint-Simonian background, but its real importance lies in the fact that it is a review of German literature by a critic who is himself a poet, and who is speaking mostly, though not always, at first hand. Heine begins by declaring his book to be, as it were, a continuation of Madame de Staël's *De l'Allemagne*, since the appearance of which a whole new literature has developed in Germany. The weakest part of her book, leaving aside its general character, is the treatment of the Romantic School, where she is following the suggestions of August Wilhelm von Schlegel. The Romantic School in Germany was something quite different from what is known by that name in France. It was nothing but the reawakening of the poetry of the Middle Ages, the characteristic tendency of which was the subjugation of matter by the spirit. So he formulates once again the antithesis of spiritualism and sensualism. We have, too, an echo of the Saint-Simonian theory of organic and critical periods. Christian spiritualism was a wholesome reaction against the colossal materialism of the Roman Empire, and beneficial for the vigorous youthful nations of the world.

In a very suggestive passage he discusses the essential difference of classical and romantic art. " Classical art had only to represent the finite, and its forms could be identical with the idea of the artist. Romantic art had to represent the infinite, and purely spiritual relationships, and it had recourse to a system of traditional symbols, or rather to the parabolic, just as Christ tried to exemplify his spiritualistic ideas by all kinds of beautiful parables. Hence the mystical, enigmatical, wonderful and extravagant elements in the works of art of the Middle Ages."

The general tone of this survey of German Romanticism is directed against the " pilgrimage to Rome " of many of the Romantics, against the re-introduction of that Catholic, feudal mode of thought, that chivalry and priestcraft, which had been preached in art and letters. Freedom of thought and protestantism have to be named in one breath, since they are related to one another as mother and daughter. This polemical tendency, and the Saint-Simonian standpoint, can be noted not only in the criticism of the school as a whole, but also in the attitude to the several poets. Lessing is touched upon, and Heine concludes his brief reference with the words that he was " of all German writers the one whom he most loved." Goethe once more occupies a good share of his attention, and we find a mixture of praise and blame. There is a good deal of personal feeling in the charge that Goethe was like Louis XI, who suppressed the great nobles and promoted the *tiers état*. " Goethe was afraid of every independent, original writer, and praised all insignificant mediocrities ; he went, indeed, so far that at last it counted as a brevet of mediocrity to have been praised by him."

He dwells at some length on the many-sided opposition to Goethe, and emphasises again that he himself has never attacked in Goethe the poet, but only the man. The truly great artist-critic speaks in the comparison he draws between Goethe and Schiller, and particularly big is his fine appreciation of a side of Goethe's creative power which he did not himself possess in a very high degree, the gift of endowing the characters of his novels and plays with a complete and rounded and independent existence.

Goethe's *Faust* he declares to have become the lay bible of the Germans, and he would be no German, he says, if he mentioned the work without adding some explanatory thoughts. His special contribution is to fit the theme into the frame-work of Saint-Simonian ideas :

" The German people is itself that learned Doctor Faust ; it is itself that spiritualist, who has at last grasped the unsatisfying nature of spirit, and longs for material enjoyments, and restores its rights to the flesh ; even though under the influence of the symbolism of Catholic poetry, in which God figures as the representative of spirit, and the devil as the representative of the flesh, that rehabilitation of the flesh was described as a falling away from God, as a pact with the devil."

The description of Goethe's appearance has already been quoted in an earlier chapter. Only one sentence might be again referred to here, since we see it in a very special light in this Saint-Simonian period of Heine's life. "This dignified body was never bent by worm-like Christian humility ; the features of this face were never disturbed by Christian contortion ; these eyes were not those of a timid Christian sinner, not turned piously heavenwards, not swimming with emotion—no, his eyes were calm as those of a God."

A good deal of the second book is devoted to the Schlegels, and August Wilhelm is treated with very scant respect, his person and character coming off even worse than his works. There is so much gall in the picture he draws of Schlegel in his later life, that we may confidently assume that something more than a mere abstract contempt for his pretensions called forth the change of front towards a man whom he had once so admired and praised. Even the treatment of him as a writer, and the statement that, apart from his metrical studies, he is only of the second or even the third rank, is generous in comparison with the mockery poured on " this fabulously ridiculous personage, who unfortunately has not yet found a Molière to put him on the stage."

There are interesting passages which show a valuable insight into the genius of many writers of the modern period, Tieck, Novalis, Uhland—who is treated much better and more justly here than in the *Schwabenspiegel*—Jean Paul and others, while Heine has nowhere surpassed his fine characterisation of *Des Knaben Wunderhorn*, or of the *Nibelungenlied*, which he associates with it as the other great and unique achievement of German literature.

Halfway through the third of the three books of which it is composed, Heine comes to the writers of *Das junge Deutschland*, who " will not make any distinction between life and letters, who will never separate politics from science, art and religion, and who are at the same time artists, tribunes and apostles." We might imagine that he was now launched on a theme whose actuality would require a very full and detailed treatment. Yet somewhat surprisingly, after a brief eulogy of Laube's " great flaming heart ", Gutzkow's " soul full of poetry ", and a mere mention of Wienbarg and Gustav Schlesier, he is, with Jean Paul, back to the subject of pure literature, and we are able to delight once more in his illuminating survey of the German poets, without being much troubled with those political themes and school maxims, which were already beginning to wear a little thin, and in which he was rapidly beginning to lose his interest. Whatever its faults may be, and it is not free from faults, especially those of bias and personal malice, one would give many volumes of his political writings for this fresh, spontaneous, witty, stimulating book, this poet's history of poetry, in which he was indebted for most of his thoughts to no one but himself, and the style of which he could have borrowed from none.

At the end of this survey of Heine's work as bilingual interpreter in the first Paris years, it is instructive to see how he appeared in the eyes of a distinguished French critic, and the place he had already conquered for himself in France. In his article of 8th August, 1833, in the *Premiers Lundis*—the *Romantische Schule* had appeared in its French dress in *L'Europe Littéraire* in the March,

April and May of that year—Sainte-Beuve mixes some
adverse criticism with his appreciation, and interestingly
enough finds Heine to suffer, from the French point of
view, from an excess of wit, but he recognises very generously the importance of what Heine had done. The
whole article is well worth reading in this connection, but
we can reproduce here only some of the most apposite
passages :

"Sous la Restauration, on se figurait beaucoup trop
l'Allemagne littéraire et poétique soumise sans contesta-
tion aux pieds de Goethe, l'Allemagne philosophique
obéissant de plein gré aux formules de Kant ou de Hégel,
l'Allemagne politique sans velléité ni chance de se déclarer.
La pensée d'outre-Rhin, qui nous avait d'abord été
révélée et préconisée par madame de Staël, continuait
d'être interprétée chez nous par des disciples et des héritiers
de cette femme célèbre. Les diverses additions qui
s'étaient faites à la première connaissance si vague et si
lyrique, les détails plus précis, les analyses et les anecdotes
se rapportaient naturellement au même point de vue. . . .

"M. Heine n'était pas connu chez nous avant la révolu-
tion de juillet, et aujourd'hui il est tout à fait naturalisé ;
il est des nôtres autant que le spirituel Grimm l'a jamais
été . . .

"M. Heine est beaucoup plus railleur qu'il ne convient
à notre indifférence acquise ou à notre religiosité renais-
sante. . . . Notre juste et droit sens a, en outre,
quelque peine à le suivre dans sa logique brisée, saccadée
qu'interceptent à chaque pas les fusées de la métaphore.
Pour tout dire, M. Heine sera davantage encore à notre
niveau de Français quand il aura un peu moins d'esprit ".

A considerable amount of space has been devoted to the

writings of these few years, but they did, in fact, represent the most important phase of Heine's work as an interpreter between the two countries, and on the whole his greatest phase as a prose-writer, and for these reasons deserve very special consideration.

Chapter Eight

GATHERING CLOUDS

If the first four or five years in Paris were a time of high hopes and confidence, when Heine felt " like a fish in the water " and was physically, in general, well and buoyant, " at the zenith of his fat," the seeds of future trouble were being sown, and the storm-clouds soon began to gather about him. He had hoped from Saint-Simonism a synthesis of the spiritual and sensuous sides of his nature, which should allow him to revel in the fullest expression of both, but he never achieved the longed-for peace of a final harmony. If the " twofoldness " failed to disappear, it was certainly not due to an excessive mortification of the flesh. Heine was always a good liver, whether he could afford it or not ; though a very moderate drinker, and never a smoker, he was fond of rich food. His way of life was costly, his whole attitude the aristocratic one, that expects as a right the best of everything. However, he was not a millionaire, and the shifts and straits, the beggings and borrowings of his German days, were merely transplanted to French conditions.

The kind of society reflected in the poems to *Verschiedene* would easily have swallowed up all the money that he could lay hands on, but towards the end of 1834 he made an acquaintance which, if from the outset on a somewhat higher plane, and financially for the moment less disastrous, was to prove the cause of his permanent and irretrievable enslavement. From that time to the end his life was a constant struggle against financial embarrassment. Sometimes he was staggering under a load of debt, sometimes he was temporarily relieved. He bore the burden, it is true, with a cynical levity, which would have formed another qualification for certain types of aristocratic society of his day, but it led him all the same into many undignified or degrading positions, and indirectly, through disappointment over his uncle's legacy, was probably the immediate cause of the final physical catastrophe.

It was in October, 1834, that Heine first made the acquaintance of Crescentia Eugénie Mirat. Mathilde, as Heine calls her, was an illegitimate child, who had come to Paris from the country four years before ; she was now nineteen and was an assistant in the shoe-shop of her aunt. Heine was almost thirty-seven, so their respective ages were very much the same as those of Goethe and Christiane at their first meeting. The comparison naturally suggests itself, for in both cases the attraction was a purely physical one, without foundation in any intellectual sympathy or understanding. It was a case of that primitive conflict of the sexes transcending all other human relationships which, in its tragic aspect, was one of Thomas Hardy's great themes. Mathilde was even lower in the social scale, and in upbringing and education, than Christiane, for she had learnt nothing before she met Heine, and she learnt nothing and cared to learn nothing afterwards. Heine tried later the experiment of sending her to a convent school, but without result. He tried to teach her German, but she never got beyond a few stock phrases. She knew her " Henri " was a poet, but nothing of his poetry, except that it was one of the sources of their income, and useful for gratifying her expensive tastes. All attempts to establish an intellectual or spiritual sympathy, therefore, failed ; and yet the attraction, the mutual attraction, did not cease with the burning out of the first flames of passion, as by all the rules of the conventional programme it should have done. After all his experience, including women of culture, whom he admired but did not love, and venal beauties whom he loved but of whom he quickly tired, he found in this typical Parisian grisette some mysterious charm of sex, which bound him to her for life.

It is customary to speak of Mathilde as Heine's fate, of the relationship as one of the calamities of his life, presumably on the assumption that if Heine had not linked his life to hers, he would have made a " sensible " marriage, or otherwise established a more suitable *ménage*. Knowing what we do of him, it is surely at least as arguable that if he had not met Mathilde he would never have married at all, and that neither morally, physically, or financially would he have been any better off. She, at any rate, brought him a good deal of happiness of a sort, and he was certainly not the type of man to be made happy by any conventional recipe. So, while his connection with Mathilde was certainly far from ideal, and though it certainly did rivet upon him for good the chains of economic slavery, it is an exaggeration to make a tragedy of it.

When Heine met her, Mathilde had, by all accounts, very considerable beauty of face and person. He himself describes her as " round and buxom, always cheerful, amiable, faithful and honest." It was no doubt that eternal cheerfulness that formed her greatest permanent charm for him, her spontaneity and artlessness, her life and naturalness, the fact that she was a near approach to that mythical being, " a child of nature ". Her chatter and noise might annoy him, her whims and caprices might rack his nerves, her parrot almost drive him to despair, but she was life and vitality. She was entire, and perhaps the most refreshing thing on earth to one who was himself torn all ways by conflict and doubt, by thought and theory, by ambition and the despair of its realisation. The very fact that she knew and cared little for his poetry was in this way an added attraction, for here was somebody who took him, not as a Christian or a renegade Jew, as a patriot or a traitor, but merely as a man. It is no use saying that he ought not to have loved her, since he obviously did, and to blame him for establishing a free union with her is correct, but meaningless in view of the circumstances of Heine's life at the time. He, of course, never thought of marrying her, while she, though not willing to be treated as one of the " Verschiedene ", was probably quite ready to accept his protection, and, to judge by the apparent evidence of one of the poems, with the approval of her aunt.

Of the passion by which Heine was carried away from the outset we have abundant evidence in his letters. The first reference is in a letter to August Lewald of 11th April, 1835, in which he begins by excusing his failure to reply, by saying that he received it at a time when he was up to the neck in a love-affair, from which he had not yet emerged. Even then he did not apparently regard it as more than a passing affair, like so many others, and later in the same letter he says that there will shortly be a change in him, and that he will get to work again. Other letters show how all-consuming it had been. " Since October nothing has been of the slightest importance to me which did not directly bear on it. I have neglected everything since then, seen nobody, and at the most a sigh has escaped me when I have thought of my friends. . . . More I cannot say to-day, for the rosy waves still surge so furiously around me, my brain is still so numbed with the intoxicating perfume, that I am unable to talk reasonably with you.

" Have you read the Song of Songs of King Solomon ? Well, read it again and you will find in it everything I could tell you."

And with that repetition, which is such a common stylistic feature of Heine's prose as of his verse, he concludes this letter to August Lewald with the words : " Read the Song of Songs of King Solomon ; I would recommend him to your notice."

It did, indeed, for a time look as though he were going to break away, for there was a quarrel with Mathilde, and for months they saw nothing of each other. He first spent some weeks as the guest of the Princess Belgiojoso, at her château near Saint-Germain. From there he wrote to Campe that his soul was calmed again and his senses tamed, and that in this cultured circle he felt his spirit purged of all its dross. His verses will become more beautiful and his books more harmonious, and he feels a true horror of everything ignoble and mean. Thence he went to Boulogne, where he stayed till December. But removed from the elevating influence of this " most beautiful and noblest and most gifted woman—with whom all the same he is *not* in love "—the old passion resumed its sway, and we find him writing to Laube on September 27th, that he is " condemned to love only the lowest and most foolish."

At the end of December he was back in Paris, and almost at once re-entered the " Venusberg ", as he describes it in the poem *Der Tannhäuser*, written in the following year, which is nothing but an allegory of this struggle between the higher and lower sides of his nature. This time the return was final, and he set up a household with Mathilde at Cité Bergère No. 3, in a "new apartment, splendid and luxurious, where he sits now warm and comfortable." It was the first stage in the pilgrimage through a series of lodgings in Paris with Mathilde, both before and after their marriage in 1841. They never made a real home, and this was probably due as much to Heine's own nature as to Mathilde's lack of all domestic instincts. Heine was born to be a wanderer on the face of the earth, with no settled home or country, with a shifting religion, and an indeterminate position in society, neither wholly Jew nor German. We have seen how at the end of the time in Hamburg he sat with his unpacked trunks around him, like a bird ready to take flight in any direction, and that was typical of his whole life. Transplanted from her natural surroundings, uprooted, with no knowledge of their actual financial position, which itself was ever changing, Mathilde took no responsibilities, and merely accepted life and its pleasures as they came. So the feckless *ménage* began, as it was to continue to the end, and in the company of Mathilde and her friend Pauline, who was brought in to run the house, to the chatter of his wife, and the screams of her parrot, and the din of narrow courtyards, Heine was to do his life's work.

Whatever his outgoings were before, his financial responsibilities were now permanent. Apart from the allowance from his uncle, which at this time amounted to four thousand francs, he depended upon the earnings of his pen, and now, when so badly needed, he saw this source of income seriously endangered. Heine had been already in bad odour with the German governments, but now a man, with whom he had hitherto been on a not unfriendly footing, was the immediate cause of an action which threatened to cut the ground from under his feet. From the autumn of 1835 Wolfgang Menzel, the notorious Goethe baiter, published in the *Literaturblatt* of the *Stuttgarter Morgenblatt* a series of articles, in which he charged the writers of " Das Junge Deutschland " with the spread of pernicious doctrines and attacks upon public morality. The attack was directed in the first place against Gutzkow's weak and tasteless novel, *Wally, Die Zweiflerin*, but outraged morality plays a less important part with the virtuous critic than fear of the competition of a new journal, *Deutsche Revue*, which Gutzkow was about to found. The result was that Gutzkow was sentenced to three months' imprisonment, and that at the instigation of Metternich the *Bundestag* in Frankfort published on 10th December, 1835, the famous resolution ordering the suppression of " the writings of the literary school known under the name of ' Das Junge Deutsch-land ', of which the most notable members are Heinrich Heine, Karl Gutzkow, Ludolf Wienbarg, Theodor Mundt and Heinrich Laube."

Heine was infuriated. The Preface to the third volume of the *Salon* contains a most violent attack on Menzel, but all its biting satire and charges of personal cowardice failed to secure Heine even the satisfaction of a duel with the " hypocrite and traitor." The harm was done, and the first of the many literary feuds which mark the rest of this period did him little good.

Another source of income at this time, and one that at the best does Heine little credit, was the pension of four thousand eight hundred francs which he received from the French government. Heine himself says that he only accepted the pension after the ruin brought on him by the resolution of the *Bundestag*, but it appears in fact that he was then already in receipt of it.

It is well known to what extent the July monarchy employed funds for the creation of opinion favourable to the government. Among those subsidised were foreign writers of note resident in France, who might in the most favourable light be regarded as receiving recognition for the sacrifices they had made in the cause of liberty, which that government was supposed to represent. Heine later described the pension as " the generous alms which the French people bestowed on so many thousands of foreigners, who had compromised themselves more or less gloriously at home for the cause of the revolution, and found a sanctuary at the hospitable hearth of France." That sounds very well, but the pension came actually, of course, from a government which was representative, not of the people as a whole, and least of all of the part of the nation for which a champion of liberty might have been expected to feel most sympathy, but of the comfortable bourgeoisie. It was given moreover, not in view of past services to any cause, but with the object of securing at least a benevolent neutrality. Heine, it is true, looked upon France as the country which was specially entrusted with the mission of liberation, but from what he knew of the régime of Louis Philippe at close quarters, he must have been very well aware that it was something very far from a realisation of those ideals of which he had proclaimed himself the champion.

When the truth about this pension was brought to light by the February Revolution of 1848, it was proclaimed as another instance of Heine's unscrupulousness, and he was decried as a traitor to his country and a mercenary of France. It is certainly one of the blots on his escutcheon, and irreconcilable with any very fine sense of honour. The most that can be said in extenuation, though not in excuse, is that that money flowed very freely, and that in accepting it he and his fellow refugees were only doing what numbers of French deputies and others did. It is probable that no definite conditions were attached to the grant, and there is absolutely no proof that he sold his convictions. And as for obligation and subservience, he doubtless felt no more and no less than in the case of his Uncle Solomon or any other of his subsidisers. He was quite frankly without principle or conscience in the matter of money, which he appeared to think the world owed to his genius, without any need of thanks on his part. He was prepared to beg or borrow money from anyone ; a peculiarly glaring instance is his letter of 8th November, 1836, to Moser, one of his best and most disinterested friends. Five years earlier he had brutally declared their friendship at an end, and now in the first letter he writes again after that interval he advances as the highest proof of his friendship the request for a loan of four hundred thalers in his dire necessity !

He is constantly thinking of ways of meeting his liabilities, always excepting the simple one that never in his life seems to have occurred to him—that of cutting down his expenses. His letters to Cotta are full of bargainings, and of requests for advances on the works he is engaged upon, or still to write. In 1837 he was planning to found a new journal, the *Pariser Zeitung*, and in writing to Varnhagen on 13th February, 1838, urging him to secure its right of admission into Prussia, declares himself willing to accept any conditions imposed. His letter, one of the worst he ever wrote, contains the amazing sentence : " The Prussian government can rest assured that, in the present state of affairs, all my sympathies, in the matter of the Rhineland, are on the side of Prussia, that I never fail to recognise the services of Prussia to this bastard land, which only through Prussia is being reconquered for Germany and raised to the level of its culture."

However, the journal never appeared, any more than a contemplated international monthly, to appear under the title of *Paris und London*, or *London und Paris*. All was of no avail, and his burden of debt grew heavy. In 1837 it amounted to twenty thousand francs, and as a last resource he sold to Campe the sole right of publishing his works for eleven years. Most of the things he wrote and published at this time are not among his best-known or most popular writings, and were largely written to order, to meet his more pressing needs. The third and fourth volumes of the *Salon*, which appeared in 1837 and 1840 respectively, contained only in part new matter. The third consisted of the *Florentinische Nächte*—which had already been published in the Stuttgart *Morgenblatt*, and in a French translation in the *Revue des Deux Mondes* —and the *Elementargeister*, which has already been mentioned as forming a part of the volume *De l'Allemagne*, published in 1835. The Preface, directed against Menzel, was refused publication by the censor, and only after difficulties was published separately under the title *Über den Denunzianten*.

The *Florentinische Nächte* belongs to the narrative group of Heine's writings, though, like all his attempts in this form, it shows his impatience with the type, and his disinclination to carry a connected story to its conclusion.

The thread of the story is indeed very thin, and it becomes once more a mere vehicle for the expression of his views on various subjects, and for many personal reminiscences. Heine's all pervading subjectivity, in short, again manifests itself. The room in which the shadowy consumptive, Signora Maria, is slowly fading away, forms only a dim background for Maximilian-Heine, and for the story of his various loves, which her morbid interest extorts from him. The whole is steeped in a wan Romantic light ; we might be in the dream-world of Novalis. Those loves include the mystical passion for marble statues, the love for little Very, which began when she had been already ten years dead, and the love for music. Maria's question, " Do you love Paganini ? " introduces the main theme of the first night, the wonderful attempt to translate into another art the magic of the master's playing, to express it through the visions conjured up in his soul by the flood of tones. It is one of Heine's great prose passages, a marvellous example of stylistic virtuosity.

The Second Night, in which Maximilian at last yields to the entreaties of Maria, and tells her the story of his love for Mademoiselle Laurence, passes over more definitely to the field of autobiography. This mysterious Laurence is met first, along with the dwarf and the poodle and the drum-playing fat woman, in a setting that is like a Heinesque parody of Goethe's Mignon. She is banished, not from Italy to Germany, but from France to England, and is seen in London by a Maximilian who is obviously the Heine of 1827. The tone of the whole work is one of mild resignation, of elegiac retrospect ; Heine meant it to be tame and entirely inoffensive to the German authorities. He had even proposed to Campe as a title *Das stille Buch* or *Märchen*. But it was as though he had to put some spirit in it, and there could be no possible harm in having another go at the English. So Maximilian-Heine pours into the listening ears of his phthisical Maria some of the most vitriolic things he ever said about England and its inhabitants—a doubtfully beneficial tonic for her in her supposed condition. No modern Englishman will grudge Heine the pleasure these sallies gave him, the more so as he can saddle anything he specially dislikes on his forbears of the early nineteenth century, but it certainly surprises us to hear that one among the many annoying characteristics of the Englishman of that day was to force his foreign languages upon the long-suffering stranger. *Quantum mutatus ab illo !*

The other part of this third volume of the *Salon*, the *Elementargeister*, elaborated the thoughts on popular superstitions, and the development of Christian daemon-ology from the heathen gods of the old Germanic myth-ology, which had been earlier begun in the *Geschichte der Religion und Philosophie*. At the end he gives his version of the Tannhäuser legend, which has already been des-cribed as an allegory of his own war of the spirit and the senses. With the satiric close the veil of allegory is completely torn aside, and Tannhäuser's return from Rome to the Venusberg is plainly the story of Heine's final sur-render to Mathilde :

> " Zu Hamburg, in der guten Stadt,
>   Soll keiner mich wiederschauen !
> Ich bleibe jetzt im Venusberg,
>   Bei meiner schönen Frauen."

The fourth volume of the *Salon* contained *Der Rabbi von Bacharach* and *Über die französische Bühne*. The

Rabbi belongs to a much earlier period of Heine's life, the early twenties, when he was for a time enthusiastically interested in the Jewish cause, and in Jewish history and antiquities. The great hopes which Heine placed upon this, his most ambitious and most promising narrative work, which cost him such struggles and toils of the spirit, were never to be realised. He had planned to include it in the second volume of the *Reisebilder*, and the work appears then to have been as good as finished. The greatest part of the manuscript perished in the fire in his mother's house in Hamburg, and the fragment here published was all that has been given to the world. It has already been discussed in Chapter III.

The work on the French theatre is in the form of confidential letters to his old Hamburg friend, the actor and journalist, August Lewald. They are announced on the title page as " written in May, 1837, in a village near Paris." From his solitude Heine looks on the tumult of Paris, and records some of the sad realisations which had followed the glowing hopes with which he had " crossed the Jordan and entered the New Jerusalem ", as he put it at the time. As a liberal and democratic régime, the government of Louis Philippe was certainly not such as to inspire the enthusiasm of a friend of liberty and democracy, and the cynicism and indifference, the haste and restlessness of its materialistic society are the theme of gloomy forebodings for the future of the country. The theatrical criticism is of no very great significance. The most interesting theme is his comparison of Alexandre Dumas and Victor Hugo, the latter of whom he proclaims to be the greatest living poet of France, whose merits, not properly appreciated in France, are better understood beyond the Rhine.

Apart from the completion of the *Salon* by the addition of the third and fourth volumes, Heine wrote in these years, on commission for the publishers, two works which were undertaken solely for the monetary return they brought. The first was an Introduction to an edition of Don Quixote produced by a Stuttgart firm, for which he got one thousand francs—Campe gave him fifty Louis d'or (forty pounds) for the perpetual rights of the *Buch der Lieder* !—and which he declared to be the worst thing he had written. It was a hasty, routine piece of work, the best part being the first two pages, which are a repetition of the sixteenth chapter of *Die Stadt Lucca.*

The other was the essay on *Shakespeares Mädchen und Frauen,* written for the French publisher Dellage, who was bringing out a French and a German edition of an English illustrated work, containing engravings of Shakespeare's heronies from works by prominent artists. He received four thousand francs for the task, which as a whole he did not take very seriously, since he saw that the illustrations would be regarded as the most important feature. He undertook it unwillingly, at a time of bad health, as he wrote to Campe, but believed all the same that it would have a good reception, while a couple of months before he had told him that it was " no masterpiece, but good enough for the purpose." Its value lies, not in the direct commentary on the illustrations, of which there is very little, but in the excursions and reflections for which they furnish the occasion. Particularly interesting are those suggested by Jessica, which show that re-awakening of the sympathy for his race which marks his later years.

The period of which we are speaking was, too, one in which Heine became more and more deeply engaged in literary and personal feuds, and added to the already considerable number of his enemies. Neither the quarrel with Platen, nor that with Menzel, had done him any good, though in both cases he had fundamentally the right on his side. Nor had he learnt anything from those experiences. His was essentially a fighting nature, and he had very provocative ways, and the gift of galling his adversaries to the quick. The quarrel with Menzel was followed by that with the Swabian poets. The whole affair began with Heine's not unappreciative remarks about Uhland in the *Romantische Schule*, to which some of the Swabians replied by refusing to write for Weidmann's *Musenalmanach*, if the proposal to include a portrait of Heine in the 1837 volume were adhered to. Heine's answer was the mockery in the strophe at the end of the Tannhäuser poem. Pfizer then appeared as their champion with an essay, *Heines Schriften und Tendenz*, which drew down on their unfortunate heads Heine's *Schwabenspiegel* in 1838. Heine never questioned Uhland's greatness in his own field, though he quite rightly treated him as the poet of a past epoch, since his verse had ceased for twenty years, and denied his claim to have founded an original school, since he was after all only continuing the Romantic tradition. His real attack was directed against the lesser poets, Kerner, Schwab, Mayer, Pfizer and others, who sheltered themselves under Uhland's great name, and for whom he employed again here the biting diminutives of that Tannhäuser verse. Heine had once more a good deal of right on his side ; he was not really the aggressor, since his remarks in the *Romantische Schule* do not exceed the bounds of perfectly legitimate criticism. But he was again unduly harsh towards some quite respectable, if not great, poets, and he lost more sympathies than he gained.

This attack was followed in 1839 by *Schrift-stellernöten*, an open letter to Campe, accusing him, Gutzkow and Wihl of the mutilation of his *Schwabenspiegel* when it appeared in the *Jahrbuch der Literatur*. It was an unpleasant affair, with various ramifications, and though it led to no break with Campe, it was the end of the long friendship with Gutzkow.

Much more serious, in fact, the most serious of all Heine's polemics, was the book on Börne which appeared in 1840. In all the other quarrels the opponents had, at any rate, been able to answer for themselves ; here Heine, whatever may have been his provocation, attacked a man no longer alive, but so recently dead that the dispute appeared in a personal and not in an historical light. The only justification that can be urged is that Börne was regarded less as an individual than as the representative head, even after his death, of that republican camp, from which Heine knew that his most bitter and implacable enemies came. From the friendship of earlier years, when they had appeared to be soldiers fighting for a common cause, they had been driven gradually and inevitably, through the fundamental difference of their natures, into opposition and open enmity. Börne was a narrow and fanatical republican, and when Heine in Paris, far from throwing himself wholeheartedly into the fray, developed a philosophical aloofness which was prepared to consider the claims of any constitutional form, and to see in politics only a means to an end, they took him for a renegade and a traitor, a man without principles, a vain trifler and frivolous wit, for whom no cause was sacred, and who had no beliefs. This was the gravamen of the charge against Heine. It was Börne who had formulated it, and though he had died in 1837, his influence still lived on. In fact, all these charges and insinuations were conveniently assembled in a book which appeared in 1840 in Frankfort, the home of Börne, and the centre of all the intrigues against Heine, *Ludwig Börnes Urteil über H. Heine*, and which consisted of unprinted extracts from the *Briefe aus Paris*. Heine especially dwells on the antithesis between character and talent which Börne had first enunciated, and the insinuations he made that Heine possessed " unprincipled poetic gifts and poetic want of principle."

In Heine's judgment their antagonism sprang from that fundamental difference of character, which figures largely in his philosophical creed. He had already emphasised the antithesis of spiritualism and sensualism ; now these yield to the better known terms, Hellenes and Nazarenes. " Not only in his utterances on Goethe, but also in his criticism of other writers, Börne betrayed his Nazarene limitations. I say Nazarene, in order not to use either the terms Jewish or Christian, although the two expressions are synonymous for me, and I use them to express, not a faith, but a natural disposition. Jews and Christians are for me synonymous terms, in antithesis to Hellenes, by which name I do not designate any definite people, but a natural and cultivated spiritual bias and philosophic outlook. In this sense I would say that all men are either Jews or Hellenes, men with ascetic, anti-sensuous, spiritualising instincts, or men of full-blooded, expansive and realistic nature. . . . Börne was entirely Nazarene, his antipathy against Goethe sprang directly from his Nazarene disposition ; his later political exaltation was rooted in that rugged asceticism that thirsts for martyrdom, which is always found with republicans, which they call republican virtue and which differs little from the self-sacrificing zeal of the Early Christians."

The book at once brought about Heine's ears a storm of criticism and abuse such as even he had never yet experienced. He had indeed delivered himself into the hands of his many enemies. The more serious aspects of the book and its undoubted merits were ignored, as with a howl of feigned or genuine indignation they declaimed against the scandalous nature of the work. The indefensible sin against decency and good taste which Heine had committed in the insinuations he made about the relations between Börne and his Frankfort friend, Frau Wohl, the recipient of the Paris letters, was naturally the subject of the most severe censure, and had an important bearing on Heine's life. Her second husband, Strauss, came to Paris, and after apparently trying to win a reputation for heroism on the cheap by spreading a baseless rumour that he had boxed Heine's ears publicly in the Rue Richelieu, finally met him in a duel with pistols, at seven o'clock on the morning of 7th September. Heine, who fired in the air, was slightly grazed by a bullet on the hip.

A week before, on 31st August, 1841, he had at last legitimised his marriage with Mathilde, in order to secure her position in case of a fatal issue, and had made her his sole legatee. He took the change in his life very seriously, and indeed made quite a ceremonial occasion of it. Meissner relates in his *Erinnerungen an Heinrich Heine* that Heine invited to the wedding only those friends who were living in similar unions, in order to encourage them to follow his example, to which he exhorted them at the end of the wedding breakfast in a humorous speech. They moved into new quarters at No. 46, Faubourg Poissonnière, which Heine described as so nice that no one would think it was the home of a German poet. And a year later he wrote : " I am living in better quarters, in fact, rather in style, since I have been legitimately married. Yes, dear friend, I am living now in the most serious bonds of wedlock. I am committing monogamy."

Later on Heine expressly withdrew his suggestions against Frau Wohl, and regretted the publication of the book as a whole, but the harm had been done, and an injury inflicted on his reputation which was irreparable.

In the next few years, from 1840 to 1843, Heine wrote for Cotta's *Allgemeine Zeitung* a series of articles, which appeared in 1854 in the *Vermischte Schriften* under the title *Lutetia*. He describes the book on the title page as consisting of " reports on politics, art and national life ", and hopes to produce by the artistic arrangement of the series of monographs a work which should give a faithful picture of the " parliamentary period " of the reign of Louis Philippe, the years which formed the prelude to the February revelation. Heine himself placed the work far above the *Französische Zustände* of 1832, which he described as monotonous and lacking in humour and movement, and it certainly was far superior in its form, upon which he took great pains, aspiring to make it a chrestomathy of prose and a model of style for popular themes. But the old enthusiasms are gone—for Napoleon, for Saint-Simonism, for France as the chosen land of freedom and the mother of revolutions. He is really tired of politics, and wishes for nothing but stability and peace, and is even prepared to defend the uninspiring oligarchy of Louis Philippe as the last bulwark against the threatening flood of his new bugbear, the thousand-headed monster of Communism. His point of view has become very much that of the bourgeoisie, which " if it does not exactly fear the republic, has an instinctive dread of Communism, of those sinister comrades who would spring forth like rats from the ruins of the present régime. . . . These shop-keepers feel instinctively that the republic to-day would no longer stand for the principles of the nineties, but would be only the form in which a new unspeakable sovereignty of the proletariat, with all its creed of community of goods, would carry the day. They are conservatives from out-ward necessity, not through inward conviction, and fear is here the pillar of all things."

With the book on Börne and these articles in the *Allgemeine Zeitung* the period of Heine's great prose works comes to an end. When he wrote the preface to the second edition of the *Buch der Lieder* in 1837, he said that for some time he had felt an aversion from all verse forms. Yet in 1840 the reaction had set in, and at the end of the Börne book, he expresses his weariness with the grey world of reality : " The desolate work-a-day spirit of the modern puritans is already spreading over Europe like a grey twilight, heralding in a harsh winter. . . . What signify the poor nightingales, that suddenly raise their melodious sobbing, more sadly but more sweetly than ever, in the German groves ? They sing a melancholy fare-well ! The last nymphs that Christianity has spared take refuge in the wildest thickets. As though the bitternesses of reality are not grievous enough, I am tortured, too, by evil visions at night."

The return to poetry is heralded by a brilliant work, that emerges clear and radiant after all the dust of battle, and the toil of uncongenial tasks. *Atta Troll* is a reversion to the romanticism of his earlier years, a flight from reality, that is explicable only by his weariness with the particular world in which he had lately been living. From it all he soars away on the wings of fancy, as in the *Harzreise* from the dull work-a-day world of Göttingen. In June and July 1841, Heine spent with Mathilde six weeks in Cauterets in the Hautes Pyrénées. It was a great change from the yearly visits to the sea, in Boulogne and Dieppe and the other places on the north coast of France. The sea had become familiar to him ; now in the novel surroundings of this splendid mountain scenery, on the borders of Spain, with its romantic associations, his spirit gained elasticity and fire, and with sovereign imaginative vigour he took all the worries and antipathies of his recent years, his Swabians and German Republicans and all the rest of them, and wove them into a fantastic " Midsummer Night's Dream." The real significance of *Atta Troll* in Heine's life is that with it he recovered his poise, and looked down with sovereign irony upon his own troubles and defeats. Here for once, at any rate, his poetry served him as a magic solvent of his own sorrows.

The story of this mock-heroic poem is of the simplest. Atta Troll, the dancing bear of the Pyrenees, escapes from his leader and returns to his children. In the tales he tells them of his experiences he develops his " bear philosophy ", and his criticism of human society. An expedition is organised to hunt him down, since he is a public danger through his revolutionary propaganda against the rule of man. He is eventually captured and shot, and his skin finally adorns the bedroom of Juliette-Mathilde in Paris.

The inscription on the supposed monument erected to him in Walhalla by the Bavarian King gives the key to his character. This bear who is at once a religious moralist and a Sansculotte, who is " a character but no talent ", represents all that multifarious opposition which raised

the outcry against Heine on moral grounds, and proclaimed him to be "a talent but no character". As a
political allegory the epic has many obscurities and difficulties ; in the political aspect it is at best only a poetic
version of those feuds which can be studied elsewhere, and
that is its least interesting side. All the figures appear in
the irresponsible phantasmagoria of a dream, and jest and
earnest are inextricably mingled.

But if we refuse to trouble ourselves unduly with the
interpretation of details, on which so much has been
written, there are beauties enough and to spare which lie
patent to all. There is the grandiose setting, the wonderful description of the scenery, of Ronceval, whose sound
is as the fragrance of the "blue flower" in the poets'
heart, and of the other places, whose names are like the
echo of romantic music in his ears. There is the bold
sweep of imagination, the sure unerring logic and con-
sistency of this bear-world, the satire on human society,
carried through with its fairy elegance and lightness of
touch. What Heine could not do in prose, he did here in
verse—he wove a consistent action and plot.

When we add to all this the dazzling, daring, superbly
insolent wit, and the marvellously skilful handling of the
Spanish Trochees, the traditional metre of the Romantic
Epic, we cannot wonder that Heine, when offering it to
Laube in November, 1842, described it as "the most
important thing he had written in verse." In the final
canto, which forms the epilogue, and at the same time the
dedication to Varnhagen, Heine speaks of its tones that are
like the dreams he dreamed in his youth with Chamisso
and Brentano and Fouqué in the blue moonlight nights,
and calls it "the last free wood-song of Romanticism."

These words are only one more instance of the way in

which his youth and the land of his birth were beginning to call to him now at the end of these first ten years in Paris. He had tasted there triumphs and pleasures to the full, but also drunk deep of life's bitternesses. It was in the summer of the same year, 1843, that he wrote the famous poem *Nachtgedanken* ("Denk' ich an Deutschland in der Nacht"), in which he expresses his longing for his mother, whom he had not seen for twelve years, and the sad realisation that she might, like so many others whom he had left behind there, sink into the grave. It is true that the poems ends with the appearance of his wife, "fair as the morning", who drives the German cares away. Yet the longing was not stilled, and in October of that year he set out for Hamburg, where he arrived on the 29th and where he stayed till the 7th December.

Though his main incentive was doubtless the desire to see his mother again, he had also important business to transact with Campe. He appears to have been well received in Hamburg, and to have enjoyed the recognition of his new standing in the town where he had suffered so many humiliations. In the first letter from Hamburg to Mathilde, he tells her that Uncle Solomon has received him very warmly, and indeed been politeness itself, and that since he sees that he has not come to Hamburg to ask for money, but only to see him and his mother again, he stands high in his favour.

Yet there was much also to sadden him there. His uncle's health is such that the next attack of his illness is likely to carry him off. And he finds his mother greatly changed. She is very feeble, shrunken with age and cares. In the great Hamburg fire, which raged from 5th to 8th May, 1842, her house had been one of the four thousand buildings destroyed, and as her insurance company proved insolvent, she suffered heavy loss. " Her greatest trouble is her pride ", he writes. " She goes nowhere, as she has not the means to entertain visitors in return."

This time Heine had left Mathilde behind, but he was already planning a long visit for the following summer, on which she should accompany him. In that first letter he enclosed a note from his nephew Ludwig, Charlotte's son, the later Baron Ludwig von Embden, author of the book, *Heinrich Heines Familienleben*, expressing the wish of all the family to see her in Hamburg, and saying that all those who had seen her spoke with admiration of her beauty and charm. Heine was obviously very pleased with the friendly attitude of the family, including his uncle, towards Mathilde, which was due no doubt to their relief that he had at last married and settled down.

This was the first time that Heine and she had been parted for any length of time since their marriage, and his letters show that Mathilde had lost none of her attraction for him, though she had not apparently inspired him with much confidence in her constancy or good sense. The tone is something between that of a jealous lover and a fussy schoolmistress. The first letter is addressed to his " schönster Schatz " and signed " Dein armer Gatte ". He writes : " You are my poor, beloved wife, and I hope you will be good and sensible. I beg you urgently not to appear too much in public." In the next he writes : " I think only of you, my dear Nonotte. It cost me a great resolution to leave you alone in Paris, that terrible abyss ! Do not forget that my eye is always on you, and that what I do not know now I shall learn later." And again : " My God ! for a fortnight I have not heard your twittering ! and I am so far away from you ! It is a real exile."

He sends her four hundred francs, with instructions as to the disposal of all but fifty francs, which he tells her to keep in her pocket, and not to fritter away on trifles. He gets impatient at receiving no letter and vainly urges her to write. He himself is writing to her constantly, in the midst of his many pressing business engagements, and in spite of the terrible headaches of which he complains in nearly every letter. He presses her to begin her German lessons as soon as possible. " Of course, you are busy now with your handwriting, which is so very necessary. Make good use of your leisure." And a week later : " What is my wife doing now, the maddest of the mad ? It was madness of me, not to bring you here with me. For heaven's sake, do not do anything that I should be angry about when I get back. Live as quietly as possible in your nest ; work, study, bore yourself properly, spin wool, like the good Lucretia whom you saw at the Odéon."

Heine's letters during this German visit, eight years after their first meeting, and two years after their marriage, are the best commentary on the relations of the two, and show the footing on which their union had become stabilised. He is still hopeful that she may learn something, and become more economical, but she never did either the one or the other. As it began, so the relationship continued to the end, with Heine as the bearer of all responsibilities and Mathilde irresponsible as a child. There is every reason to believe that she was faithful to him during his life, and to his memory after his death, but beyond this passive rôle she never got. No doubt in her eyes, and in those of her aunt and her own real associates, she had done very well for herself, but the source of the comparative luxury in which she lived was a matter of indifference to her.

The business on which Heine was engaged in Hamburg

while he wrote these rather pathetic pleas for a line from her, concerned her very closely. He had concluded a contract with Campe, by which he transferred to him the perpetual right in his works in return for an annuity of twelve hundred marks, which passed to his widow in case of his death. Heine reports to her this transaction, with which he was greatly pleased, with the simple words that to provide for his wife's future is " no merit, but a duty ". Heine's record in matters of finance is not on the whole a very pleasing one, but this action, and the way it was done, can at any rate be set down to him on the credit side of the balance.

The literary fruit of this Hamburg visit was the narrative poem, *Deutschland : Ein Wintermärchen*. As he could not get a visa to pass through Prussian territory, Heine had gone by way of Brussels, and from Bremen to Hamburg by water. On the return journey he took his chance with the Prussian authorities, and this return journey in inverse order forms the background of the poem. It was written rapidly, without interruption, in the beginning of 1844, and was finished in April. He himself described it to Campe as a " humoristisches Reiseepos, versifizierte Reisebilder." He deliberately gave it a Shakespearean sub-title, and so challenged the comparison with *Atta Troll*, but the two are not to be mentioned in the same breath. To read it after the other is to experience a plunge from the realms of serene humour and airy romantic phantasy to the level of ruthless and rather vulgar polemics. This " Winter's Tale " is one of Heine's most offensive works, for all the coruscations of its dazzlingly brilliant wit. It was a great success in certain quarters it is true, for it showed him still as the hard fighter, who could deal the shrewdest blows of any of them. The new polemical fire, after the abdication of *Atta Troll*, may well have been due to the influence of his new acquaintanceship with Karl Marx. At the same time he was writing some of the most pungent of the *Zeitgedichte*. It looked now as though he had stepped again into the ranks of the " party ", and he was not stinted with applause from the republican side.

In the Preface he scornfully repudiates the charge that he is a despiser of the fatherland, and a friend of the French, ready to cede to them the Rhine. That he would never do, " for the Rhine belongs to me ; by inalienable right of birth ; I am the free Rhine's far freer son ". And he proclaims a faith in the great mission of Germany, expressed not here alone :

" The whole world will become German ! Of this mission and this universal dominion of Germany I dream often when I walk beneath the oaks. This is *my* patriotism." It certainly was patriotism of a sort, and honestly meant in a poetic way, but a rather cheap patriotism all the same, for it took the easy path of postulating an ideal state, instead of attempting to understand and build upon that which, with all its faults and its virtues, already existed. As a matter of fact the Germany he flagellates has little relation to the actual Germany of 1843 ; it was rather a resurrected bogey of the early twenties.

In the opening Caput he announces it as " *Ein neues Lied, ein besseres Lied* ", but there is not really a new constructive idea in the whole work. The programme given here at the beginning is nothing but the well-known Saint-Simonian doctrine, with a somewhat stronger emphasis on the newer Socialistic demand for immediate dividends on earth in place of drafts on heaven. Most bitter of all are the tirades against Prussia, the old well-known grievances having probably been stimulated to new and more vigorous life by the recent humiliation of having to sneak like a thief round or through its territory. The sight of the Prussian eagle on the post at Aachen drives him into a fury. That might pass; but it is unpleasant, to say the least of it, to find in Caput VIII Heine, who only a few years before had been writing to Varnhagen of the great cultural mission of Prussia in the Rhineland, describing these very Prussians as mere exploiters who had grown fat on their extortions.

In his love for the ideal Germany of the future, this " patriot " goes out of his way to besmirch with coarse mockery things that were dear to the heart of many sections of the people, irrespective of their political or religious connections. Whatever he might think of Becker's *Rheinlied*, it was not easy to hear much patriotism in the wish he puts in the mouth of Father Rhine for the return of the French. One did not need to be a Catholic to resent his prophecy that, instead of being completed, Cologne Cathedral would be turned into stables, or his desecration of the shrine of the Three Kings.

His re-telling of the Barbarossa story is witty enough, but the legend is too good to be turned into a burlesque, leading up to another bitter attack on Prussia. As for the scene in which Hammonia reveals to him the future of Germany, it may have the coarseness of Aristophanes, and some of his wit, but one cannot wonder if his fellow-countrymen saw little love in it for this Germany whose faithful son he boasts himself to be.

The epic is, as a whole, amazingly clever, extremely witty, wonderfully fluent, with a brilliant command of its easily cantering strophes, and a most masterly use of rhyme for achieving humorous and other effects. But with all that, one finishes it with a feeling that Heine had nothing new to say in it, that he achieved nothing beyond making himself offensive all round, and that if he had not written it, it would have been better for himself, and that apart from a few hearty things, such as the reference to his mother, his uncle Solomon, and the Westphalians, the world would not have lost very much.

Towards the end of July in the following year, Heine again paid a visit to Germany, this time taking Mathilde with him. She did not however stay long, alleging as the reason of her departure the illness of a friend, and on 12th August, Heine is already writing to her of his despondency at her absence. No doubt she was hopelessly bored in this strange world, and in the company of people whose language she could not speak. She appears all the same to have made a good impression, at any rate according to Heine's account, for he tells her in that same letter that everybody, and especially his mother, were disconsolate at losing her. She even seems to have found favour with the mighty Solomon, who treated his " poor kitten " very generously, as he wrote to sister Charlotte.

When she is gone, Heine's letters to her take on the same tone as those of the year before—expressions of long-ing and devotion, exhortations to circumspection in her life in Paris, fear for the safety of his " Lamm ", his " brebis," among the wolves of Paris, a mixture of cajolery and veiled threats. He has to wait a fortnight for his first letter from her, and then he is beside himself with joy. " At the mere sight of your letter my heart leapt, I sang and danced, and went to the theatre to revel in song and dance. . . . Whether the acting was good I cannot say, for I was so full of my thoughts that I completely forgot the play."

The nine or ten weeks of the second visit to Germany cannot have been on the whole either a very restful or very happy time for Heine. Apart from his anxiety for Mathilde, he was troubled about his own health, which made it more difficult to expedite the serious business of seeing his new volume with Campe through the press. The letters to Mathilde have frequent reference to his headaches, and the trouble with his eyes. On 14th September he writes to Detmold that he can hardly write, and that he is three-quarters blind, while a week later he tells him that his left eye is completely closed, and the right one very dim. One has to bear these facts in mind when considering the collapse of his health in the following year. His condition was obviously very uncertain, and not such as to withstand any physical or mental shock. All the same, in spite of ups and downs, his spirits and his courage were still high, and there was nothing about him of a man who was conquered by fate. "The future is ours," he writes to Mathilde on 11th September, and he had indeed hitherto, whatever blows he had suffered, never been overwhelmed by catastrophe. The oil-painting made of him, from a couple of sittings, by Isidor Popper during this visit, shows us a man who is wonderfully youthful looking for his forty-seven years, and whose general expression is that of a confident acceptance of life.

Nothing, indeed, spoke to him of impending calamity, for these various cares were such as could be met and surmounted. It is true he was anxious about his uncle. "My old uncle is much worse," he wrote to his wife on 16th August. "There are so many things I should have liked to say to him, but it looks as though he will not have time to hear them in this world. Heavens, what a misfortune! He will not outlive this year." His mother, on the other hand, he found "wonderfully well." He was never to see again either of these two people, who had played such an important part in his life. And when on the 9th October, he went on board the Dutch steamer that was to take him to Amsterdam, whence he travelled by way of Brussels back to Paris, he was never to set foot on German soil again.

Heine's second German visit of 1844 denotes, in more respects than one, the close of an epoch in his life. It is the final break with the land of his youth, and the definite end of that feeling of ultimate security within the fold of the clan, which, whatever his immediate difficulties, had always up till now differentiated his lot from that of the mere literary and political adventurer. What the loss of that feeling meant to him is expressed in the bitter outbursts which occur ever and again down to the end of his days.

Chapter Nine

NEUE GEDICHTE

At the end of this middle, prose period of his life, Heine appeared again before the public with a collected edition of his poems, the second of the three which he himself prepared. Seventeen years had passed since the appearance of the *Buch der Lieder* when he presented to the world his *Neue Gedichte* in 1844. Their publication was a symptom of that return to poetry which we have already noted. It is true that, as with the earlier volume, most of the individual poems had previously appeared elsewhere, and several of them have been already discussed. He had planned to publish them as early as 1838, but Campe, on Gutzkow's advice, was then unwilling to proceed with the venture.

Once more the whole is greater than the sum of its parts, for it furnishes a valuable survey of Heine's poetic productivity during these years. Not that one finds the same degree of " composition " as in the *Buch der Lieder* ; this time the collection is more heterogeneous. Moreover, no distinct advance, and no new pervading tone, is to be noted ; for that one had to wait for the elevation lent by suffering to the last and in many ways greatest period of his poetic life. The *Neue Gedichte* would not have added very greatly to Heine's reputation as a poet, if his production had ceased with their appearance.

To some extent we have a repetition of the earlier lyric

of the *Buch der Lieder*, without in general the freshness of those earlier songs. The poem *Prolog* presents in graceful imagery a picture of Heine, the champion of the "idea", the fighter, who, when going forth to do battle, is robbed of lance and sword, and bound with garlands by the Goddesses of Love. That conflict within his soul between the call of poetry and the call of the "idea" runs through the whole collection, which, in so far as it is novel at all, is a poetic reflection of the years of his active political life.

The *Neuer Frühling*, the opening section, stands nearest to the *Buch der Lieder*, of which it might well be a continuation. It does in fact follow chronologically, for the poems it contains were written before the migration to France, some indeed going as far back as the year 1822. A few, whose theme is the love for Therese, were written before her engagement in February 1825; but the majority were inspired by the Countess Bothmer, who consoled him in Munich, and for whom he felt on the rebound a very tender interest. It contains at least one pearl, "Leise zieht durch mein Gemüt", a tiny poem of ethereal lightness, dainty and fairy-like, for which Heine has with wonderful skill stolen the very heart of a well-known folk-song of the *Wunderhorn*. Two others have perhaps a special interest for us, since they refer to his Ramsgate visit, one of them being the only prose poem which he included in his collected editions. Another has gained prominence because Heine himself inscribed its two opening lines beneath the Byronic portrait made of him by Ludwig Grimm in 1827:

"Verdrossnen Sinn im kalten Herzen hegend,
    Reis' ich verdriesslich durch die kalte Welt."

N

Yet as a whole, little is to be said of them, in respect either of matter or form, which has not already been said of the poems of the *Buch der Lieder*.

With the next section, *Verschiedene*, it is a very different story. With these poems Heine dropped one of the many bombs which it was his fate to land, often half-unwittingly, among the unsuspecting populace, and which frequently wounded and scarified impartially friend and foe. He certainly never put together a more remarkable mixture, and it is calculated to add considerably to the labours of those tidy folk who endeavour to place him in his proper literary niche. The strangest bedfellows here keep company. The first cycle, the fifteen poems to Seraphine, of whose texture love and the sea form warp and woof, were written perhaps in 1827, and in any case not later than the early thirties. They are morally quite unexceptionable, and many of them beautiful, notably that favourite of Lenau, " Es ragt ins Meer der Runenstein." Another, " Das Fräulein stand am Meere," is sometimes quoted as an instance of Heine's culpable frivolity. It is certainly surprising to find this very amusing little poetic quip in the place where it stands. Was it a mere *jeu d'esprit*, put in here for want of a better place? To assume that with Heine would be dangerous, for he was one who calculated his effects, and especially his transitions. It is difficult to appreciate his feeling in this instance, though it is probably to be taken as the sardonic reaction of the poet to the sentimental gush of the mistress who can look on unmoved at his sufferings.

A notable instance of Heine's sense of composition is the poem found in the very middle of this Seraphine group, which, out of place almost as it might appear, strikes the dominating note of the section as a whole. This poem,

Auf diesem Felsen bauen wir, the manifesto of his new found Saint-Simonian faith, was undoubtedly written at the beginning of the thirties, whatever may have been the origin of the rest of the group. That emancipation of the senses, which is symbolically expressed in the final line, is the theme of the bulk of the poems which follow. Most of the portraits in the gallery belong indeed to the fleshly school, and the beauties painted to a very venal company. And yet—whom do we find there? Not only Therese, but Friederike Robert, and even the Princess Belgiojoso, for whom Heine felt such unbounded admiration! What grotesque tastelessness, what unpardonable insults, some might feel inclined to exclaim. His answer would have been that, by his creed, the senses were justified of themselves, and there was no longer any barrier between them and the world of spirit.

The longest, and in many ways the most notable poem in the collection is Heine's modernised version of the Tannhäuser legend, of which mention has already been made. He takes it as a setting for his own experience, and the return of Tannhäuser to Venus symbolises his final surrender to Mathilde. At the end, with the mischievous, irresponsible humour that is characteristic of him, he makes Tannhäuser's return from Rome to the Venusberg carry him through various German towns, of whose inhabitants he gives a satiric picture to Frau Venus over the soup she has cooked to welcome her prodigal. It is one of the most remarkable twists that even Heine has given to the tail of an ancient story.

To add still more to the heterogeneity of this strange assortment, one finds at its close the three moving poems united under the title *In der Fremde*, which had been written as far back as 1833, and which appeared in the

Salon of the following year. It is notable that even in these earliest Paris years, when all looked rosy to him, and he was " at the zenith of his fat ", he could yet write a poem of such deep longing as is expressed in the famous lines : " Ich hatte einst ein schönes Vaterland."

The poems entitled *Romanzen* have in many cases no claim to that title, and only a few are of any special interest. A striking difference of mood is reflected in the two called *Anno* 1829 and *Anno* 1839. In the former is poured out all his hatred and contempt for the smug, self-satisfied, successful Hamburg citizens, who are for him, along with the English, the typical representatives of the bourgeois in his romantic antithesis of artist and philistine. In the other the poet in exile pours out all his longing for the Germany of his dreams. It is a Germany of no particular place or time, though doubtless the images that mainly inspired his imagination were Düsseldorf and his beloved Rhineland. What he loved most in Germany was that which formed a complete contrast to France. After the light, bright, clear intelligence of Paris, he felt the charm of that brooding, dreamy, old-world simplicity, of which the traces are not by any means obliterated even in the Germany of to-day.

Among the few real *Romanzen* which go to justify the title, two or three are very good, *Frau Nette*, *Begegnung* and others, and one, *Ritter Olaf*, may safely be reckoned among Heine's masterpieces, and as a perfect specimen of its type. It combines, it is true, various well-known motives, even though no direct source is traceable, but whatever Heine may have borrowed, it cannot lessen our admiration for the supreme mastery displayed in every movement of this miniature epic. Again we have the tripartite form, the whole leading up to a climax that is the more effective for being suggested rather than expressed. All Heine's characteristic qualities are found here, his command of antithesis, the direct movement of the action, the wonderful concentration and suggestiveness, the use of haunting repetition and refrain. It is a genuine little trilogy, fulfilling the requirements of every work worthy of the name—unity of the whole and independence of the parts. Each poem is entirely different in tone. In the first we have the grim trochees befitting the procession from the church to the scaffold, in the second a lilting measure fitted to its theme of banquet and dance, while in the third the soaring lines are such as befit the final stage of this tragedy, in which the mood grows ever brighter and more sunny as it approaches its inevitable climax. The poem, first printed in 1839, and probably written shortly before, shows that, for all his political cares and other distractions, Heine had lost none of the creative power that produced *Der arme Peter* nearly twenty years before.

The ten poems of the small section *Zur Ollea* were only inserted in the third edition of the *Neue Gedichte* in 1852, and they could without any great loss have been omitted indefinitely, since they are as a whole comparatively uninteresting and commonplace. As the name, which is wrongly employed for *Olla Potrida*, implies, it is a mixed dish, and it in fact consists of fragments not incorporated in *Romanzero* in 1851.

Only when we come to the *Zeitgedichte* do we find the important new note of the whole collection. They were, when the volume appeared, really modern, for most of them were written at the beginning of the forties. These twenty-four poems, together with the six which were kept back at the time and only subsequently published, represent Heine's contribution to the political lyric of

1840. It was then that he wrote his poem *Deutschland*, inspired to genuine patriotic fervour by the threat of a French invasion. But the Heine who in 1840 joined in the chorus of patriotic bards and wrote his fiery song, " Deutschland ist noch ein kleines Kind," and warned his French hosts of the terrible fury of an awakened German Siegfried, had cooled down by 1844 ; and that enthusiastic praise of an abstract Germany could now find no place in the volume which contained such biting satire of Germany's concrete parts and actual personalities.

On the publication of the volume he kept back as well the *Lobgesänge auf König Ludwig*, with their wealth of coarse abuse, and pungent wit, and ingenious rhymes. Yet even if he left out the most provocative—he himself described the poem to Ludwig as the most vitriolic (" das Sanglanteste ") he had ever written—some of those retained were in all conscience provocative enough. Prussia, and its King, Friedrich Wilhelm IV., the " Romanticist on the Prussian Throne ", are very roughly handled. His dilettante Liberalism and sentimental democracy, his empty phrasemaking and timid retreat in face of all concrete demands, his wavering and inconsistency, awakened Heine's bitterest scorn. An interesting example is the poem *Georg Herwegh*. In spite of the outspoken poem, " An den König von Preussen " in his *Gedichte eines Lebendigen* in 1841, Herwegh was graciously received in audience by the king during his journey through Germany in the following year, and assured that " we will be honest foes ". Yet when the same poet addressed an equally outspoken letter to the King on the suppression of the paper he was planning to produce, he found that the rôle of Marquis Posa before this particular Philip was an uncertain and incalculable one, for he was escorted by the

gendarmes over the Prussian frontier, and his journal suppressed unborn. The poem, in which Heine deals with
the episode, is a good instance of one of his satiric styles,
that of cold and ironic contempt. Another, *Der Kaiser
von China*, barely troubles to conceal behind a transparent
pseudonym the most outspoken ridicule of the royal person
and his entourage. Most bitter of all is the dreadful
effusion we have already spoken of, *Der Wechselbalg*,
which vilifies in execrably bad taste the whole Prussian
State, including Frederick the Great. Treitschke describes it as " the mad howling rage of Jewish hatred ",
and declares it to be unthinkable that any English, French
or Italian Jew would ever have the insolence to fling dirt
at the country of his birth in the way Heine did in his epic
Deutschland and here. If anything could excuse the lack
of fair treatment from which Heine often suffers at German hands it would be such hopeless lapses as these.

Very telling in an entirely different style are the two
poems on Dingelstedt, whose *Lieder eines kosmopolitischen
Nachtwächters* appeared in 1840, and who in November,
1841 arrived in Paris as correspondent of the *Allgemeine
Zeitung*. The first, entitled *Bei des Nachtwächters
Ankunft zu Paris*, draws in reply to the rhetorical question :
" Ist schon befreit das Vaterland," a picture of a Germany
which is the best of all possible worlds for those willing to
be lulled to sleep by blessings and bounties from above, and
to trust the promises of its ruler. It is more subtle, but no
less biting, in its indictment of the King for the non-
fulfilment of the promise of a constitution made by Frederick William III. so long ago as 1815. In the second,
Dingelstedt, who meantime had gone as Librarian to
Stuttgart, is ironically defended against those who charged
him with treason to the cause of freedom—" Verhof-

räterei" as Heine calls it, with a play on his new title of Hofrat.

Another poem, *Das neue Israelitische Hospital zu Hamburg*, probably written in 1841, is interesting, apart from the repetition of the words used in the *Stadt Lucca* on "das tausendjährige Familienübel" (the misfortune of being a Jew), for the warm tribute it pays to the benevolence of his uncle Solomon, who founded the institution in memory of his wife. Heine's relation to his uncle was altogether more cordial in these years, especially so at the end of his second Hamburg visit.

At the end of the group stands, in strange company, the famous poem *Nachtgedanken*, in which Heine expresses in moving tones the longing for his native land, or rather for the mother who dwelt there, and which was written in the summer of the year, 1843, when he was to see her again after the lapse of twelve years.

Taken as a whole the *Zeitgedichte* form undoubtedly the most interesting part of the volume, and as political poetry they compare very favourably with the best of the countless effusions of 1840 and the following years. Along with some personal gall and malice, there is much genuine moral indignation at the faithlessness of the reactionary rulers, and much genuine sympathy with the peoples who were the dupes of their promises.

With what fire Heine could be inspired by a story of suffering and distress is shown by the poem, *Die schlesischen Weber*. It was written before the *Neue Gedichte* appeared, though not published there, but in the socialist *Vorwärts*, to which Heine was a frequent contributor at this time. It was not included in *Romanzero* either, and may well stand here at the close of this chapter, since it belongs directly to the political lyric of the forties, and is one of the most

vigorous poems written by Heine or any of the political
poets of the day. Treitschke has pointed out that the
attack on the King was unfair, since he showed himself
throughout more sympathetic than his officials, but the
weavers could not be expected to know that, and Heine's
poem is psychologically true. Hauptmann has treated
the same theme in his *Weber*, but even that dark picture
does not convey more effectively the impression of gloom
and bitter hopelessness than these few pregnant strophes :

" Im düstern Auge keine Thräne,
   Sie sitzen am Webstuhl und fletschen die Zähne :
   Deutschland, wir weben dein Leichentuch,
   Wir weben hinein den dreifachen Fluch—
   Wir weben, wir weben !

" Ein Fluch dem Götzen, zu dem wir gebeten
   In Winterskälte und Hungersnöten ;
   Wir haben vergebens gehofft und geharrt,
   Er hat uns geäfft und gefoppt und genarrt—
   Wir weben, wir weben !

" Ein Fluch dem König, dem König der Reichen,
   Den unser Elend nicht konnte erweichen,
   Der den letzten Groschen von uns erpresst,
   Und uns wie Hunde erschiessen lässt—
   Wir weben, wir weben !

" Ein Fluch dem falschen Vaterlande,
   Wo nur gedeihen Schmach und Schande,
   Wo jede Blume früh geknickt,
   Wo Fäulnis und Moder den Wurm erquickt—
   Wir weben, wir weben !

" Das Schiffchen fliegt, der Webstuhl kracht,
Wir weben emsig Tag und Nacht.
Altdeutschland, wir weben dein Leichentuch,
Wir weben hinein den dreifachen Fluch—
Wir weben, wir weben ! "

Chapter Ten

ILLNESS AND TURN OF FORTUNE

When Heine returned to Paris in the middle of October 1844, there was at first nothing to foreshadow the coming storm. He found everything at No 46, Faubourg Poissonnière in the best order, and Mathilde had " followed his instructions with exemplary obedience," as he wrote to his mother the day after his return. That letter gives one of the best impressions of the relationship between this strangely assorted pair. Heine might be suspicious, jealous, distrustful of her discretion, and anxious about her extravagance when away from her. He might rate her for her neglect to write to him, warn and threaten and exhort. She was undoubtedly empty-headed and vain and extravagant, and wholly indifferent to his intellectual interests. But when they were together again, all these distinctions between the intellectual giant and the uneducated grisette were as nothing, and they met merely as man and woman, for whom the polarity of sex submerged all other forces. " We are both still as it were dazed with the joy of meeting. We stare at one another, laugh, embrace, speak of you, laugh again, and all the while the parrot screeches like mad. How glad I am to have my two birds again. You see, dear mother, I am as happy as it is granted to a man to be, since nothing is perfect on this earth ; the only thing wanting is a healthy head, and to have my good mother and my good Lottchen near me." He tells her that in spite of the bad trouble with his head he is gay and cheerful.

We might think this merely his usual practice of veiling his troubles from his mother, if we did not find him a week later telling Campe, with whom he never minimised his sufferings, that apart from his eyes, he was in good health. His eyes to be sure troubled him a great deal ; he has been blind four weeks, can scarcely read what he has written, but comforts himself with the thought that the trouble is periodic, and that he will be free of it from time to time. And on 28th November he writes to Charlotte that he is otherwise quite well, has a good appetite, is quite at peace, and happy in his domestic life. His great anxiety is for his uncle, and he asks to be kept constantly posted as to his condition. So it goes on through the rest of the year, the trouble with his eyes and head being an ever-present threat to a state of affairs, which would have been otherwise a not unhappy one.

It was on 28th December, 1844 that he received from his sister Charlotte the news of Solomon's death. Although he was prepared for it, he was deeply moved—more than by anything since his father's death, he writes. His sympathy goes out in the first place to the children, Therese, and poor Karl. His uncle has played a great rôle in his life, and shall be described in unforgettable manner. His grief was undoubtedly genuine, but it was unaccompanied by any inquietude as to his own position: " I have long been free from any anxiety as to the conditions of his will, he has given me plenty of plain indications concerning them." Before the first visit to Hamburg, his uncle had sent him his portrait, with a quaint, fairly cordial, rather pathetic letter. During the second visit, Solomon appears to have given him the rough side of his tongue at first, and once even to have struck him with his stick, though later a better understanding was established between them.   Heine wrote to his wife on 12th August, 1844 that he had just received a letter from his uncle almost begging his pardon for his grumpiness, due to ill-health and over-work.   On 2nd September he wrote to her that his uncle was better and more sociable.   " I am in high favour at court."

Since his marriage the old pension of four thousand francs had been raised to four thousand eight hundred, and he had been promised that the half of it should be continued to his wife in case of his previous death.   Moreover, apart from the pension, there is no doubt he had been reckoning on receiving some really substantial sum on the death of his uncle; he writes to Laube that he might expect his future to be brilliantly assured.

What then was his amazement and indignation to receive a week after his uncle's death a letter from his cousin Karl, written as he says apparently on the day of the funeral, in which he informed him bluntly that his father had left him in his will only four thousand marks, while there was no mention of the pension, though he was himself willing to make him an allowance of two thousand francs, on the condition that if he wrote anything about his father he should first submit the manuscript for his inspection.

Heine's first step was to write Karl a contemptuous letter threatening him with legal action ; his next to look round for allies in the war, which he was at once preparing to wage for what he regarded as his legal rights.   The first to whom he turned was Campe, and that in spite of the dispute about fees—one of many—which he had just been having with his publisher.   He sent him Karl's letter, and his own reply for dispatch to Karl, enjoining on him the greatest secrecy with regard to both.

"You will see," he writes, "that I am entering on a struggle to the death, and mean to get on my side not only the courts, but also public opinion, in case Karl Heine does not give way. I insist upon my rights, though I should have to seal it with my death."

He is obviously in great agitation, and uncertain which of many courses he shall pursue.

Threats of legal action, intimidation and compromise—those were the alternatives between which Heine wavered throughout the course of this unsavoury affair. He ranges from a blind fury against Karl, that Karl whom once during a plague of cholera in Paris he had nursed at the risk of his own life, which drives him to the wildest abuse, to hopes of a favourable settlement, which urge him not to go to lengths that may make all negotiations with his cousin impossible. His passion and his interest are in conflict, and now one and now the other carries the day.

He has in short entirely lost his balance ; we never find him so jumpy and changeable as in this affair. He is touched to the very quick ; the material foundation of his existence is shaken. And Mathilde does not appear to have made things any more pleasant. "For two days my wife has been sitting by the fire like a marble statue, and does not utter a word ; she is as though petrified by the catastrophe", he writes in that letter to Campe. And a few days later to Detmold : "My domestic volcano, that has been quiet for three years, is again active ; Mathilde is in the most excited state, a consequence of the Hamburg affair ; she is ill with fear and vexation." His programme is most clearly expressed in a letter of 9th January. "Perhaps they expect that I shall approach them as a suppliant," he writes to Detmold, " and I should then perhaps get the money again as before. But I believe I shall have more effect with threats, and that they will lead more quickly to the goal. The legal action is no threat ; I can very well bring it. But if I show a serious front they will no doubt get frightened and give way. The press can do most in the way of intimidation, and the first word flung at Karl Heine, or better still at Adolf Halle, will settle the business. They are not used to that sort of thing, whilst I can stand whole dung-carts, which forsooth, as is the case with flower-beds, only make me flourish the more."

Therese's husband, Halle, was especially to be worked upon. He was President of the Chamber of Commerce in Hamburg and hoping to become a Senator, and it was to be pointed out to him how harmful the sort of scandal now brewing would be to his chances. And yet at the same time, Heine is not sure whether Halle is not the best of the lot, even if he did " stand calmly by while they were murdering me ". He is even soon after writing to Campe that, after mature consideration, he has resolved to place his interests confidentially in Halle's hands, and make him the mediator between himself and Karl Heine.

In one letter it is only his pension that matters ; in another on the same day his sense of outrage. " I am ready to make any declaration or apology to satisfy their outraged pride ; I care nothing for paper, for a printed pillory ; when one has great fame one can sacrifice a little ' point d'honneur'. But my pension I must have, in full and irrevocable, and unattached to any condition. Please act in accordance with this admission.

> Contemnere mundum,
> Contemnere se ipsum,
> Contemnere, se contemni——

so the old monks taught, and I arrive at this maxim by way of disgust, disgust of life, contempt for humanity, and for the press, of illness,—Mathilde—a confused marasmus, a weariness of feeling and thought, a yawning—the pen falls from my hand." So to Detmold on 13th January, 1845, while to Campe he writes on the same day : " I am sustained only by my moral consciousness, scorn of baseness, and my outraged sense of justice. The last I will satisfy at any cost, and it is here not merely a question of money."

Our interest in this whole sorry business is not so much its material issue, as its effect upon Heine's physical and moral health. That its effect could only be a destructive and well-nigh annihilating one, is obvious from the feverish restlessness of his movements as they appear from the letters of the time. The quarrel drags on and on. Heine engages new recruits for his cause ; along with his old friend and enemy Campe, who is his chief ally and commissioner, Laube is urged to " beat the drum " against the family, and especially against Halle, and Heine sends him two articles for the press, one an attack on Halle, and the other a defence, " as stupid as possible, and in the wretched style that rich people are usually defended in." They are to be copied, and Heine's manuscript at once destroyed.

At the beginning of 1846 he is planning to go to Hamburg, and writes to Baron James Rothschild and to Alexander von Humboldt, asking them to secure for him from the Prussian authorities the assurance that he will not be molested, if he makes a brief excursion from Hamburg to Berlin for the purpose of seeing old friends and of consulting the doctors there. Humboldt did his best, but the official reply was that Heine was charged under several counts with lèse majesté, and accordingly would be arrested as soon as he set foot on Prussian soil; that moreover there was the less reason for extending special favour or protection for him, since his attacks on the King had been continued up to the present, an instance being the poem *Der neue Alexander*, which had just appeared in the *Telegraph*, and was certainly from his pen.

It is another amazing instance of Heine's naïve belief that he could have it both ways—launch the most reckless insults and expect the injured party to forget them as soon as he chose to forget them himself. As a matter of fact that drastic poem had appeared first in the *Vorwärts* in 1844, and so he probably did think it belonged to the " past, in relation to which no accusations should be brought up against me ", and that little as his request might be in accord with administrative customs, " in an exceptional time they might perhaps be ready to enrich the old records by a special rubric for exceptional contemporaries."

Varnhagen, Lassalle, and Prince Hermann von Pückler-Muskau are urged to intervene with Karl on his behalf, and the Prince writes a letter to him, but is politely but very firmly told that it is a family matter which outsiders cannot appreciate, and that he does not wish to discuss the question. Heine, to be sure, is enraptured with the Prince's letter, of which he sees a copy. " What a grand seigneur ! " he writes to Lassalle. " His letter is not merely a literary masterpiece, but also a significant document, more important than may appear to him himself, in relation to our social conditions and transformations. . . . Here one of the last knights of the old aristocracy of birth gives the upstarts of the new aristocracy of wealth a lesson on the point of honour in the interests of outraged genius."

Nothing avails, neither the intervention of friends, nor the " de-und wehmütige Briefe " (the humble and pathetic letters) which he himself addresses to Karl, and for the humiliation of which he blames those friends, Meyerbeer, Varnhagen and others, whose advice he had followed in writing them. Karl Heine stood firm against the combination of threats and cajolery. As late as February 1846 Heine is speaking in a letter to Varnhagen of appeals to the generosity of his cousin, and a further press campaign against him in the shape of sham attacks upon himself: " Karl Heine will see that he will have in fact to pay the pension in any case from fear of manifestations in the press, but narrow-mindedness and the tyrannical pleasure of letting me constantly feel his despotic caprice will restrain him from doing the only sensible thing, namely, pacifying me by a definite undertaking."

That is Heine's way of putting it, and it is usual with those who defend Heine through thick and thin to represent him without qualification as the injured party. However, if one looks at the matter impartially, it is hard to see how the blame can be put all on one side. As a matter of fact Karl did pay him the amount of the pension all the time, as Heine himself admitted. It was only towards the end of the year, after the false news of Heine's death had spread in Germany, that the quarrel was at last patched up. " Karl Heine has written me the most affectionate and friendly letter ", he writes. . . . " But the confidence in my family is gone. . . . We have both committed great follies, but I pay for them more dearly with the remnants of my health."

In the end Heine only got what he could have had all along, the assurance of his pension on condition of writing nothing concerning the family without submitting it first to their censorship. The breach was formally healed, yet Heine neither forgave nor forgot, but nursed the sense

of injury in a mind embittered by illness and disappointment. He had given, it is true, an undertaking to publish
nothing against the family, but that did not prevent his
writing poems which have handed down to posterity his
flaming passion and fury at all the wrongs, real and imagin-
ary, which he had suffered at the hands of the old
" Brummbär Boreas " Solomon, at his house " Affrontenburg " in Ottensen, and all the treachery of his " Magen
und Sippen."

Meantime the effect of all this agitation had been disastrous for Heine's health. It had been giving him grave
trouble in the immediately preceding years ; especially
during the second German visit of 1844 there are constant
complaints of his eyes, and of the headaches from which he
had suffered from his early days. All the same he had
been able hitherto to carry on his life in fair comfort, but
it is not long after the outbreak of the quarrel before other
serious symptoms begin to make their appearance. In
March, 1845 he is complaining to Campe of paralysis of
the chest. In the summer he spends some weeks in the
country at Montmorency, but without any permanent
benefit. In October he writes to Campe the moving
words : " Once sweetest life, now gloom and longing for
death." He cannot read at all ; his left eye has been
completely closed since January, and he is afraid of total
blindness.

At the beginning of 1846 he tried, unsuccessfully as we
have seen, to get permission of the Prussian authorities to
go to Berlin to consult there a friend of his youth, the
famous surgeon Professor Dieffenbach. In February his
lips are often so paralysed that he sits silent whole evenings
through by the fire with his wife. " Quelle conversation
allemande ! " she often exclaims with a sigh. The tongue,

too, is attacked, he tells Varnhagen ; it and the palate and tongue are so dead that everything tastes like earth. In March he writes to Campe that his illness has made terrible strides in the last fortnight.

In June he goes again to the Pyrenees, but after a temporary improvement his condition grows worse than ever. The news spreads indeed in Germany that he is already dead. On September 1st, he writes to Campe from Tarbes that he cannot speak, and that he has not been able to eat for four months on account of the difficulty of swallowing and the absence of taste. Also he is terribly emaciated ; his poor paunch has lamentably disappeared, and he looks like a withered one-eyed Hannibal. He thinks there is no hope for him, though he may drag on a painful existence for one or at most two years. And there follows the characteristic passage : " Well, that is not my affair ; that is in the hands of the eternal gods, who have nothing to reproach me with, and whose cause I have always championed on earth with courage and love. The pleasant consciousness of having lived a fine life fills my soul even in this troublous time, and will I hope accompany me in the last hours to the edge of the white abyss." Only from his mother does he conceal his true state ; as he tells Campe, his reports to her contain the exact opposite of the truth. As a Christmas greeting he sends her the message that he is better, is eating and drinking with a good appetite, and has got rid of all his doctors ; though on the very same day he tells Campe that his health is in a pitiable condition.

During the year 1847 he grew rapidly worse. In April he tells Campe that if it were not for his wife and parrot he would put an end to his misery like a Roman. He again spent the summer months in Montmorency, where he was visited by many friends, Meissner, Laube

and others. The change appears to have been considerable even during the time spent in Montmorency.
Meissner gives at the beginning of his *Erinnerungen*
a description of Heine as he saw him for the first
time in the February of that year. " He was far from
being the invalid we came to think of a few years later.
His right eye was closed to be sure, but no other traces of
the stroke were visible in his face. That face was of
peculiar beauty, the brow high and broad, the nose fine and
nobly formed ; the delicate mouth was shaded by a beard,
which also covered the whole chin. This beard was
already streaked with white, while the brown hair, which
hung low on his neck, showed in its fullness no trace of
age."

Meissner draws, too, an interesting picture of the parties
which Heine gave on Sundays to the numerous guests in
his villa at Montmorency, and of the expansive mode of
living of this invalid poet, who even now refused to abdicate
his place at the table of life. That is one form of the courage which Heine so freely displayed.

" Almost every Sunday the omnibus that goes from
Enghien to Montmorency had to halt at the house in the
Châtaigneraie and deposit there a troupe of guests. . . . We
found Heine lying out of doors, portfolio and pencil in
hand, writing and composing. Mathilde's parrot had not
been left behind in the city, his cage stood at the window,
and as often as the bell of the garden-door rang, he greeted
the arrivals with a loud *Bon jour !* The big room on the
ground floor was used as dining-room ; on the neatly-
appointed table a giant bouquet was never lacking, each
place had its little arsenal of glasses for the madeira, médoc
and sauterne, with the champagne glass towering above
them. What a pleasure to sit down to table in the cool

shady garden-house, amid the scent of acacias in bloom, with beautiful Frenchwomen as neighbours and Heine as host ! When the presence of friends he liked distracted his thoughts momentarily from his sufferings, and he was stimulated by the conversation of pretty women, he was inexhaustible in witty sallies, and they flew rocket-like in all directions."

But bravely as he fronted it, the end even of such qualified sociability was near. A few days before he left Montmorency for Paris, on 20th September, Heine wrote to his old friend, the Princess Belgiojoso, that the paralysis had now attacked his feet and legs, so that for a fortnight he had been unable to move. He would gladly have wintered in the south, in the hope of securing some relief, but his finances would not permit it, and he spent the next months in Paris, with physical calamity closing down upon him. Only painfully could he hobble about, with the help of a stick, half-blind, through the streets of Paris.

At the beginning of February he went to a private hospital in the Rue de l'Ourcine, out beyond the Jardin des Plantes. From there he had driven on the 24th February, the very day the Revolution broke out, to his home in the Faubourg Montmartre, and on the return journey his carriage was seized by the insurgents. He had to make his way back as best he could. Trapped in a street between two barricades, he had one of the best places for seeing the performance, he said, " a place in the stalls, so to speak."

The Revolution brought Heine only discouragement and further troubles. Of his political attitude more will be said later. On the financial side alone he was badly hit. Not only did the bank in which his savings were deposited fail, but he lost the pension which he had been drawing from the government of Louis Philippe. That was more

than a merely financial matter, for among other disclosures
in the archives of that régime, the matter of these political
pensions came to light. It is true that Heine was in good
company, but it was a thing which his best friends found it
hard to defend, and with which his enemies were able to
make deadly play, and which was indeed used with effect
to discredit him still further in those quarters in Germany
which already were sufficiently embittered against him.

For the half-blind cripple the upheaval was only an
added complication of his already sufficiently complicated
existence. It was in the turbulent Paris of those revolutionary days that he sallied forth for the last time, alone and
unaided, as a free man among his fellows, into that world
which he had loved so well. It was the end of all his
journeyings, by sea and by land ; after that the world was
to narrow down for him to three successive bedrooms,
and the transport of his helpless carcase from one to the
other of them. Meissner tells the story as he heard it
from Heine's lips, and we have it in the poet's own words
in the Epilogue to the *Romanzero* which he wrote in
1851 :

" It was in May, 1848, on the day when I went out for
the last time, that I took farewell of the gracious idols that
I had worshipped in the days of my prosperity. With
difficulty I dragged my steps to the Louvre, and I well-
nigh broke down when I entered the stately hall, where the
blessed goddess of beauty, Our Lady of Milo, stands on her
pedestal. I lay long at her feet, and I wept so bitterly, that
it would have melted the heart of a stone. The goddess
indeed looked down pityingly upon me, but at the same
time disconsolately, as though she would say: ' Cannot
you see then, that I have no arms and therefore cannot
help ? ' "

Whatever basis of fact the story may have, it is a good poetical allegory of the close of one phase of the poet's life.

Towards the end of May he went to Passy to escape the noise and feverish excitement of Paris. It was here, in the "peaceful little town", that the enemy which had been testing him for years finally swooped down and overwhelmed him. On 7th June he writes to Campe : " I have been living here in the country now for twelve days, wretched and miserable beyond words. My illness has made horrible strides. For the last week I have been completely paralysed, so that I am confined to my armchair and my bed ; my legs are like cotton, and I am carried like a child. The most horrible convulsions. My right hand, too, is beginning to die, and God knows whether I shall be able to write to you again. Dictating is painful on account of my paralysed jaws. Blindness is the least of my afflictions."

To his brother Max he writes on 12th September : " In the last three months I have suffered more tortures than ever the Spanish Inquisition was able to invent. . . . Even if I do not die at once, I am robbed of life for good and all, and I love life with such fervent passion. For me there are no more mountain peaks to climb, no more women's lips to kiss, not even a good joint of beef in festive company."

A week later he returned to Paris, since, as he said, he did not want to be buried in the cemetery at Passy, which must be very dull, but wanted to be near Montmartre, which he had long chosen as his last resting-place.

His new quarters in Paris were at No. 50, Rue d'-Amsterdam, on the fourth story, looking out at the back on a small courtyard. He never saw the sky, and the sun but rarely found its way into his room. There he lived for six years, perhaps the most famous period of his life, for the tragic contrast of this setting with the rich country of his imagination has impressed itself upon the mind of the world, and made even the personality of the youthful poet of the *Buch der Lieder* shadowy in comparison. The stairs were so narrow that it was a matter of the greatest difficulty to carry a helpless invalid up and down them. He could not afford the expense that would have been involved in transportation to the country or the sea, and so he never left those cheerless quarters till he made the last double move in 1854. He suffered from all the assortment of noises that reverberate in the courtyard of such a barracks ; for years he was tortured by the strumming of some ladies in an opposite flat. Nor was it too restful in his own home. Mathilde was no manager and no nurse, and beside the cook, he had to have a nurse, a mulatto woman, to carry him from the bed to his chair. Most of the time he could not lie on any ordinary bed, but his mattress had to be piled up with cushions, the famous " mattress-grave."

In the first winter his condition grew even more terrible; it looked as though he could not possibly long survive. Meissner, who saw him again in January 1849, was appalled at the ravages which his disease had made in the two years since he saw him last in Montmorency. However, in the course of 1849 some slight temporary improvement showed itself, thanks to the treatment of a Hungarian doctor, Gruby, who appears to have been the first to diagnose his disease as a softening of the spinal column. That view has been disputed by later authorities, notably by Rahmer. Heine himself described it as a family inheritance. If he did inherit it, he inherited with it a most amazing tenacity of life, for few constitutions could have stood his sufferings so long.   But as we have seen, the Heine family was a very long lived and vigorous one.   He was able to take pleasure once more in his food, which had always played an important rôle with him.   To some extent also he became inured to his sufferings, and attuned to this narrow world. The thoughts of suicide, which had tempted him, but which he had thrust aside, partly from a feeling of duty towards Mathilde, partly from his irrepressible love of mere existence, attacked him less.   There was occasional alleviation, and some variation in the intensity of his pains, but yet, scattered through these eight years, we hear ever and again the tortured cry of a man tried well-nigh beyond human endurance.

What could be expected of this emaciated cripple, who was carried about in the arms of his black nurse like a baby, with legs hanging down like those of a big doll ; who was half-blind and often half-speechless, barely able to write ?   No one could have blamed him if he had given up the fight, and left the rest of the battle to others.   But he did nothing of the kind.   Whatever the cause of the illness may have been, he was a perfect prodigy of fortitude in enduring it.   Far from handing over the responsibility, this wreck of a man carried the whole establishment on his shoulders, the nurse who tended his puny frame, and the cook, and the housekeeper, and his secretaries and the doctors—to say nothing of his wife.   One wonders whether any other patient in so serious a plight ever paid his own way !

This cripple was indeed a tornado of energy.   He ran his business affairs with no less keenness than before, wrangled and quarrelled and bargained with Campe throughout these years.   He was struggling desperately the whole of the time with financial difficulties, as his fixed income, consisting of the pension from Karl and the yearly payment from Campe, which he had secured during that Hamburg visit of 1843, only covered about half his expenses. The rest had to be earned by his pen, or borrowed from his brothers, or anyone else, like the Rothschilds, who would assist him directly, or through allotment of shares in their undertakings. He had always dabbled in speculation since he had been in Paris, and his illness made no change in this respect either.

In spite of his partial blindness he read a great deal, both in German and French. He received many visits from German men of letters who were staying or living in Paris. Of French writers Béranger, and Dumas and Gautier were among the visitors. He always had a German secretary, the best of them being Karl Hillebrand and Richard Reinhart, and sometimes a French one as well. But he only dictated his letters to them. He wrote the works himself, and so it is little to be wondered at, if for that reason alone, that prose plays a less important part in this period of his life. His poems he wrote, mainly in the long, sleepless nights, in pencil on big sheets of white paper, in large letters, which, considering everything, are surprisingly clear and easy to read. This life of his was one that would have broken most people, but it was at any rate free from distractions, and in his solitude the inward-turning eye of the poet ranged to heights and depths that it would never have reached amid the stir of that outside world that he had loved so well, and whose temptations he could never resist.

The work of Heine in this last period bears the general character of a literature of escape, of withdrawal from the active present, and flight to the lands of memory, and those far distant horizons that could be visited only in imagina-

tion by the " Europe-weary " poet. In politics he had
been losing touch even before the final banishment to his
living grave. The famous letter of 3rd January, 1846 to
Varnhagen is one of the most important documents we
possess on Heine's change of feeling at this period, and a
most illuminating self-criticism of his whole political life.
He sees himself now as having been all along nothing but
the romantic dreamer in politics, the amateur, who is being
replaced by men of a sterner mould, clear-sighted, ruthless,
objective, who will look at things, not through a poetic
haze, but in all their crude reality, who will not dream, but
organise and act. Lassalle, to whom he is giving a letter of
introduction to Varnhagen, is in his eyes characteristic of
this younger, more scientific generation :

" Lassalle is in truth a typical child of the new age, who
has no use for that renunciation and moderation with which
in our time we idled and dreamed along more or less hypo-
critically. This new generation means to enjoy and make
good in the Visible world ; we of the older bowed humbly
before the Invisible, snatched at shadow kisses and the scent
of blue flowers, renounced with tears, and were yet perhaps
happier than those hard gladiators, who go so proudly into
mortal combat. The thousand-year-old Holy Romantic
Empire has come to an end, and I myself, its last fabled
king, was dethroned. If I had not snatched the crown
from my head and pulled on the smock, they would have
beheaded me without a doubt. Four years ago, before I
became a renegade to my own cause, the longing overcame
me to roam once more in the moonlight with my old dream
friends—and I wrote Atta Troll, the swan-song of the age
that was passing away, and I dedicated it to you. It was
only your right, for you have always been my closest and
nearest brother-in-arms, in jest and in earnest ; like me you

helped to bury the old age and to bring the new to birth—yes, we have brought it into the world and are frightened at the result. We are like the poor hen that hatched the duck's egg, and saw with horror its young brood plunging into the water and swimming merrily about ! "

In June, 1847 he tells Campe that he cannot enter into the political "expectorations" of his last letter, since his own tub-thumping days are over—a very illuminating phrase for his change of attitude. It is true that the February Revolution aroused in him once more a temporary interest, and after a lapse of five years he took up again his old rôle of tribune. But the articles for the *Allgemeine Zeitung*, the last he wrote for it, collected in his works under the title *Die Februarrevolution*, show little of the flaming enthusiasm with which in Norderney he had greeted that earlier rising. He complains that his head is quite dizzy with the constant drumming and shooting, and that the everlasting Marseillaise almost drives him mad. Then, in 1830, it " filled him with fire and joy, and kindled in him the glowing stars of inspiration ". He is filled with mild regrets for Louis Philippe, " the only possible king for the French ", as he says and, no republican himself, maliciously adds that the French are now condemned to republicanism in perpetuity.

More and more he grows weary of the disturbance, and sceptical of any genuine democracy in the Paris world as he knows it. " Of current events I will say nothing," he writes to Campe in July. " It is universal anarchy, sheer topsy-turveydom, cosmic muddle, most patent heaven-sent delirium." These words were written in an hour of many trials and great depression, but the word he uses (" Gotteswahnsinn ") sends his lively fancy off, and there follows the characteristic quip : " If it goes on so, He will have to be shut up. It is all the fault of the atheists for driving Him mad!"

In 1849 Meissner reports that he rarely spoke of politics, in which he had lost interest, and that his literary work occupied the first place, while the religious question was gradually obtruding itself into his thoughts. This last period of his life was indeed, in more ways than one, a return from the middle period of prose and politics and positivism to the interests of his youth and to his own fundamental nature. Verse predominates, he dwells in the past, and writes up his memories; and he abandons both Saint-Simonian dogma, and metaphysical abstractions, for the belief in a personal God, the God of his Fathers.

Much has been written about Heine's "conversion", and it has been turned by his enemies, like everything else, to his discredit. It is nothing but a death-bed repentance, they say; the attempt of a conscious reprobate to escape his well-deserved doom. There were many by this time for whom Heine could do nothing right, and who saw only further degeneracy in the return of this baptised Jew to the God of the Hebrews under stress of suffering and fear of death. The case itself is not so simple, and it is not made simpler by a study of Heine's own statements on the matter. It was certainly not a blind, humble, submissive surrender of all personal will and opinion to the teaching of a definite church, such as has sometimes been seen in the return to the fold of avowed unbelievers. Heine never becomes pious and devout in the ordinary sense, never curbs his mischievous wit, or fears that the deity in whom he believes will take amiss the sallies of his wayward and paradoxical humour.

There is a good deal of pose even here, as in everything he did his whole life through, and the mood of the moment and the circumstances colour his presentation of this change of mind. Yet on the whole it is true that the Jewish faith, which had been nothing more than the conventional religion of his youth, becomes the very real refuge and strength of his years of adversity. Unwillingly as it were, and with mockery at his own weakness, he watches the change taking place, the cynical spectator and the subject at once of this experience. A typical confession of this change of heart, made in the very year that saw the final triumph of his disease, is to be found in a letter written to his brother Max on December 3rd, 1848 :

"There has come over me a tearfulness and a sighing that is foreign to my inmost nature, and which fills me with special alarm as a mysterious phenomenon. (It is as though his earlier words concerning Schelling had occurred to him.) You must not be surprised if one of these fine days my Muse appears to you in the guise of a penitent. In my sleepless nights of torture I compose very beautiful prayers, which I do not have taken down, and which are all addressed to a very definite God, the God of our fathers. My old nurse told me last night that she knows a good prayer for cramp in the knees, and I begged her earnestly to offer it for me while she wrapped the hot bandages round them. The prayer was successful, and the cramp left me. But what will they say of me in heaven ? I can already hear many a high-principled angel saying contemptuously of me : ' here's an unprincipled fellow, who, when he's ill, gets old women to intercede for him with the very God whom he mocked so bitterly in his time of health.' "

The most famous statement is probably that contained in the communication which Heine sent in April of this year to the editor of the *Unparteiischer Korrespondent* in

Hamburg, in correction of false rumours as to the state of his health and his financial position :

" At many moments, especially when the spasms in my spinal column are raging all too fiercely, the doubt flashes through my mind, whether man is really a two-legged God, as the late Professor Hegel assured me twenty-five years ago in Berlin. In May of last year I had to take to my bed and I have not left it since. In the meantime, I will candidly confess, a great change has taken place in me. I am no longer a divine biped ; I am no longer ' the freest German since Goethe ', as Ruge called me in healthier days ; I am no longer the Great Heathen Number Two, who was compared with the vine-wreathed Dionysius, whilst my colleague, Number One, was given the title of the Grand Ducal Jupiter of Weimar. I am no longer a plump Hellene filled with the joy of life, looking with smiling condescension on gloomy Nazarenes—I am now nothing but a poor Jew, sick unto death, an emaciated image of misery, an unhappy wretch ! "

One of the most remarkable letters that even Heine ever wrote is that to Campe of 1st June, 1850, in which he blames him for the delay in bringing out his poems, since his religious views have changed in the meantime. Now, from a sense of straight dealing with his new-found God, he has had to " tear out with resolute hand the most beautiful passion flowers from the earlier blasphemous period ", whereas if they had been already printed he " would have been able to let them stand and say ' quod scripsi, scripsi.' " That letter must be read in connection with his most famous manifesto, the recantation found in the *Nachwort zum Romanzero* written on September 30th, 1851 :

" Poems which contained anything even approaching personalities against God, I have consigned to the flames with the most scrupulous zeal. It is better that the verses should burn rather than the versifier. Yes, I have made peace, not only with His creatures, but also with the Creator himself, to the great offence of all my enlightened friends, who reproached me with this relapse into the old superstition, as they chose to call my return to God. . . . Yes, I have returned to God like the Prodigal Son, after I had long tended swine with the Hegelians. Was it distress that drove me back? Perhaps a less miserable reason. I was overcome by a divine nostalgia, which drove me forth through forest and ravine, over the dizziest mountain-peaks of dialectics. On my way I found the god of the pantheists, but he availed me naught. This poor chimerical being is interwoven and intertwined with the world, imprisoned in it as it were, and is but a yawning emptiness, powerless and without a will. To have a will you must have a person, who must have his elbows free for its manifestation. When one wants a God who can help—and that is after all the chief thing—one must accept, too, His personality, His extra-terrestriality and His sacred attributes, All-Goodness, All-Wisdom, All-Justice, and so on. . . . Yet I must expressly deny the rumour that my retrogression has led me to the threshold of any church, much less into its fold. No, my convictions and views have remained free of all ecclesiasticism ; no bells have allured me, and no candles dazzled me." Almost at the end of his life, in the *Geständnisse* in 1854 he said the same thing in nearly the same words.

Amid all the variants, that is the dominant note. He did not formally return to the Jewish faith, and apparently never thought of abandoning the protestant confession into which he had been baptised, and which now as ever sat lightly upon him. He returned unreasoningly and instinctively to the God of his childhood, the God of the old Testament, to the humble faith of the common man. " I, who used formerly to quote Homer, am now quoting the Bible like Uncle Tom ", he says in the *Geständnisse*. " In truth I owe much to it. It has re-awakened religious feeling in me ; and this rebirth of religious feeling suffices the poet, who perhaps far more easily than other mortals can dispense with positive dogmas. He possesses grace, and the symbolism of heaven and earth is revealed to his eyes ; he needs for that the key of no church."

Meantime, from his sick-bed his eyes were turning back, not only in religion, to the things of his youth. " Cut off by my physical state from the pleasures of the outside world ", he writes to the younger Cotta on 26th March, 1852, " I seek for compensation in the sweet dream-world of memory, and my life is nothing but a backward groping into the past." Much of his work in this last period is an escape from the complex philosophy of the modern world to the simple theogony of ancient Palestine, from the grey realism of nineteenth century Paris to those exotic lands which he and his contemporaries clothed with all the gay colours of romance, from sickness and age to the golden days of childhood.

It is characteristic that of the prose works of the period the most important are autobiographical—the *Geständnisse* and the *Memoiren*, written at the very end of his life. Several others appeared in the first of the three volumes of the *Vermischte Schriften* in October, 1854, namely, *Die Götter im Exil*, *Die Göttin Diana* and *Ludwig Marcus*. The second and third volumes consisted of a collection of older essays, written for the *Allgemeine Zeitung* in the years 1840 to 1843, to which he here gave the title *Lutetia*.

Die Götter im Exil, which appeared as an article in the *Revue des Deux Mondes* in 1853, and in an unauthorised German re-translation in the same year, took up again a favourite theme of Heine's, which he had already treated in the *Salon*, that of the transformation of graeco-roman mythology into daemonology and witch-craft under the influence of Christianity.

Die Göttin Diana had been written in 1846, and like *Doktor Faust*, written in 1847, was due to the suggestion of Benjamin Lumley, the director of Her Majesty's Theatre in London, who required some subjects suitable for ballets. *Die Göttin Diana* never got beyond the brief scenario, and no use was made of it, any more than of his *Faust*, though he received for the latter the respectable fee of six thousand francs. Heine had, like most poets of the age, dreamed in his youth of writing a Faust, and it was the mention of that plan that helped to alienate Goethe's sympathy during the famous visit of 1824. Heine, whose most important source was Scheible's *Kloster*, claimed as a great merit of his *Tanzpoem* its greater truth to the Faust of the legend than is found in Goethe's work. He had for a time extravagant notions of its value, placing it above the *Romanzero*, with which for a time he intended to publish it, though eventually the two appeared separately in the same year, 1851. When trying to persuade Campe to give him one thousand marks for it in June, 1847, he described it as a poem which is a ballet only in form, and as one of his " greatest and most highly poetical productions." Campe did not make the offer, and few have been found to share Heine's view of his work.

The real reflection of his inner life is found in this period not in his prose, but in his poetry. If he was not a poet now, helpless on his mattress-grave, he was nothing.

" As you well know, dear Reader ", he wrote in the *Geständnisse*, after drawing the fantastic picture of himself as pontiff, " I have not become a pope, nor a cardinal, nor even a Roman Nuntius ; I have won neither office nor dignity, either in the temporal or the spiritual hierarchy. I have come to no good, as they say. I have come to nothing, nothing but a poet."

Hence the great event of these years is the publication in 1851 of his third great collection of poems, under the title of *Romanzero*. Other poems were written right up to the end, some of which appeared in the second edition of the *Neue Gedichte* in 1852, some in the *Vermischte Schriften* of 1854, but most only after his death. We shall consider at the end as a whole the poetic production of this last phase of his life. The success of *Romanzero* was immense, such as no collection of lyric poems has ever had in Germany before or since. Within a few months four editions, comprising some twenty thousand copies, had been sold. He received a good fee from Campe, but not enough to affect materially his financial position. It was only the success of the *Vermischte Schriften* in 1854 that enabled him at last to escape from the prison house of the *Rue d'Amsterdam*.

The cholera was raging then in Paris, and his fear of it was one of the reasons for the move. He went first to Batignolles, where he took a house with a large garden, and there for the first time for six years he could be taken out of doors, and would sit in fine weather under the trees. For a time he was delighted with the change. " You have no idea," he writes to his mother, " how much good the fresh air and the sunshine that I missed in my old quarters are doing me." He did not even grudge the very heavy expense, he wrote, since his health was the most important thing of all, more important even than Mathilde, his "Verbrengerin," (squanderer), to whom he could not in any case leave enough. He sat in his own garden, feeling better than ever, and eating the plums that almost fell of themselves into his mouth.

It is pathetic to see his joy at this last vision of the free and open world, and the hopefulness that no sufferings could ever entirely kill. However, his joy was short-lived, for the new home proved cold and damp and more unhealthy than the old one ; he suffered greatly with his throat, and from an ulcer in the back, for which he had to undergo a painful operation. A second move, and further heavy expenses, proved necessary, and on 6th November he had made his last and final journey, and was back in the heart of Paris. His new home was at 3, Avenue Matignon, off the Champs Elysées. It was at the top of the building, removed from the din of the street, was light and airy, and had a balcony to which he could be carried on fine days, and see something of the busy world from which he was an exile. There he spent the remaining fifteen months of his life, and though the long illness had thinned the circle of his acquaintances, some admirers, relatives and friends still found their way up the many steps to his flat.

The first summer in the new home brought him the visit of many German friends, who had come to Paris for the great exhibition, Adolf Stahr, Fanny Lewald and others. In the autumn of that year his sister Charlotte came with Gustav to visit him. Gustav soon returned to Vienna, for he felt a dislike, fully-reciprocated, for Mathilde, whom he regarded as the cause of all his brother's troubles. Charlotte on the other hand apparently got on quite well with her, and she stayed two months as her brother's guest, leaving only at the beginning of December on receiving news of the sudden illness of one of her children, and with the solemn promise to return the following spring. Her son, Baron Ludwig v. Embden, records in his book, *Heinrich Heines Familienleben*, a long account given him by his mother of this meeting, the last that Heine had with any member of his family. After the reports she had heard of his illness, Charlotte had been dreading the first sight of him : " But since I saw only the head, which was of a wonderful, transfigured beauty, and his smile, I was able to abandon myself to the first joy of meeting. Yet when, towards afternoon, the nurse carried my brother in her arms to a couch, in order to make up the bed, and I saw his shrunken body, from which the legs hung lifelessly down, I had to summon up all my strength to endure the terrible sight." Her presence was a very great comfort to him, and he sat long, with his sound right hand in hers, talking in his German mother-tongue of far-off, happy youthful days.

Heine was engaged then with his autobiography, and this visit of the playfellow of his youth must have been a very great stimulus in the work. He was only carrying out a long-cherished plan. He had been occupied with the *Memoiren* off and on throughout the twenties and thirties. He told Campe in a letter of 1st March, 1837, when there was a question of writing his autobiography as an appendage to his works, that he was planning to write " not a dry summary, but a big book, perhaps of several volumes, which should form the conclusion of the Collected Edition, and should comprise the whole history of my times, in whose great moments I have played a part, along with the most notable people of my day, the whole of Europe, the whole of modern life, German conditions up to the July Revolution, the results of my sojourn in the lobby of the political and social revolution, the fruits of my most costly and painful studies, the book that is very specially expected of me." " Even if I were to die to-day," he wrote to Campe in 1840, " I should leave four volumes of Autobiography or Memoirs."

Then at the end of the forties, partly owing to the undertaking he had given his cousin Karl not to publish anything against him or other members of the family, and partly owing to the change in his religious views, he had destroyed half of what he had written. At the beginning of 1854 he set about the task of re-writing them. Alphonse Trittau, in a letter to Campe of 1st February, 1854, quotes him as saying that he had already got so far that a volume would be able to appear in a year.

He first of all wrote the *Geständnisse*, which he described as a precursor of his *Memoiren*, written in a more popular and more picturesque style, and which appeared in a French translation in the *Revue des Deux Mondes* in the September of that year. There they made " the most tremendous furore ", in spite of the changes and mutilations which had been made in his version. A few days afterwards they appeared in an unauthorised German version in the Augsburg *Allgemeine Zeitung*, adding another to the vexations which the little work caused him.

In the *Geständnisse* he says : " In another place, in my *Memoiren*, I relate more fully than I could here, how I migrated to Paris after the July Revolution." The little fragment we possess does not get so far ; it is mainly co-cerned with his parents, and ends with the melodramatic version of the Sefchen episode. The beginning is missing, having been destroyed by his brother Max. What became of the other half of the original *Memoiren* is not known. He may have destroyed it himself, as he tells us in the introduction he might be driven to do. Alfred Meissner describes how, after Heine's death, Mathilde showed him in an unguarded moment a thick pile of folio sheets, which she admitted in answer to his question to be the *Memoiren*. He surmises that they were ready to be despatched to some purchaser, some member of the Heine plutocracy. If so, it may have been Karl, or possibly even Gustav, who frequently asserted that he possessed the manuscript. Wherever it went, it was probably bought in order to be destroyed, and there is very little likelihood of its ever being seen again. The fragment which we now possess was published only in 1884 after Mathilde's death.

Apart from Charlotte, there were three other women whose visits were, in their different ways, of special interest in these last years. In the June of 1853 Therese was in Paris, and in spite of the opposition of the family insisted on coming to see him, though " only in the company of Karl, who was sent with her as sentry, so that I should say nothing that she ought not to hear ", as Heine wrote to his mother. His sufferings and the courage with which he bore them obviously made a deep impression on her. His image remained constantly before her, and on 10th August she wrote him a letter, which is touching in its naivety. She obviously knew little of the real state of affairs between Heine and her side of the family, and the whole tone of that letter lends colour to the view that in giving up her cousin she was obeying the family influence against the promptings of her heart. The poem in the cycle *Zum Lazarus:* " Ein Wetterstrahl, beleuchtend plötzlich Des Abgrunds Nacht, war mir dein Brief," may well have been called forth, as Elster suggests, by the effect produced on Heine by that letter, though one can hardly agree with Elster that it is like the final word of reconciliation in a

Shakespearean tragedy. If that poem means anything, it surely means that her letter was a measure, not of her tenderheartedness, but of his misery, which could move even her to pity, and that her visit as little re-awakened the old feelings as did the meeting with Amalie in 1827.

Another visitor, who revived more pleasant memories, was Lady Duff Gordon, (Lucie Austin), whom he had met as a child of eleven in Boulogne in 1833, and with whom he liked to talk in German of those happier times, and of the fairy stories which he had told her then. She visited him in 1853 and again in 1855. Descriptions of her visits to Heine are incorporated in *Monographs, personal and social*, by Lord Houghton (Monckton Milnes).

Very apt is her account of the impression made on her by Heine's appearance on the first of these visits : " his face was as full of pain and as emaciated as would be found in the *Ecce Homo* of any old German painter"—a description that might well apply to the portrait of him by Lots which appeared in the *Revue des Deux Mondes* in the previous year. Interesting, too, are the words she quotes Heine as saying in reply to her remark that he had never been able to stand her countrymen :

" Why, upon my soul, I don't know what I had against the English, that I was always so spiteful against them ; but to tell the truth, it was only a mischievous pose, for I never really hated them, and, in fact, never knew them. I was once in England many years ago, but I knew nobody there, and found London very dull, and the people in the streets looked awful to me. But England has taken a fine revenge ; it has sent me some excellent friends—you and Milnes, good Milnes !—and others besides."

More important than these visitors, whose presence

served above all to arouse memories of that past world from which he was for ever cut off, was a fresh acquaintance, whose coming opened up for him a new world on the very brink of the grave. It was in June, 1855, that " Camilla Selden " paid her first visit to Heine. She was known to Alfred Meissner, and it was probably through him that she came to call on the poet, whose fervent admirer she had long been. Her life is still something of a mystery, which the book she published in 1884, *Les derniers Jours de Henri Heine,* does little to clear up. It is doubtful how much she let even Heine or Meissner know of the real facts of her life. Though still young, probably in the late twenties, she had, it seems, already gone through many unpleasant experiences. She was born in Germany, but brought when quite young to France. She had been married to a certain Krinitz, apparently a rascal, from whom she was separated, after he had attempted to get her shut up in an asylum in England, and was at this time earning her living as a teacher in Paris. After Heine's death she disappeared again, and it was only with the publication of her book that the world learnt that she was still alive, and earning her living in Rouen by teaching German in a girls' school.

Heine had then just lost Richard Reinhart, who had been for many years his trusty secretary, and was unable to find any suitable successor. This Swabian girl with a command of French was then very welcome to him. She had a soft and pleasing voice, and read much aloud to him, and he discussed with her his poems and the translations of his works.

Charlotte, who met her during her stay in Paris, gives a very sympathetic account of her. She describes her as youthful and charming, rather graceful than beautiful, with a delicate face framed in brown hair. With her lovely blue eyes, and small mouth, that showed when she smiled her brilliant teeth, she must have possessed an attractiveness of which the one poor portrait we possess gives no suggestion. Heine was very anxious to know what Charlotte thought of her, and was doubtless much pleased at her approval. Mathilde on the other hand did not approve at all, and was, not altogether unnaturally, jealous of this bright little person, and took every opportunity of showing her dislike. Mouche was frail and sensitive, and Mathilde in her robust health probably despised her, in addition to being suspicious of qualities she could not understand. That the antipathy was mutual is very obvious from Mouche's book.

Mouche, as Heine called her from the fly engraved on her signet, soon became indispensable to him. There is no doubt that she was intellectually sympathetic to him, and even though he probably overrated her gifts, she was more to him than a mere literary adviser and partial substitute for his paid assistants. We have only to read the letters he wrote to her, and the poems she inspired, to see that this hopeless cripple, hovering on the very brink of the grave, half blind and paralysed, physically a mere shell of a man, was swept away by a love, that, while more etherealised perhaps than any of his other loves, was yet by no means platonic, but as sensuous and passionate as that of a youth. More wonderful still, there seems little doubt that he inspired a like feeling in her. Soon he would not have her out of his sight ; he would have liked to see her as a guest at their table, but that Mathilde refused to permit.

In the eight months of life that were left to him this was the great outstanding experience. His life had come full circle ; he was dwelling on the memories of his youth, and here he found himself actually in love once more, and this time with someone who did not ask for wealth or position, but for whom he was rich beyond compare in the things of the spirit. His letters to his " Mouche " are full of whimsical, fanciful, half-teasing, yearning expressions of his affection, inexhaustible in the invention of ever-new terms of endearment. In the first letter of 20th June, 1855, she is his " sehr liebenswürdige und charmante Person ! " The next is addressed to " Ma chère enfant ! " She is his " Liebste Seele ", " Liebe süsse Seele ", his " Lotosblume ", " Allersüsseste fine mouche ! " And the great phrase-maker is so pleased with some of these that we find them in the poems too— the " Lotosblume " indeed twice over. The refrain of a song of Mendelssohn is constantly ringing in his brain, " Komme du bald ! ", and that is the constant refrain of his letters. That impatience for her coming receives its final pregnant expression in the poem : *Lass mich mit glüh'nden Zangen kneipen.* One significant letter is addressed to his " Liebste Helöise ", and contains the English words, " My brain is full of madness and my heart is full of sorrow ! " " Never ", he adds, " was a poet more wretched at the summit of fortune, which seems to make mock of me."

When he wrote these words he obviously felt that he had met too late a woman who could have given him all that he had sought in vain throughout his life. The poem beginning " Worte ! Worte ! keine Taten ! " is nothing but a poetic version of the phrase in his New Year's letter : " Leider kann ich nichts für Dich thun, als Dir solche Worte, ' Gemünzte Luft ' sagen. Meine besten Wünsche zum neuen Jahr—ich spreche sie nicht aus, Worte ! Worte ! " How characteristic is another sentence : " Du bist nicht so dumm, wie Du aussiehst ; zierlich bist Du über alle Massen und daran erfreut sich mein Sinn."

The letters go on through these few months, right into the new year. Heine's condition was meantime growing worse. He has more often to tell his Mouche that the " *maître-d'école* " is so ill that there will be " no school to-day ". She visited him for the last time on 14th February, and when she went he begged her to return on the morrow. However, the end of his sufferings had now really come at last. He had often spoken of dying in these last weeks ; in January for instance he sent his card to Alexander von Humboldt with the words : " To the great Alexander the last greetings of the dying Heine." He warned people that if they wished to see him again they must not delay, as he might pass away any time. All the same he probably never thought his end was actually so near ; he had been threatened so often. And now when the end did come, it was in a sense a minor trouble that carried him off—a sickness that began the night after Mouche left him, and went on for three days. Even in this state he still tried to work. He began to draft a new will, but did not get beyond the first paragraph. Meissner, in his account of these last days, tells the oft repeated anecdote of the friend who rushed into his room a few hours before his death, fearful that he might be too late, and hardly over the threshold, asked the dying poet how he stood with God. His wit was ready as ever and he answered with a smile : " Do not worry ! *Dieu me pardonnera, c'est son métier !* "

Meissner does not give the name of the officious friend, and the setting of the story is no doubt apocryphal, though

Heine may well have used those words on another occasion. When Dr. Gruby visited him the last night, Heine asked whether he was dying, and when told the truth, received the news calmly. The end came at four o'clock on the Sunday morning, the 17th February. Mathilde was not present when he passed away, and Mouche only saw him late in the morning. "He was in death more beautiful than anyone had ever seen him in life," says Meissner. "Even his physician declared that he had never known death to cast such serenity even on the faces of the young. The death-mask has preserved a faithful and lasting impression of those features." Mouche describes her last impression as that of an antique mask, a pale, marble face, whose beautiful lines recalled the most sublime masterpieces of Greek art.

In accordance with his own repeated wish, the poet was buried, not in the famous Père Lachaise, but in the cemetery of Montmartre. He had desired that his burial should be simple, without any funeral address, and without religious ceremony. It took place on 20th February, on a cold and misty morning. Some hundred people were present, four-fifths of them Germans. Alexandre Dumas and Théophile Gautier were the most notable mourners. His grave was marked by a simple grave-stone, without any ornament, bearing merely the name "Henri Heine". Strodtmann describes that grave in the early eighties, while Mathilde was still alive, with its one upright and one horizontal slab of sand-stone, and no trace of wreath or flower. Mathilde refused the offer of his brother Gustav to erect a more imposing memorial, and only after her death did German and Austrian admirers unite to pay a tribute to his memory. Now there rises, since 1890, above the grave which from 1883 Mathilde had shared with him, the monument of the Danish sculptor L. Hasselriis. The column of white marble bears a lyre, on which is entwined a wreath of roses, and is surmounted by a bust of the poet.

On it are inscribed the beautiful words of that poem, to which the answer is furnished by this grave in a foreign land :

> "Wo wird einst des Wandermüden
> Letzte Ruhestätte sein?
> Unter Palmen in dem Süden?
> Unter Linden an dem Rhein?

> "Werd' ich wo in einer Wüste
> Eingescharrt von fremder Hand?
> Oder ruh' ich an der Küste
> Eines Meeres in dem Sand ?

> "Immerhin ! Mich wird umgeben
> Gotteshimmel, dort wie hier,
> Und als Totenlampen schweben
> Nachts die Sterne über mir. "

Chapter Eleven

ROMANZERO AND LAST POEMS

The title which Heine gave to the last of the three collections of his poems, *Romanzero*, was not his own invention, but was due to a suggestion of his publisher Campe.
It was in fact due to Campe that they appeared at all at
this time ; Heine himself professed indifference, and said
there was no knowing when they would have been published, if Campe had not " put the thumb-screw on
him." At the beginning of the famous *Nachwort zum
Romanzero* he says the title is used because the predomi-
nant tone of the whole is that of the romance, and lays
great stress on the unity of mood and colouring. This
claim of his is, in fact, well founded. The word is a
Spanish one, denoting a collection of romances, and two-
thirds of the book consists of poems in those four-foot,
Spanish trochees, which Herder had first introduced in his
Cid, and which were so beloved of the Romanticists.
Five only of those poems, *Vitzliputzli*, *Spanische Atriden*
and the three *Hebräische Melodien*, occupy almost exactly
one half of the book.

It is then clear that we have to do with something quite
different from the *Buch der Lieder* or the *Neue Gedichte*.
Here Heine is above all the epic poet, and from the concentration of the ballad is drawn more and more to the
broader sweep of the mock-heroic or the longer romance
in verse. The poems were, unlike those of the two

previous books, mostly unknown. They had mainly been written in the three preceding years, under manifold physical disabilities and sufferings, he tells us. They represent for him largely the poetry of escape.

The poet of these years looked out on the world from an angle of vision that it has been given to few poets to occupy. Face to face with death, he reviews his own fate and human destiny ; looks back on his own past and compares it with the dark present. It is no wonder if the colouring is on the whole sombre. It would be true in a sense to call his *Romanzero* a great elegy, a great epic of renunciation. He himself described it as a miracle, since with the exception of a few small poems, he wrote the whole book in a state in which he cannot himself understand how such a manifestation was materially possible. It was a characteristic of the day that, weary of political struggles and disappointments, men turned to distant climes, and sought a golden age in the life of a more primitive humanity. Heine, too, sought that relief ; he writes in November, 1851, that he now reads mostly descriptions of travel, and for two months has not been out of Senegambia and Guinea. " Disgust with the whites is the reason why I immerse myself in this black world, which is really very entertaining. I like these negro kings better than our native rulers, though they likewise know little of human rights and look on slavery as a natural institution." He is " europamüde," to employ that term which he invented in the *Englische Fragmente*, and uses twice over here. The flight takes us not only to Persia and Mexico, but in the last and greatest section of the three to the world of his childhood's religion.

In the *Nachwort* he says that he has with zealous care committed to the flames all the poems which contained anything even approaching blasphemy. He tells Campe, too, that he has suppressed every poem which might give political offence. There is, indeed, an almost complete absence of the political lyric here ; Heine has abandoned his office of tribune. After being for thirty years a forlorn hope, " Enfant perdu," in the Wars of Liberation, now " Ein Posten ist vakant," and he hands on the torch to others, the younger men such as Lassalle, of Heine's admiration for whom we have already spoken. One of the finest, most spirited and most buoyant poems in the whole is that entitled *An die Jungen*, in which he hails these new protagonists. But that belongs to an earlier time, and had appeared already in 1846. Personalities and literary polemics are, to be sure, not avoided ; *Der Ex-Nacht-wächter* is full of coarse jibes at the obscurantism of the Munich school, while *Plateniden* is wittily drastic and effective in its ridicule of the pretentiousness of the progeny of his old antagonist.

The middle section, *Lamentationen*, consists mainly of a number of brief poems, in which the poet's utter disillusionment finds poignant expression. Notably is this the case with the twenty poems of *Lazarus*, the text of which is given in the brief introductory *Weltlauf*—" To him that hath shall be given and from him that hath not shall be taken away even that which he seemeth to have." If you have nothing you are a rogue, and had better get yourself buried. The rich are triumphant and arrogant, and can be won only by servile flattery, so swing your censer boldly before the golden calf ! The second, *Rückschau*, contrasts the hopeless present with the rosy promise of younger days, and the poet, "getränkt mit Bitternissen," looks into a yawning chasm of despair, and would fain find rest in the grave.

When he dreams of the friend of his youth, Wilhelm Wisetzki, who was drowned in trying to save a cat, he thinks now that his was the happier lot in dying before he fell ill of the sickness of the world. The hero perishes, " doch die Katze, die Katz' ist gerettet ! " Yet that mood does not always prevail. Even now, " Unjung und nicht mehr ganz gesund," his longing for life and love is not stilled, and though he may be " Der Abgekühlte ", with passions calmed, he dreams of the rapture of loving some blond and placid beauty with soft moonlight eyes. But vain are all such golden wishes, and sweet hopes ; they are but bubbles, that burst and vanish like his life. In *Gedächtnisfeier* he sees himself already buried in the cemetery of Montmartre, after a funeral bare of Christian mass or Jewish kadosch, and on a fine mild day, Mathilde comes to lay a wreath of immortelles upon his grave. She has had a long climb to his lofty dwelling, and he has no chair to offer her, and his dear plump girl must not drag her weary feet the long way home, but find herself a fiacre at the barrier. Playfully there, but more seriously in the poem *An die Engel*, he voices his anxiety for the wife he will soon have to leave behind. He already hears the hoofbeats of the pale horse, on which the dark rider, " der böse Thanatos," is rapidly overhauling him, and he implores the angels in the heights to guard her whom he will leave behind, as widow and orphan, when he shall have descended into the shades.

He sees in spirit the end of his life's tragedy. " Der Vorhang fällt, das Stück ist aus ; " the house grows still and dark ; the last light of all splutters and goes out : " das arme Licht war meine Seele." There follows then a poetic testament, *Vermächtnis*, on the lines of a well-established tradition. He bequeaths to his enemies all his tortures and pains, and as in *Nicht gedacht soll seiner werden* in the *Lamentationen*, he utters, as " the flower of all curses ", the wish that their very memory may for ever perish among the sons of men.

Apart from these, the volume consists mainly of the shorter poems contained in the first section, the *Historien*, and the six long narrative poems, upon which the justification of the title depends. These shorter ballad-like poems are very varied in character. A few only have the directness and naive sincerity of those earlier ballads which Heine had written in the spirit of the folk-song. He has never himself surpassed *Der Asra* in pregnant brevity and restraint ; it is universally acknowledged as one of his masterpieces. That, however, dates from a somewhat earlier period, for it had appeared in 1846 ; at the same time he wrote *Der Schelm von Bergen*, which is also in his best tradition. The legend is a Rhenish one, though Heine is himself responsible for placing the scene at Düsseldorf. It belongs to the sphere of his early associations, and the world of Red Sefchen, and has a freshness and vigour that make it worthy to compare with such a masterpiece of his younger days as *Der arme Peter*. *Schlachtfeld bei Hastings* deals also on a serious note, and in an objective, uncommentated narrative style, with the theme that underlies the whole book—the tragic fate of heroism and beauty in this pitiless world. These, however, are some of the exceptions, for in general the mock-heroic tone and the satiric spirit prevail.

The six long poems are *Der Dichter Firdusi, Vitz-iputzli, Spanische Atriden* and the three *Hebräische Melodien*, and of these the first four, at any rate, are all in their various ways among the finest things that Heine ever wrote. In all of them his own experiences are reflected, and often behind a very transparent veil.

Der Dichter Firdusi is the story of a poet cheated of his reward; who when he finds pieces of silver in place of the promised pieces of gold, spurns the gift with a superb pride that Heine would no doubt only too gladly have indulged in similar circumstances of his own life. The middle poem of the three, with its very obvious reference to his Uncle Solomon, his admiration for whom made what he regarded as his treachery the harder to bear, is one of the more restrained, but not least effective expressions of his enduring bitterness at that great disappointment of his trust. The final poem, which has the form and much of the spirit of his great ballad *Belsatzar*, shows all the lavish wealth of colour and imagery in which Heine's oriental fancy loved to run riot, while its effective close displays once again his masterly gift of carrying us with him to the culminating point of the action, and leaving the rest to our imagination.

Vitzliputzli is a flight of the " Europe-weary " poet to the New World, to that America discovered by Columbus, not as he says the Europeanised America of to-day. The form is the mock-heroic ; we find that common feature of the epic apparatus, the address to his winged steed, which Heine was so fond of employing. The verse is the Spanish Trochee, and Heine has never employed it more effectively than here. Trochees readily incline in German to slip over into a rising, iambic rhythm, and they do so frequently with Heine, as, for instance, in *Spanische Atriden*. Here, however, Heine keeps them down to a regular heavy tread, to a tom-tom-like beat, which is the most effective rhythmic form possible for the tale of barbaric horrors which he unfolds.

He displays a wonderful skill in the employment of long heavy words and weighty compounds, which reminds us of the mastery of his *Nordseebilder*. A considerable number of the lines are filled by two compounded tetra-syllables, which leave no possible doubt as to the rhythmic movement. One could find few finer examples of plastic imagery in verse than the description he gives of Mexico, the island city, lying in the midst of a great lake, and of the desperate sally of the Spaniards fighting for their lives over the bridges, rafts and fords. " Über Brücken, Flösse, Furten "—through the grim story these words ring like a passing-bell, tolling for the fugitives. It is, with *Bimini*, the best of all his longer narrative poems.

The next of these tales of horror, *Spanische Atriden*, gets its effect by quite different means. The gruesome recital is presented as the report of a story told by that entertaining raconteur, Don Diego Albuquerque, at a banquet given on the third of November, 1383, in his castle at Segovia by King Henry of Castile, and ends with the polite enquiry of the seneschal whether the guests had dined well. But in the studied realism of this setting is unfolded a grim history of family feuds and passions. It rises in an ascending scale of horrors from the murder by Pedro the Cruel of his brother Fredrego to the brutal revenge of Henry on Pedro's young sons, whom he keeps like dogs in a cage in the royal kennels, whither after the banquet the narrator is led out to view them. Heine first labelled the poem *Familiengeschichte*, and it is undoubtedly one of the various settings which he has given to his sense of family wrong. The end of the Siegfried-like Fredrego within this clan of ruthless egoists is another variant of the theme that pervades the whole. He deals with the historical facts very freely, and the two most striking features are his own invention, the treatment of the children, and the appearance of the dog Allan with the bloody head of his master, for the latter of which he himself challenges comparison with the scene at the feast of Belshazzar.

Of the *Hebräische Melodien*—a title borrowed from Byron—the finest by far, and one of the most striking things Heine has written, is the first, *Prinzessin Sabbat*. The high poetic seriousness underlying this poem reminds us of his earlier prose narrative, the *Rabbi von Bacharach*. If the latter was written in the flush of a youthful enthusiasm for the history of his race, the former shows the late awakening of a sense of community with his own people. The greatness of his subject, the tragic contrast between the inner wealth and external humiliations of the life they lead, give Heine here a dignity and singlemindeness that we too rarely find with him, and which show that he did not, in fact, depend for success on those glittering, paradoxical, and ironic qualities with which his fame is often associated.

Under the fiction of borrowing his allegory from a story of the *Arabian Nights*, Heine presents to us Israel as an enchanted prince, who lives the whole week through in his shape of a dog, but ever on the Sabbath eve regains the dignity of human form, and with uplifted head and heart is wedded to Princess Sabbath. The festal day moves on in a calm world of ceremonial and traditional joys, but with the approach of evening the hour of bewitchment draws near, when the Prince, after receiving from the hands of the Princess one last parting cup, will again suffer his hated metamorphosis.

The other two Melodies, *Jehuda ben Halevy* and *Disputation*, are much longer, but for all their interest less fine and less satisfying than the briefer opening poem. *Jehuda ben Halevy*, the twelfth century Jewish poet of Toledo, who in his old age, overcome by longing, made a pilgrimage to Jerusalem and there died, is Heine's great prototype and becomes for him a symbol of his own hereditary longing for the home and religion of his fathers, re-awakened at the end of his days. There ring constantly in his ears the words : " If I forget thee, O Jerusalem, let my right hand forget her cunning ; " ghostly bearded figures pass before him, and he recognises among them the great poet who with his song went before the suffering caravan of Israel, in the desert of their exile, like a singing pillar of fire. The poem contains many very beautiful passages, but it is somewhat diffuse as a whole ; when the story is really ended it rambles on, through a humorous reference to his wife, to a final section that leads nowhere. Heine rightly laid stress with Campe on placing the word " Fragment " at the end. Such epic breadth and even discursiveness, in place of the pregnant brevity and epigrammatic close which were earlier such noticeable features, is one of the outstanding characteristics of the poet of *Romanzero*.

The subject of the third poem, *Disputation*, is a dialectic tourney, before Pedro the Cruel at Toledo, between a Rabbi and a Franciscan, on the question which is the true God, the vanquished being pledged to adopt the religion of his victor. The battle rages twelve hours, and each does his best to outbid the other, more in vituperation than in argument, but the satiric close gives the victory to neither, expressing an equal distaste for both forms of bigotry.

With the appearance of *Romanzero* in 1851 Heine's poetic productivity by no means ceased ; for the remaining poems form a collection rather larger than either of the two preceding ones, and surpassed in bulk only by the *Buch der Lieder*.

Ten of them appeared under the title *Zur Ollea* in the third edition of the *Neue Gedichte* in 1852, more than thirty in the first volume of the *Vermischte Schriften* in 1854, and the rest after his death, partly in various periodicals, and partly in a volume published at Hamburg by Hoffmann and Campe in 1869 under the title *Letzte Gedichte und Gedanken*.

Gathy, Campe's plenipotentiary in Paris, quotes Heine on 13th September, 1853, as saying : " Campe thinks he has got the whole of the poet Heine, but he is wrong. Here (pointing to his portfolio) there are many more poems, the inspiration of the moment, with which I chase away my sufferings, death-bed poems. I am not yet dead." His unabated confidence in his powers is expressed in a letter to Campe in October of the same year, in which he says he can surpass the *Neue Gedichte* and even the *Romanzero* by " a later vegetation."

A special place among this latest harvest is occupied by the collection, about a third of the whole, which appeared in 1854 under the title *Gedichte 1853 und 1854*, since Heine arranged and published them himself. Had he lived long enough, he would doubtless have incorporated them in a fourth volume, with the same care for its artistic composition as he had displayed in the three that went before. Of this particular group may be said, as indeed of these last poems as a whole, that we have, in general, variations on the themes of the *Romanzero*, with at times an intensification even of the tones of weariness and despair, of harsh mockery at life's injustices and man's brutality to man.

239

Ruhelechzend, the opening poem, ends with the last word of all pessimism :

> " Der Tod ist gut, doch besser wär's,
> Die Mutter hätt' uns nie geboren."

The next, *Im Mai*, with its refrain, " O schöne Welt, du bist abscheulich," draws a grim contrast between his suffering state and the blossoming spring without and the joyous song of the birds :

> " Für leidende Herzen ist es viel besser
> Dort unten am stygischen Nachtgewässer."

The new *Lazarus* poems strike the same note as the older ones : it is not the bankruptcy of the world that he bewails, but its injustice :

> " Warum schleppt sich blutend, elend,
> Unter Kreuzlast der Gerechte,
> Während glücklich als ein Sieger
> Trabt auf hohem Ross der Schlechte ? "

Like a refrain at the end of most of them comes the longing for death, the desire to end " die schreckliche Tragödia ".   And yet, so great is the tenacity of life of this sufferer on the rack, that resignation and the desire for extinction do not always prevail.   His pessimism is a quali-fied one ; happiness of a sort is possible for humanity, for all the hardness of his individual lot.   And so at the end of this cycle, all grey in grey, the songs of a poet gazing into the black nothingness of despair, his humour and love of life break out in spite of all.   Though this life may be a vale of tears, he would be prepared to renounce all the fame of this world and all glories of the next, if he might but live on, in slippered comfort, with his wife *in statu quo* ! This is the other form of his renunciation, the renunciation of all aspiration in the clinging to mere naked life. " Better a live donkey than a dead lion ! " Such is the note of the *Epilog* with which he concluded this last collection ; better to live here in the light as the meanest slave than by the Stygian stream as a hero vaunted in Homer's song.

Political satire and polemical lyric do not play a very prominent part in these final years, and there is little new or of special note in this field, though at the same time there is no falling off in his wit and inventiveness, nor in his striking power. In his own compilation there are two or three poems which show Heine the humorist at his best : *Erinnerung aus Krähwinkels Schreckenstagen*, with its delightful burlesque of the language of bumbledom, *Die Audienz*, in which he treats again with malicious parody the relations of Herwegh to Frederick William IV., and *Kobes I.*, in which he turns Venedey, his former Paris friend and present light of the Frankfurt National Assembly, into a figure of fun.

Among the posthumous poems, too, are several of the same type, but they treat mainly the old themes and often the same people—Herwegh again (*Simplicissimus I.*) Frederick William again (*Der neue Alexander*), Massmann, Meyerbeer and others. *Die Menge tut es* is a general satire on Berlin, which shows that time and distance had not mellowed his views of that city. " *1649—1793—? ? ? ?*," one of the most interesting, shows Heine as a prophet. His view of the terrors that might be expected when the sleeping German giant awakened have now undergone a radical change, and he pictures the German monarch of a future revolution being driven to the place of execution, in coach and six, by a weeping coachman, and there respectfully guillotined. It was not a bad forecast, although, as things have turned out, still too drastic. *Die Wanderratten* is a poetical version of that dread of communism which greatly occupied him at this period, and to the expression of which in prose attention has already been called.

If these last poems present few really new aspects, we have a wonderful, inexhaustible power of variation on the old themes. In his long sleepless nights of pain he revolved in his mind his chief preoccupations—his anxiety for Mathilde, his bitter sense of family wrong, and his own tortures, and the brooding thoughts took on ever new poetic forms. He dwells on Mathilde's imprudence and defencelessness, and the thought of dying and leaving her alone in Paris fills him with dread. He would fear less to leave her at the mercy of wolves in a wild forest :

> " Viel grimmere, schlimmere Bestien enthält
> Paris, die leuchtende Hauptstadt der Welt."

And so he writes *Babylonische Sorgen.* Or again he sees her as a lamb, whose fleece must be protected from the thorns, and her feet from the quagmire, and another poem takes shape : *Ich war, O Lamm, als Hirt bestellt.* The grievance against his family burned and rankled within him ; to his own greatest misfortune he could never rise above it. And so we have in these last years poems of a concentrated bitterness, which reveal a sheer intolerable sense of injury. *Affrontenburg,* the most impressive of them all, gives a truly dreadful picture of human servility in face of tyrannical power, and the poet as the victim of sordid family jealousy and intrigue. In *Orpheisch* his uncle Solomon is arraigned as his murderer ; like Orpheus the poet will descend to the nether world, and tear off the mask of his false munificence. Even when he is dead they will not be satisfied, but will cut the tongue from out his dead body—a reference to the condition under which alone the payment of his pension would be continued by Karl to his widow.

But if those two rankling cares occupied a good share of his thoughts, his own personal tragedy of suffering was ever present with him. Now at grips with death in this endless seeming struggle, he had time to get familiar with his face, and estimate all earthly gains and aspirations in the light of eternity. He pierced all the conventional, comfortable trappings with which society has agreed to drape the naked facts of life, and uttered ruthlessly his final thoughts on the great enigma—his questionings and doubts and fears.

The thoughts recur endlessly, and endless is the variation of their expression. Most painful reflection of all is the contrast between then and now. In the poem, *Mir lodert und wogt im Hirn eine Flut*, he dreams that, still a student at Bonn, he is lusty and strong as ever. But then, even as he drinks, he sees a pale, emaciated wretch, who assures him that they are really one, and are not in an inn by the Rhine, but in a sick-room in distant Paris. That poem spans the road that Heine travelled over and over again in these last years. Life drags on at a snail's pace— *Stunden, Tage, Ewigkeiten*—and though at times a golden light emerges from the misty sea, the moment of rapture is quickly past, and he sinks back into the leaden consciousness of his dread misery.

Over and over again, like a refrain, rises the lament that what is Great and Good and Beautiful must perish. The prevailing note is that of despair, and he prays for the relief

of death. In one of the poems best exemplifying the
" laughing tears " so often associated with his name, *Die
Söhne des Glücks beneid' ich nicht*, he envies those who are
mown down when seated at the banquet of life, with roses
in their hair.   Theirs is a happy lot, compared with a life
like his, culminating in eight years of torture, and he accuses
God of inconsistency in creating the most joyous of poets,
only to rob him of his good spirits, and so ruining " the best
of humorists ".   Yet, in spite of it all, ever and again
there rise up before his eyes the possibilities that life
possessed for him, and the man who shortly before had been
craving death as a boon, and acclaiming as the greatest
happiness never to have been born at all, is overcome by his
unconquerable love of existence, and would gladly live on as
the humblest Philistine in that very " Stukkert am Nec-
kar " that he had ridiculed so often.

As we know, at the very end of his days, life and grace
and love did come to him once more, in the form of Elise
Krinitz, awakening in him the thoughts and imagery of his
sensuous youth.   The most famous of the poems she
inspired is that entitled *Für die Mouche*, of which it has
been vainly attempted to prove Alfred Meissner the author.
One of the last, perhaps the very last he wrote, it would be
remarkable among his work of any period for its vigour and
power, while in its profound sincerity and depth of feeling
it has something which only this final period conferred.

He sees himself lying on a moonlight night, in a field of
ruins, dead in a marble coffin, while at his head stands a
passion flower, which, by the magic of dreams, turns into a
female form, in which he recognises his beloved.   His eye
is closed, no sound is uttered, but they hold a wordless com-
munion closer than any speech, as elemental as wind and
wave.   Yet even in a dream he is not secure, even there he

is pursued by the dissonance that had destroyed the harmony of his whole life ; the figures on the bas-relief of his tomb range themselves in the two perennial factions of Hellenes and Nazarenes, and a wild tumult begins. Not even the dream of perfect understanding which he sought in the company of the Mouche could assure him real peace after all ; it could be hoped for only in the grave :

" O Tod ! mit deiner Grabesstille, du,
　　Nur du kannst uns die beste Wollust geben ! "

This mournful conclusion of all his philosophy is that, too, of *Bimini*, the finest and most moving poem which Heine wrote in these concluding years, and perhaps the finest and most tragic in all his works. Narrative poetry does not play so prominent a part at the very end of his life, as in the brief preceding period which produced the *Romanzero*. Yet here—as also in the drastic and gruesome realism of *Das Sklavenschiff*—he showed himself possessed as a narrator of no diminishing powers.

Heine learnt the story of Juan Ponce de Leon from Washington Irving's *Voyages and Discoveries of the Companions of Columbus*, which appeared in 1831, and we can well imagine how it would appeal to him as an allegory of his own fate. The *Prolog*, with its fine, richly-coloured disquisition on the age of wonders, and that wonder in particular which always so greatly fascinated Heine, the rising of a whole New World from out the sea, even though we would not gladly miss a verse of it, might at first sight appear out of scale. Particularly beautiful is his description of the ship—a Ship of Blissful Fools—in which he invites all who will to sail with him for Bimini.

The first section, with the hero's account of the stormy

lives of himself and his fellow-adventurers, shows the relief poor crippled Heine found in these years in the poetic flight to the active life and to exotic climes. One might describe him in this period as a Romantic Realist. Ponce de Leon is now Governor of Cuba, and laden with riches and honour, but he would gladly give it all in return for his lost youth, and in profoundly moving words he prays the Virgin for that boon :

> " Du o Jungfrau, bist ein Weib,
> Und obgleich unwandelbar
> Deine unbefleckte Schönheit,
> Weiblich klugen Sinnes fühlst du,

> " Was er leidet, der vergänglich
> Arme Mensch, wenn seines Leibes
> Edle Kraft und Herrlichkeit
> Dorrt und hinwelkt bis zum Zerrbild !

> . . . .

> " Rüttle ab von meinen Gliedern
> Dieses winterliche Alter,
> Das mit Schnee bedeckt mein Haupt,
> Und mein Blut gefrieren macht—

> " Sag der Sonne, dass sie wieder
> Glut in meine Adern giesse,
> Sag dem Lenze, dass er wecke
> In der Brust die Nachtigallen—

> " Ihre Rosen, gib sie wieder
> Meinen Wangen, gib das Goldhaar
> Wieder meinem Haupt, o Jungfrau—
> Gib mit meine Jugend wieder ! "

With wonderful changes and modulations of tone the epic goes on its way, through the song of Kaka, and the fitting out and departure of the little armada, led by Ponce de Leon, who has already dressed himself in anticipation in the height of youthful foppishness. There is a wonderful lightness and sureness of touch, a sovereign command of language and verse, a skilful use of haunting echoes and repetitions. Heine has never surpassed this blend of laughter and tears at the pathos of all human aspiration.

It appears as though he originally intended to give some account of the actual search, such as he found in his source, and on the other hand he at one time obviously contemplated the substitution of a much briefer version for the present spacious prologue. If so he was finally guided by his better artistic instinct, for the very abruptness of the ending, in contrast to all the wealth and fulness of description given to the plans and hopes that launched this cruise of life, makes it but the more poignant and striking:

" Während er die Jugend suchte,
  Ward er täglich noch viel älter,
  Und verrunzelt, abgemergelt
  Kam er endlich in das Land,

" In das stille Land wo traurig
  Unter schattigen Cypressen
  Fliesst ein Flüsslein, dessen Wasser
  Gleichfalls wunderthätig heilsam—

" Lethe heisst das gute Wasser !
  Trink daraus, und du vergisst
  All dein Leiden—ja, vergessen
  Wirst du, was du je gelitten—

"Gutes Wasser ! gutes Land !
Wer dort angelangt, verlässt es
Nimmermehr—denn dieses Land
Ist das wahre Bimini."

Chapter Twelve

CONCLUSION

What shall we say then of Heine at the end of the story ? As it was from the outset an impossible task to capture all the complexity of his genius and character within the space of one small volume, how shall one hope to sum up the effect in a few brief pages ?

If the work of any poet can be considered in the void, detached from all circumstances of time and place, that poet is certainly not Heine, for he is in much that he wrote very peculiarly of his own time. That he was the last to wish for a verdict on his poetry alone, we know from his own words ; he says himself in the *Memoiren* : " the inter-action of external events and of the inner history of my soul reveals the signature of my whole life and being."

Two chief dangers confront the writer of a life of Heine ; one that he should let his estimate of the man colour his judgment of his poetry, the other, and perhaps more subtle, that he should sentimentalise his character for love of his poetry.

To write of Heine at all without perfect frankness would be a mere waste of time, and in this work no facts have been ignored merely because they were either pleasant or un-pleasant. No biographer should start with a fixed idea, but should let his conception grow out of his study on the basis of all available evidence.

Germany is roughly divided, in relation to Heine, into the two camps of his admirers and partisans and his hostile critics and opponents. There are few real neutrals, and the hostile camp contains many weighty and notable champions. Lichtenberger, writing in 1905, gave a list of names of the chief leaders on the two sides, and has discussed the whole question at length. He points out that Heine has against him the defenders of the established order, the champions of Imperialistic Germany, those whose minds are governed by respect for tradition in politics, morals and religion ; and that fundamentally the opposition is due above all to his Jewish birth and his French sympathies. To the Germany of that day, realist and positivist, robust and well-disciplined, he seemed indeed a bad prophet.

It is not to be wondered at that the herald of triumphant Prussianism should furnish us the most scathing indictment of this presumptuous scoffer. Along with some grudging praise, Treitschke gives us a pretty full catalogue of his crimes. He treats him as a typical representative of the preference for France displayed by Jewish cosmopolitanism : " To a nation, which for centuries had possessed no political history, nothing was more foreign than the historical sense. The filial piety of the Germans seemed to it ridiculous. Modern France on the other hand had broken with its history ; here it felt itself more readily at home, for here the state was brand-new, apparently a pure product of the reason." In that sentence is given the fundamental cause of Heine's rejection and condemnation by German patriots, but with Treitschke we find also most of the other accusations commonly brought against him. He has talent, but no character—that antithesis sums up the charge which had been launched against Heine so frequently in his life-time : " Intellectually gifted but without depth, witty without conviction, egoistic, licentious, untruthful, and yet sometimes irresistibly charming, he was as a poet without character, and therefore strangely unequal in his work." It is even brought up against him that he was the only German lyrical poet who had never written a drinking song ! " His heaven was stocked with almond-tarts, purses and prostitutes ; the Oriental did not know how to carouse in German fashion. It was some time before people saw that Heine's ' esprit ' was far from being wit in the German sense. Everywhere when he spoke seriously he was found to be a false prophet ; what he thought to be dead lived on, what he called living was dead. Of the true signs of the times, which Thomas Carlyle then already clearly recognised in his profound book on the French Revolution, of the decadence of France and the steadily growing strength of Prussian Germany, Heine had no presentiment."

That is, of course, only one side of the picture. There were, even before the War, doughty champions in the other camp too, such as Strodtmann, Heine's earliest biographer, and Elster, the editor and life-long student of his works. Some of them even in their loyalty are led into the opposite failing of uncritical partisanship. Since the War the picture has changed somewhat. For one thing, Heine's errors of prognostication do not appear in quite so glaring a light ; while a nation that has been driven by tribulation to introspection and self-analysis, is not so sensitive to criticism of its institutions as one in the full flush of success and power. In the shattered harmony of its existence it has found more echo of its own feelings with the great poet of life's broken tones and dissonances.

Yet there still remains, and there seems likely to remain,

a remarkable contrast between the estimation in which Heine is held in Germany and in the rest of the world. Or perhaps one ought to say in official Germany, for his songs have always been favourites with the mass of the people, which is indifferent to the authorship of the words it sings. Many English people would be surprised to find the place occupied by him in the official presentation of German literature, as represented by the manuals composed for the initiation of youth into its treasures. One of the best of these to-day, a history of German literature of some three hundred pages, is rather more than normally generous in giving Heine a page and a half, when his contemporaries, Otto Ludwig and Friedrich Hebbel, each get three times as much.

Whatever Germans may think, for the rest of the world Heine is the representative German poet after Goethe ; Heine was not a bad prophet when he said in 1827 that nothing Goethe could do would prevent his great name being one day coupled with that of Heinrich Heine. Patriotic Germans may feel that Heine ought not to be so famous, but that cannot alter the facts.

It is interesting to compare the fate of Heine with that of Byron, whose castigation of British hypocrisy the Germans never minded, and who, like Heine, enjoys a far greater reputation abroad than in the land of his birth. In England, Pharisaism and puritanism have now at any rate, whatever may have been the case in his lifetime, little to do with the appreciation of Byron. In Germany many have never forgiven Heine for his moral laxity, and for the Rabelaisian element in his work, although even on that score one could enumerate many recognised classics in ancient and modern times, who have exceeded in frankness anything that he ever wrote. He was probably, like

Rousseau, not worse, but only more outspoken than many of those who condemned him.

In England Heine's popularity is great, but it is based mainly upon his early poetry, and is accompanied by very little real knowledge of his life and character. Generally speaking, his life has been sentimentalised in harmony with the conception of his poetry. That is largely true of Sharp's brilliant but imaginative impromptu, while his other best-known interpreter, Matthew Arnold, presents, in his usual pontifical style, a one-sided view of him from a political and social aspect, using him largely as a whip to lash his hated Philistines.

Of Heine the Man so much has been said in the course of the volume that little need be added here. He had many good qualities; love for his family, strange streaks of gratitude, and a somewhat careless generosity, and, especially in his last years, astounding strength of will and wonderful courage and endurance. Yet, on the whole, it is very doubtful whether even the most broad-minded of us would have found him an easy person to live with.

It has been said that vanity was his dominating quality, and it is probably true. He was proud and ambitious, and his whole attitude to life was conditioned by the fact that, born with those instincts, he found himself a member of the " Urübelvolk ", a Hebrew in the midst of a Gentile race, that looked down upon him for the mere accident of his birth. He was the son of an outcast race, and he wanted a place in the sun ; to escape from the figurative, as he had escaped from the actual ghetto, into the world of accepted Gentile society.

He was instinctively an aristocrat, and would have been perfectly happy if born under a propitious star. It is strange where this aristocratic strain came from—not only the desire, but with it a good deal of the ability to play the part, which showed itself in various forms in one member of the family after another. The urge to play the rôle was there with the poet, but not the easy means, and it was this conflict of impulse and outward circumstance which brought him into some of his most indefensible positions. His two great handicaps were his Jewish birth and his poverty. The Jewish stigma he tried to get rid of by baptism, with what disastrous results we know. His poverty led him into an ignominious dependence on his uncle Solomon and his family all his life long. The four things that did him most harm in his life were his apostasy, the Börne book, the Platen affair and his French pension. For all of them he repented, and might well now be forgiven, even though a biographer cannot overlook them in attempting to arrive at an unbiassed estimate of his character.

Heine's world was a very different one from that of Goethe ; he rightly felt that Goethe and he were representatives of two different orders. The " Kunstperiode", the aesthetic age, of which Goethe was the typical representative, was over ; it was no longer possible to see and represent life and the world as one harmonious whole. " Perhaps Goethe himself feels ", he wrote in 1828, " that the beautiful objective world, that he has created by word and example, is of necessity collapsing, even as the ' Kunstidee ' is gradually losing its sway. New spirits are being brought forth by the new idea of a new age, and, like northern barbarians sweeping over southern lands, are overthrowing the civilised Kingdom of Goethe, and founding in its place an empire of the most unfettered subjectivity ".

Heine grew up in an age of reaction, of the bankruptcy

of the idealism of the French revolution, of the disillusionment of the Metternich régime, and he lived on into the
age which saw the rise of industrialism and materialism in
Europe in life and art. Goethe established himself
firmly with the aristocratic bearers of German culture of
his day ; he was a Wilhelm Meister, who entered that
magic ship, in which the privileged by birth made, with
favourable winds, the passage of this earthly life. Heine
had no roots, and no traditions. A Hebrew in Germany
and a German in France, a Jew among Christians and a
convert recognised by neither, he had no definite place and
no fatherland. His only footing was in that newly-
emancipated Jewry, of which he was financially only a
hanger-on, even though intellectually one of its most
shining lights. Both of them had their full share of pride
and consciousness of their own worth, but while Goethe's
found its satisfaction, Heine's met only with humiliation.

It is little wonder that such a man never made of his
life a thing of harmony, never succeeded in resolving the
inherent dissonances of his nature, or in attaining to a
serene mastery of his own fate. What he probably
envied Goethe most of all was the firm central core of his
being, however much he might decry it as coldness and
want of feeling. We know from his repeated assurances
that the German men of letters whom he most admired
were those two characters, Lessing and Herder, who were
in most things his opposites.

Heine never made peace between the sensuous and the
spiritual elements of his own nature, between the Hellene
and the Nazarene, as he put it. His ideal undoubtedly
was the life of devotion to a great cause. He had a certain
ambition to live for the " Idee ", as we have seen, but little
aptitude, and his constant asseverations only serve to show

his need of self-conviction. It is quite vain to represent him as the martyr of his own devotion ; he had noble visions and great dreams, but he was a creature of impulse and swayed by emotion, and had not the steadfastness and perseverance for a sustained effort, as a reformer any more than as an author. Once he dreamed an intoxicating dream of a synthesis of sense and spirit, which would require the sacrifice of neither, but the Saint-Simonian dream was not of long duration, and he found nothing to replace it till he sought, at the end, a refuge with the Old Testament God of his fathers.

Heine was not in fact, either politically or socially, a constructive thinker. He had plenty of original ideas, but no system. Revolution for him was a negative idea ; he had little to put in the place of what he would have pulled down. His whole political genius was critical, not positive. He only took part all his life in two constructive movements, the " Verein für Kultur und Wissenschaft der Juden ", and Saint-Simonism, and his active share in both was but short. He was, it is true, a champion of " Emancipation ", to which, in his more enthusiastic moments, he was ready to devote his whole life, but it is doubtful whether he ever had any consistent idea of what he meant by it, or whether it was ever more than a general spirit of revolt. He had no real sympathy, either with his fellow-Jews or his fellow-democrats, and some of his worst quarrels arose from the fact that his nominal allies realised that he was not with them at heart. He was not a natural revolutionary, and right up to the end of his German period was ready to become a henchman of the existing feudalistic order. He had no real faith in the political salvation of mankind through its own efforts. He never believed in the equality of man, but in the government of the masses by their superiors.   He was an aristocrat and hero-worshipper.   It was only late in life perhaps that he recognised this himself, when his dread of communism made him ready to accept any form of absolute rule.

His importance as a thinker is not to be found in the field of formal philosophy, or religion, or politics, but in his criticism of society and of life.   Here again his approach is that of the artist and poet, not of the cool and dispassionate thinker.   Heine was an artist before all, a lover of beauty in all its forms, and from the conflict between the exaggerated demands he made of life, and the possibility of their satisfaction in the world of reality, sprang that disappointment and disillusionment with which we are familiar in the period under various names.   Yet Heine's *Weltschmerz* is never fundamentally that most hopeless type, which denies the possibility of happiness in the world.   Heine was a hedonist, with a robust love of life, in contrast to the morbid Romantics.   The world of sense came first and foremost with him, and he found it very beautiful. It was never his lament that life held nothing desirable, but only that he was denied a place at its rich board. Even at the end he is not consistently nihilistic, but still has at times a longing for that comfortable world, where he could be quite happy " with health and a financial rise ! " This attitude is poles apart from that of the true pessimist, for whom life itself is in all circumstances a gift not worth the acceptance.

Such was Heine's fundamental disposition, and if he had been one of the favourites of fortune, he would have made a very charming addition to the aristocratic society of various European capitals.   Fate, however, treated him otherwise, and with all his gifts he had not the strength of character to stand the test. He was no Lessing to write a serene dramatic parable out of the heart of his bitterest sorrows. And so the conflict between the real and the ideal, the dissonances in his own life, sharpened his sense for the hypocrisies of life around him, and made him that for which he stands above all, the exponent in prose and verse of the restlessness and questioning and doubt of the modern spirit.

He is a critic of life, a satiric beholder, who sees through the conventional façade of civilised society, and exposes its shams with a ruthless hand, and with dazzling wit and brilliant ironic humour. A disillusioned child of his age, he does not hug his sorrow to him, but voices aloud all those intangible woes and shades of feeling, all those subtleties of grief and transient flashes of perception, that were waiting for their adequate expression. He spares nothing and nobody ; he even takes a delight in shocking the Philistines. Like Shaw he loves to " épater le bourgeois ", and like him possesses the power of lashing to fury serious and solemn opponents. He refuses to follow the laws of the game ; to speak seriously of serious things, and keep jokes to their proper place. What he himself called his "satiric gift and the urge of his wanton love of parody " ran away with him, and he often forgot till too late the inevitable results of his provocative wit. He was a great phrase-maker ; we see him revolving some happy turn in his letters, till it receives its final crystallisation in a poem. He simply could not resist the temptation of saying a good thing ; we have seen the risks he took even with his Uncle Solomon. His works, like his letters and his conversation, abound in mischievous, daring, impudent sallies, relieved by astounding wit and fertility of invention, by unsurpassed skill and audacity in phrase and rhyme.

If Heine is of no great importance as a political thinker, his social thought and criticism has been of the highest value, as a corrective to all complacency, and easy acceptance of things as they are. He is not to be hypnotised by any of the ready-made nostrums, and pours ridicule on the pretensions of pompous self-sufficiency. He is too Mephistophelean to be a pleasant companion for the timid and conventional ; only the stout-hearted feel better for that bold tearing down of the veils of convention which is his peculiar contribution. For that reason he will always arouse the antagonism of all upholders of the dogmatic presentations of life.

Heine has often been charged with inconsistency, and the charge is in a sense true, though this very inconsistency is often only a higher degree of poetic and aesthetic truth. He responded to every impulse, uncontrolled by the usual restraints of common sense and expediency. He was the artist who reflected every changing aspect of life, and was, for his very indifference to contradictions, the more faithful recorder of passing moods. He was the more true to the impression of the moment, because he did not feel the necessity of making all he said conform to some preconceived and consistent philosophy of life.

Whatever may be the verdict on Heine as man and as thinker, that verdict leaves untouched the field in which he is greatest of all. When we come to Heine the singer, the pure lyric poet, we rise above all the dust of conflict, above any limitations of his life and surroundings, and can only be thankful that from a soil of such little promise there sprang flowers of such rare and surpassing beauty. At the end of his life, in the *Geständnisse*, Heine said that he had made of himself nothing but a poet, but that it was much to be a poet, and to be forsooth a great lyrical poet in Germany, among a people which has surpassed all other nations in two things, in philosophy and lyric song. Though that statement is not to be taken literally, Heine did there see his life's work in its true perspective. It is not a little to have been one of the most brilliant stylists and one of the wittiest writers of Europe, but it is in the end upon his songs that Heine's immortality will depend.

That immortality seems well assured, both inside Germany and without. Yet, while other nations have a perfect right to accept Heine as a lyric poet of supreme rank, they cannot ignore the German contention that he does, in fact, lack some essential German qualities. Above all he has none of that simple piety and childlikeness, of that brooding, mystic dreaminess, which, ever since Wolfram's *Parzival*, has found its reflection in German poetry.

When all has been said, what is the note on which we shall take leave of Heine ? He was a human phenomenon that has attracted an amazing amount of interest. This Rhenish Jew, a sick man for most of his life, has enriched the world by a legacy of beauty, of which we cannot estimate the price. The world has always forgiven the great lovers and the great conquerors, and shall it not forgive Heine ! A passionate lover of the beautiful world, and of all forms of beauty, he has fashioned words and melodies, in which the troubled modern spirit can find the relief of expression for some of its most subtle and complicated woes. He, the poet of half-tones and broken chords, of all subtle shades of thought and emotion, has voiced the dissonances of the modern world in verses of delicate and ethereal beauty. Linked with great composers, he has given mankind songs to sing that help to soothe its jangled nerves.

CONCLUSION

We have followed him from the cradle to the grave ; traced the circumstances that helped to mould him, and the factors that counted for most in his life. Now we are at the end, and must leave the essential unexplained. We have cast up the total, but one item is missing. Whence did it come, that wonderful and inexplicable gift of song ?

CHRONOLOGICAL LIST OF WORKS

The date of composition of the longer works is alone given, as it is impracticable to consider here Heine's shorter prose writings and his thousand odd poems. The titles of collected works are given in italics, and the date is that of their publication.

Die Romantik	1820
Almansor	1821
Gedichte	1821
Ratcliff	1822
Briefe aus Berlin	1822
Über Polen	1822
Tragödien, nebst einem lyrischen Inter-
mezzo	1823
Memoiren	1823*ff.*
Die Harzreise	1824
Der Rabbi von Bacharach	1824-6
Nordsee III	1824-6
The " Curriculum vitae " (to the Dean
of the Faculty of Laws in Göttingen)	1825
Nordsee I	1825
Das Buch Le Grand	1826
Nordsee II	1826
Reisebilder I	1826
Buch der Lieder	1827
Englische Fragmente	1827-30

Reisebilder II	1827
Beers Struensee	1828
Die Deutsche Literatur, von Wolfgang Menzel	1828
Reise von München nach Genua	1828-9
Die Bäder von Lucca	1829
Die Stadt Lucca	1829-30
Reisebilder III	1829
Änderungs–Vorschläge zum " Tulifäntchen "	1830
Reisebilder IV	1831
Einleitung zu " Kahldorf über den Adel "	1831
Französische Maler	1831
Französische Zustände	1831-2
Die Romantische Schule	1832-5
Französische Maler. Nachtrag	1833
Salon I	1834
Zur Geschichte der Religion und Philosophie in Deutschland	1834
Salon II	1835
French Autobiographical Sketch (to Philarète Chasles)	1835
Florentinische Nächte	1835-6
Elementargeister	1836
Über den Denunzianten (Vorrede zu Salon III)	1837
Einleitung zum " Don Quichotte "	1837
Salon III	1837
Der Schwabenspiegel	1838
Shakespeares Mädchen und Frauen	1838
Schriftstellernöten	1839
Ludwig Börne	1839

Salon IV	1840
Lutetia	1840-4
Thomas Reynolds	1841
Atta Troll	1842
Neue Gedichte	1844
Deutschland : Ein Wintermärchen	1844
Ludwig Marcus	1844
Die Göttin Diana	1846
Der Doktor Faust, Ein Tanzpoem	1847
Die Februarrevolution	1848
Romanzero	1851
Nachwort zum Romanzero	1851
Vorrede zu Salon II (second edition)	1852
Die Götter im Exil	1853
Geständnisse	1853-4
Vermischte Schriften	1854
Memoiren	1854-6

Letzte Gedichte und Gedanken von Heinrich Heine. Aus dem Nachlasse des Dichters zum ersten Male veröffentlicht.   A. Strodtmann, Hamburg   1869

BIBLIOGRAPHY

The literature concerning Heine has attained such proportions that any attempt at completeness is here entirely out of the question. The following list aims only at giving the more important works, or those which have a special interest for English readers. For fuller information, the two chief bibliographical works to be consulted are :—

Karl Goedeke, *Grundriss zur Geschichte der deutschen Dichtung*, 2nd edition by Edmund Goetze, Dresden, 1905, Vol. 8, pp. 526-564.

Friedrich Meyer, *Verzeichnis einer Heinrich Heine Bibliothek*, Leipzig, 1905 ; with the additions, *Namen-und Sachregister zu dem Verzeichnis einer Heinrich Heine Bibliothek*, and *Heinrich Heine und das Junge Deutschland*, Leipzig, 1910.

Valuable bibliographical information is also given in some of the biographies and editions, notably in the first volume of the second edition of Ernst Elster, *Heines Werke*, Leipzig, 1924.

The bibliography at the end of William Sharp's *Life of Heinrich Heine*, London, 1888, is of special value for English translation and criticism, and for the composition of Heine's songs.

For other countries the following should be noted :—

HEINE

Louis P. Betz, *Heine in Frankreich,* Eine literar-historische Untersuchung, Zürich, 1894.
Carlo Bonardi, *Enrico Heine nella letteratura italiana avanti la revelazione di T. Massarani,* Livorno, 1907.
H. B. Sachs, *Heine in America,* Philadelphia, 1916.

I.—*Editions of the Works*

Heinrich Heine's Sämmtliche Werke, 6 volumes, Philadelphia, Verlag von John Weik, No 195 Chesnutstrasse, 1856-7 ; *Heinrich Heine's Sämmtliche Werke,* Rechtmässige Original-Ausgabe, 21 volumes, edited by Adolf Strodtmann, Hamburg, Hoffmann und Campe, 1861-66 ; *Heinrich Heine's Gesammelte Werke,* 9 volumes, edited by Gustav Karpeles, Biographical Introduction by C. A. Buchheim, Berlin, G. Grote, 1887 ; *Heinrich Heines Sämmtliche Werke,* 7 volumes, edited by Ernst Elster, Leipzig, Bibliographisches Institut, 1887-1890 ; 2nd edition, *Heines Werke,* 1924ff. ; *Heines Werke,* 10 volumes, edited Oskar Walzel, Leipzig, Insel-Verlag, 1910-15.

II.—*Letters and Conversations*

Heinrich Heines Briefwechsel, edited by Friedrich Hirth, 3 volumes, München, 1914-20 ; *Gespräche mit Heine,* edited by H. H. Houben, Frankfurt, 1926.

III.—*Biographies*

Adolf Strodtmann, *H. Heines Leben und Werke,* Hamburg, 1867-9, 3rd edition, 1884 ; William Stigand, *The Life, Work and Opinions of Heinrich Heine,* 2 volumes,

London, 1875 ; Robert Proelss, *Heinrich Heine. Sein Lebensgang und seine Schriften*, Stuttgart, 1886 ; William Sharp, *Life of Heinrich Heine*, London, 1888 ; Heinrich Keiter, *Heinrich Heine : Sein Leben, sein Charakter und seine Werke*, Köln, 1891 ; 2nd edition. Köln, 1906 ; Gustav Karpeles, *Heinrich Heine. Aus seinem Leben und aus seiner Zeit*, Leipzig, 1899 ; Rudolf Fürst, *Heinrich Heines Leben, Werke und Briefe*, Leipzig, 1910 ; Hermann Wendel, *Heinrich Heine. Ein Lebens- und Zeitbild*, Dresden, 1916 ; 2nd edition, Berlin, 1926 ; Max J. Wolff, *Heinrich Heine*, München, 1922 ; Ernst Elster, *Heines Leben und Werke*, Leipzig, 1924 (as introduction to the first volume of the new edition) ; Hartwig Jess, *Heinrich Heine*, Leipzig, 1924 ; Michael Monahan, *Heinrich Heine. Romance and tragedy of the poet's life*, New York, 1924 ; Lewis Browne, *That Man Heine*. A Biography, New York, 1927 ; Henry Baerlein, *Heine : the strange guest*, London, 1928.

IV.—*Biographical Detail and Memoirs*

Adolf Stahr, *Zwei Monate in Paris*, Oldenburg, 1851 ; Alfred Meissner, *Heinrich Heine. Erinnerungen*, Hamburg, 1856 ; Friedrich Steinmann, *Heinrich Heine. Denkwürdigkeiten und Erlebnisse aus meinem Zusammenleben mit ihm*, Prag and Leipzig, 1857 ; Maximilian Heine, *Erinnerungen an Heinrich Heine und seine Familie*, von seinem Bruder, Berlin, 1868 ; Rocca, Principessa della, *Erinnerungen an Heinrich Heine*, von seiner Nichte, Hamburg, 1881 ; Alexander Weill, *Souvenirs intimes de Henri Heine*, Paris, 1883 ; Alfred Meissner, *Geschichte meines Lebens*, Wien, 1884 (various references to

Heine) ; Camilla Selden, ("Mouche"), *Les derniers jours de Henri Heine*, Paris, 1884 (Translated into English by C. Brune, *The Last Days of Heinrich Heine*, London, 1884) ; Fanny Lewald, *Erinnerungen an Heinrich Heine*, In "Zwölf Bilder nach dem Leben," Berlin, 1888 ; Baron Ludwig v. Embden, *Heinrich Heines Familienleben*, von seinem Neffen Baron Ludwig v. Embden, Hamburg, 1892 ; Hugo Lachmannski, *Düsseldorf und Heinrich Heine*, Berlin, 1893 ; J. Nassen, *Heinrich Heines Familienleben*, Fulda, 1895 ; David Kaufmann, *Aus Heinrich Heines Ahnensaal*, Breslau, 1896 ; Eugen Moos, *Heine und Düsseldorf*, Neue Beiträge zu einer Heine-Biographie, Düsseldorf, 1909 ; Eduard Wedekind, *Studentenleben in der Biedermeierzeit*, Ein Tagebuch aus dem Jahre, 1824, edited by H. H. Houben, Göttingen, 1927. (Interesting references to Heine as a student at Göttingen).

V.—*Criticism and Appreciation*

Matthew Arnold, *Heinrich Heine*, In "Essays in Criticism," London, 1865 ; Paul Beyer, *Der junge Heine*, Eine Entwicklungsgeschichte seiner Denkweise und Dichtung (Bonner Forschungen), Berlin, 1911 ; M. Bienenstock, *Das jüdische Element in Heines Werken*, Ein Kritisch-ästhetischer Beitrag zur Heine-Frage, Leipzig, 1910 ; Michael Birkenbihl, *Die orientalischen Elemente in der Poesie Heinrich Heines*, Amberg, 1906; Wilhelm Bölsche, *Heinrich Heine*, Versuch einer ästhetisch-kritischen Analyse seiner Werke und seiner Weltanschauung, Leipzig, 1880 ; Georg Brandes, *Ludwig Börne und Heinrich Heine*, Leipzig, 1896 ; W. A. Braun, *Types of Weltschmerz in German Poetry*, Columbia

University Germanic Studies, Volume 2, no. 2., New York, 1905 ; E. M. Butler, *The Saint-Simonian Religion in Germany*, Cambridge, 1926 ; George Eliot, In "Essays and Leaves from a Note-book", (" *German Wit : Heinrich Heine* "—from the *Westminster Review*, 1856), London, 1884 ; Erich Eckertz, *Heine und sein Witz*, Berlin, 1908 ; Ernst Elster, *Das Vorbild der freien Rhythmen Heinrich Heines*, Euphorion, volume 25. 1924 ; August Walter Fischer, *Über die volkstümlichen Elemente in den Gedichten Heines*, Berlin, 1905 ; Karl Hessel, *Die metrische Form in Heines Gedichten*, Zeitschrift für den deutschen Unterricht, 1889 ; Karl Hessel, *Die Nordsee. Meeresdichtungen von Heinrich Heine*, Norden, 1893 ; Hermann Hüffer, *Heinrich Heine*, Gesammelte Aufsätze, ed. by Ernst Elster, Berlin, 1906 ; Jules Legras, *Henri Heine poète*, Paris, 1897 ; Henri Lichtenberger, *Henri Heine, penseur*, Paris, 1905 ; Otto zur Linde, *Heinrich Heine und die deutsche Romantik*, Freiburg, 1899 ; Felix Melchior, *Heinrich Heines Verhältnis zu Lord Byron*, Berlin, 1903 ; Georg Mücke, *Heinrich Heines Beziehungen zum deutschen Mittelalter*, Berlin, 1908 ; Wilhelm Ochsenbein, *Die Aufnahme Lord Byrons in Deutschland und sein Einfluss auf den jungen Heine*, Bern, 1905 ; Alexander Pache, *Naturgefühl und Natursymbolik bei Heinrich Heine*, Ein Beitrag zur Würdigung seiner Kunst und seiner Persönlichkeit, Hamburg and Leipzig, 1904 ; Georg Plotke, *Heinrich Heine als Dichter des Judentums*, Dresden, 1913 ; S. Rahmer, *Heinrich Heines Krankheit und Leidensgeschichte*, Berlin, 1901 ; G. Ras, *Börne und Heine als politische Schriftsteller*, Groningen, den Haag, 1927 ; Paul Remer, *Die freien Rhythmen in Heinrich Heines Nordseebildern*, Heidelberg, 1889 ; Paul Remer, *Zu Heines Verskunst*, Neue Zeit VIII, 1890 ; Heinrich von

Treitschke, *Deutsche Geschichte im Neunzehnten Jahr-
hundert*, 5 volumes, Leipzig, 1879-94. New edition,
Leipzig, 1927. (A classified list of references to Heine in
the index at the end of the fifth volume.)

VI.—*Heine in English Translation*

(For this list I am indebted to one of my students, Miss
Kathleen Kirby.)

A.—*Verse*

Edinburgh Review, 1832, Poems by anonymous trans-
lators ; Athenæum, 1833, Poems by anonymous trans-
lators ; *Ballads and other Poems*, Mary Howitt, Long-
man's, London, 1847 (contains translation of *Die Wall-
fahrt nach Kevlaar*) ; *Selections from the Poetry of Heinrich
Heine*, translated by John Ackerlos (J. S. Smith), John
Chapman, London, 1854 ; *Book of Songs*, translated by
J. E. Wallis, Chapman and Hall, London, 1856 ;
Edinburgh Review, 1856, Poems translated by Monckton
Milnes ; *The Poems of Heine, Complete*, translated in the
original metres, with a sketch of Heine's life, E. A.
Bowring, Longman's, London, 1858 ; *Six Poems from
Heine*, translated by E. B. Browning, dated Rome, 1860
(Poetical works, Smith Elder, London, 1906) ; *Poems
from the German*, translated by Richard Garnett, Bell and
Daldy, London, 1862 ; *Ballads from the German*, by Henry
Inglis, William Blackwood and Sons, London, 1864 ;
Heine's Book of Songs, translated by C. G. Leland, Trüb-
ner, London, 1864 ; *Translations from Heine* (written
in the sixties) in " Poetical Works of James Thompson,"
edited by Bertram Dobell, Reeves and Turner, London,

1895 ; Fortnightly Review, 1870, Poems translated by Robert, Lord Lytton (in his article on " *Letzte Gedichte und Gedanken*.") ; *Poems by Heine*, translated by the Honourable Julian Fane, privately printed, Vienna, 1854 (reviewed by Monckton Miles in the *Edinburgh Review*, 1856) ; Also in *Julian Fane, a Memoir*, by Robert, Lord Lytton, Murray, London, 1871 ; *Anthea*, Poems and Translations, the latter chiefly from the German poet Heine, with sketch of his life, William Stigand, Kegan Paul, London, 1907 ; (the translations originally appeared in the *Life of Heine*, 1875) ; *Atta Troll and other Poems by H. Heine*, translated by T. S. Egan, Chapman and Hall, London, 1876 ; *Exotics*, by George Macdonald, Strahan and Co., London, 1876 ; *Selections from the Poetical Works of H. Heine*. (Alma Strettell), Macmillan and Co., London, 1878; *Poems and Ballads*, by H. Heine, translated by Theodore Martin, Blackwood and Sons, Edinburgh, 1878 (the third edition with additions appeared in 1894) ; *Translations from Heine* (in a book entitled *Quarterman's Grace and other Poems*), by Emily Pfeiffer, Kegan Paul, London, 1879 ; *Translations from the German Poets*, by E. S. Pearson, Sampson Low, London, 1879; *Translations from Heine and other Verses*, by Ernest Radford, E. Johnson, Cambridge, 1882 ; *The Book of Songs*, by H. Heine, translated by "Stratheir," (Colonel H. S. Jarrett), Constable and Co., London, 1882 (new edition, 1913) ; *A Romance in Song*, Heine's Lyrical Interlude, translated by Franklin Johnson, D. Lothrop and Co., Boston. (Mass. 1884) ; *Poems and Translations*, by Elizabeth Craigmyle, J. & J. P. Edmond & Spark, Aberdeen, 1886 (contains 16 translations from *Heine*) ; *Poems selected from H. Heine*, by Käthe Freiligrath-Krœker (translated by K. F. Krœker and others), Walter Scott,

London, 1887 ; *Songs and Lyrics* by H. Heine and other German Poets, done into English verse by James Geikie, James Thin, Edinburgh, 1887 ; *The Love Songs of Heinrich Heine*, Englished by H. B. Briggs, Trübner, London, 1888 ; *Translations from Heine*, by Lady Lucie Duff Gordon, Murray's Magazine, 1891 ; *German Ballads*, translated and edited by Elizabeth Craigmyle (contains 7 translations from Heine), Walter Scott, London, 1892 ; *Lyrics and Ballads of Heine and other German Poets*, translated by Frances Hellman, G. F. Putnam's Sons, New York, London, 1892 (2nd edition, 1895) ; *Choice Poems of Heinrich Heine*, translated by J. W. Oddie, Macmillan, London, 1896 ; *Poems of 1848 and earlier Days*, translated by E. Robinson, Sherratt and Hughes, London, 1904 ; *Heine's Book of Songs*, translated by John Todhunter, Clarendon Press, Oxford, 1907 ; *Versions and Perversions of Heine and Others*, by G. Tyrrell, Elkin Matthews, London, 1909 ; *Heinrich Heine. Poems and Ballads*, done into English by Robert Levy, Andrew Melrose, London, 1909 ; *The Poetical Works of Heinrich Heine* : now first completely rendered into English verse in accordance with the original forms by John Payne, 3 volumes, Villon Society, London, 1911 ; *Translations from Heine and Goethe*, by Philip G. L. Webb, A. C. Fifield, London, 1912 ; *Atta Troll*, from the German of H. Heine, by Herman Scheffauer, with some pen-and-ink sketches by Willy Pogany (with an introduction by Dr. Oscar Levy), Sidgwick and Jackson, London, 1913 ; *Vision*. A Book of Lyrics (with 5 translations from Heine), Elkin Matthews, London, 1914 ; Heine's poem *The North Sea*, translated by Howard Mumford Jones, German and English, Open Court Publishing Co., Chicago, London, 1916 ; *More Translations from Heine*, by Philip G. L. Webb, Allen and Unwin, London, 1920 ; *Songs and Ballads,* chiefly from Heine (in the Scottish dialect), by Alexander Gray, Grant Richards, London, 1920 ; *Poems by Heine,* translated by Louis Untermeyer, Broadway Translations, London (revised edition), printed in U.S.A., 1923 ; *Translations from Heine,* by Monica Peveril Turnbull, A. L. Humphreys, London, 1923 ; *Heine's Dream Pictures,* translated by W. G. Waters, H. L. Glaisher, London, 1927 ; *Poems from Heine,* a revised and enlarged edition of *Translations from Heine,* and *More Translations from Heine,* by P. G. Webb, Nisbet & Co., London, 1927 ; *Songs from Heine*—Schumann's *Dichter-liebe,* by Alexander Gray, Porpoise Press Broadsheets, Series 4, No. 4. Edinburgh, 1928.

B.—*Prose*

Letters auxiliary to the History of Modern Polite Literature in Germany, by Heinrich Heine, translated from the German by G. W. Haven, Munroe and Co., Boston. (Mass)., 1836 ; *Scintillations from the Prose Writings of Heinrich Heine,* 1. Florentine Nights, 2, Excerpts, translated from the German by Simon Adler Stern, Henry Holt and Co., New York, 1873 ; *Prose Miscellanies from Heinrich Heine,* translated by S. L. Fleishman, J. B. Lippincott and Co., Philadelphia, 1876 ; *Wit, Wisdom and Pathos from the Prose of H. Heine, with a few pieces from the Book of Songs,* selected and translated by J. Snod-grass, Trübner, London, 1879 ; *English Fragments,* translated from the German of H. Heine, by S. Norris, R. Grant and Sons, Edinburgh, 1880 ; *Ludwig Börne : Recollections of a Revolutionist,* by H. Heine, abridged and translated by Thomas Selby Egan, Newman and Co., London, 1881; *A Trip to the Brocken*, (from *Die Harzreise*), translated by R. McLintock, Macmillan, London, 1882; *Religion and Philosophy in Germany, a Fragment*, translated by John Snodgrass, Trübner, London, 1882; *The Romantic School, by H. Heine*, translated by S. L. Fleishman, Henry Holt and Co., New York, 1882; *The Memoirs of Heinrich Heine, and some newly-discovered fragments of his writings*, with an introductory essay by T. W. Evans, George Bell & Sons, London, 1884; *Ideas, "Buch le Grand" of the Reisebilder of Heinrich Heine*, 1826, a translation by I. B., Macmillan and Co., London, 1884; *Ideen. Buch le Grand of the Reisebilder of H. Heine*, 1826, translated by R. McLintock, London, 1884; *Travel Pictures including the Tour in the Harz, Norderney, and Book of Ideas, together with the Romantic School*, Bell, London, 1887; *The Prose Writings of Heinrich Heine*, edited with an introduction by Havelock Ellis, Walter Scott, London, 1887; *Heine as Novelist and Dramatist, being a selection from his longer works*, translated into English by R. McLintock, Roper and Drowly, London, 1890; *The Works of Heinrich Heine*, translated by C. G. Leland vols. 1-8; by T. Brooksbank, vol. 9, *The Book of Songs*; by Margaret Armour, vol. 10-12, *New Poems, Germany, Romancero, Last Poems*, 12 volumes, Wm. Heinemann, London, 1892-1905; *Heine's Italian Travel Sketches, etc.*, translated by E. A. Sharp, Walter Scott, London, 1892 (New edition published by Foulis, London, 1927); *Heine in Art and Letters*, translated with prefatory note by E. A. Sharp, Walter Scott, London, 1895; *Heine on Shakespeare*, a translation of his *Notes on Shakespeare's Heroines*, by Ida Benecke, A. Constable & Co., Westminster, 1895; *Pictures of Travel (Reisebilder)*, a new translation by Russel Daris Gillman, Sampson Low

& Co., London, 1907 ; *The Poetical Works of Heinrich Heine*, volume 1. *The Book of Songs*, translated by T. Brooksbank, volume 2. *New Poems*, volume 3. *Germany, Romancero*, Books I. II, volume 4, *Romancero*, Book III., translated by Margaret Armour, (Cheaper issue from *The Works of Heinrich Heine*), 4 volumes, Wm. Heinemann, London, 1917 ; *Florentine Nights*, from the translation of C. G. Leland, with 12 illustrations by Felix de Gray, Methuen & Co., London, 1927.

APPENDIX

Chapter I, p. 11 (*Mein Kind, wir waren Kinder*) :

My child, we once were children,
Two children, small and gay ;
We'd creep off into the hen-roost,
And hide among the hay.

We'd crow, and the people passing,
Who heard us, never knew
But what it was cocks a-crowing :
" Cock-a-doodle-do ! "

The cases in our courtyard
We papered with odds and ends,
And there we two together
Kept open house for our friends.

And when our neighbour's tabby
Came over to pay us a call,
We made her bows and curtsies
And compliments and all.

We asked of her health politely
And gravely again and again ;

We've said the same things often
To other old tabbies since then.

And there we'd sit on talking
With sober elderly ways,
Of how all things were better
By far in our own young days.

How faith and trust had vanished,
And love, from off the earth ;
Of the terrible price of coffee,
Of money how great the dearth !—

Gone are the toys of childhood,
And all things have their day—
Time, tide and faith and money
And love all pass away.

Chapter V, p. 82 (*Ein Jüngling liebt ein Mädchen*) :

A youth once loved a maiden,
But she for another sighed,
Who'd given his heart to another,
And led her home as his bride.

The lovelorn maiden married
Straightway, in pique at the slight,
The very first man who woo'd her,
The youth was in evil plight.

It is an old, old story,
But one that is always new ;
And ever again it only
Breaks some man's heart in two.

Chapter V, p. 84 (*Die Grenadiere*) :

Two grenadiers were tramping home
To France from their prison in Russia,
And at last with hanging heads they came
One day to their quarters in Prussia.

And there they heard the sorrowful tale
That France was forlorn and forsaken,
Beaten and crushed her mighty host,
And the Emperor captive taken.

Then wept together the grenadiers,
Their hearts in their bosoms turning.
The one of them said, " Ah, woe is me !
I feel my old wound burning."

The other said, " The game is up !
I'd welcome death, ne'er doubt me.
Yet I have wife and child at home,
Who'd perish in want without me."

" And what care I for wife and child.
My heart with grief is shaken ;
What matter it though they beg their bread
When my Emperor's captive taken !

" Grant me this one request I pray :
An I die here, as you love me,
Take me and bury me, brother, in France,
With the good French earth above me.

" Over my heart on its ribbon red
The cross of the legion clasping,

My good sword girded about me withal,
In my hand my musket grasping,

" There I'll tarry and listen still,
In my grave like a sentry lying,
Till I hear above me the thunder of guns
And the neighing horses a-flying.

" And when over my grave my Emperor rides,
And the swords are clanging and clashing,
I'll rise full-armed from my grave once more
To guard him with sabre flashing."

Chapter V, p. 86 (*Belsatzar*) :

The midnight hour was drawing on ;
Deep silence brooded o'er Babylon.

And only the palace windows bright
Told of wild revelry by night.

There on high in his banquet hall
Belshazzar feasted his captains all.

His captains line on shimmering line
Drained the goblets of foaming wine.

And the laughter loud and the goblets' ring
Fell sweet on the ears of the stubborn king.

And as to his cheek the red wine flew,
His heart more overweening grew.

And goaded on in his blinded pride,
With sinful word he God defied.

And bolder grown blasphemed more loud,
To the brawling cheers of the ribald crowd.

The king called out, and a servant sped,
And quick returned, and on his head

Full many a golden vessel he bore,
Robbed from the temple's sacred store.

And before them all the king took up,
With impious hand a brimming cup,

And cried aloud, as the wine he quaffed,
To the very dregs at a single draught :

" Jehovah ! so my taunt I fling—
Here in Babylon I am king ! "

Yet scarce the awful words were said,
When the king was seized with a mortal dread.

One heard the laughter ebb and fall,
And a ghostly silence filled the hall.

And lo ! and lo ! on the wall so white,
A shape, a hand, was seen to write.

It wrote and wrote there, on and on,
In letters of fire, and wrote, and was gone.

The king sat still with frozen look,
Pale as a corpse, and knees that shook.

And cold with horror sat around
The lords and captains without a sound.

The sages came, but none of them all
Could read the letters of fire on the wall.

But Belshazzar the king in his pride and might
Was slain by his men that selfsame night.

Chapter V, p. 89 (*Ein Fichtenbaum steht einsam*) :

> A pine-tree sad and lonely
> Stands on a northern height.
> It sleeps ; and the snow-flakes falling
> Weave it a mantle white.
>
> It dreams of a lonely palm-tree,
> That far in an eastern land
> On barren crag stands mourning
> Amid the burning sand.

Chapter V, p. 90 (*Du schönes Fischermädchen*) :

> Oh lovely fisher-maiden
> Steer now your skiff to land,
> Come hither and sit beside me,
> We'll whisper hand in hand.
>
> Your head upon my heart, dear,
> May safely pillowed be,
> When daily without tremor
> You trust to yon wild sea.

My heart is like that ocean,
With storm and ebb and flow,
And many a pearl lies hidden
Far in its depths below.

Chapter VII, p. 135 (*Auf diesem Felsen bauen wir*) :

Upon this rock where now we stand
A new church shall be founded ;
Now for the third new testament
The hour at last has sounded.

This twofoldness has overlong
Befooled and duped the nations ;
The flesh shall now no more endure
These vain mortifications.

Dost hear God's thousand voices speak
Where yonder waves are dashing ?
And seest thou above our heads
His thousand candles flashing ?

God dwells above us in the light,
As in the dark abysses ;
And God is everything that is ;
He is in these our kisses.

Chapter IX, p. 191 (*Die schlesischen Weber*) :

With tearless eyes, in sullen gloom,
With flashing teeth, they sit at the loom ;
And " Germany ", they cry aloud,
" We're weaving curses into your shroud—
        We're weaving, we're weaving ! "

A curse on the idol to whom of old
We've prayed in our hunger and bitter cold ;
We've hoped in vain and we've waited in vain,
He's fooled us and tricked us again and again—
  We're weaving, we're weaving !

A curse on the king, who's brought us low,
And knows no pity for all our woe ;
He's squeezed us and robbed us—the king of the rich,
And has us shot like dogs in a ditch—
  We're weaving, we're weaving !

A curse on our faithless Fatherland,
With its shame and squalor on every hand,
With its stunted flowers and its blighted lives,
Where the worm on rot and corruption thrives—
  We're weaving, we're weaving !

In the creaking loom the shuttle flies,
And never the sound of the weaving dies.
" Old Germany ", it calls aloud,
" We're weaving your thrice-accursed shroud,
  We're weaving, we're weaving ! "

Chapter X, p. 229 (*Wo ?*) :

  Where at long last, travel-weary,
  Shall the poet lay him down ?
  Under palms ? or 'neath the branching
  Lindens of a German town ?

  Shall I rest in some far desert
  Buried by a stranger's hand ?
  Shall my grave lie where the waters
  Break upon a northern strand ?

Little matter ! God's high heaven
Will enfold me there or here,
And the stars as funeral candles
Shine at night above my bier.

Chapter XI, p. 246 (*Bimini*) :

Thou, O Virgin, art a woman,
And although immaculate
And immutable thy beauty,
Wisely, woman-like, thou feelest,

What he suffers, man—poor, transient,
Perishable—when his body,
All its noble power and splendour,
Shrivels to a thing of scorn !

.   .   .

Shake, O shake from off my members
Wintry age, so cold and frosty,
Age that crowns my head with snow,
Age that makes my blood turn frozen—

Tell the sun to set his fiery
Touch once more upon my pulses,
Tell the spring to re-awaken
In my breast the nightingales—

Give again, O give the roses
To my cheeks, and give the golden
Hair back to my head, O Virgin—
Give me back my youth again.

Chapter XI, p. 247 (*Bimini*) :

So his quest of youth pursuing
Daily he grew old and older,
And all wrinkled, furrowed, withered,
Came at last unto that land,

To that silent land, where, eerie,
Underneath the cypress shadows,
Flows a little stream, whose water
Has, too, wondrous power of healing.

Lethe, so they call that water !
Drink thereof, and you forget
All your sorrows—ay, all sufferings
Ever suffered, you'll forget.

Blessed water ! blessed land !
Who sets foot there leaves it never,
For this land, indeed, none other,
Is the real Bimini.

INDEX

Alexis, Willibald, 45, 75
Allemagne, De l', 137, 139, 160
Allgemeine Zeitung, Augs-
 burger, 122, 169 *f.*, 189, 211,
 216, 221
Almansor, 39, 41, 50 *ff.*
Archenholz, 70
Arme Peter, Der, 84, 187, 234
Arnold, Matthew, 253
Atta Troll, 170 *f.*, 176 *f.*, 210
Ausland, Das, 96

Bäder von Lucca, 9, 100 *ff.*, 104,
 106, 108, 113, 131, 134
Bazard, 138
Becker, 178
Beer, Michael, 45, 51, 112
Belgiojoso, Princess, 44, 155,
 185, 204
Belsatzar, 40, 84, 86, 235
Benecke, 40
Béranger, 209
Beughem, Fritz von, 39
Bimini, 92, 236, 245
Blücher, 29
Boccaccio, 56
Bopp, Franz, 43
Börne, 27, 63, 95, 111, 124, 128,
 166 *ff.*, 170, 254
Bothmer, Gräfin, 97, 183
Brentano, 68, 172
Breza, Graf von, 49
Briefe aus Berlin, 43, 66, 70
Brockhaus, 41
Buch der Lieder, 45, 50, 55, 65,
 79, 80, 83, 91 *ff.*, 97, 164,
 170, 182 *ff.*, 230, 238
Buch Le Grand, viii, 13, 15, 22,
 65, 70 *f.*, 84, 117

Bundestagsbeschlüsse, 126,
 157 *f.*
Bürger, 79
Burns, 34
Butler, E. M., 133
Byron, 22, 34, 39, 46 *f.*, 75, 86,
 237, 252

" Camilla Selden " (" Mouche"),
 44, 224 *ff.*, 244
Campe, viii, 66, 79, 102, 155,
 160 *f.*, 164, 166, 173, 176,
 180, 182, 194 *ff.*, 201 *f.*, 206,
 208 *f.*, 211 *f.*, 214, 217 *f.*,
 220 *f.*, 230, 232, 238 *f.*
Canning, 75, 78, 105
Carl Theodor, Elector, 3
Carlyle, 251
Chamisso, 45, 172
Charles V., Emperor, 116
Christiani, 53, 55, 57, 59
Cornelia Goethe, 10
Cornelius, 3
Cotta, 94, 96 *ff.*, 102, 122 *f.*, 137,
 159, 169
Cumberland, Duke of, 4

Delacroix, 129
Delaroche, 129
Dellage, 164
Denunzianten, Über den, 160
Detmold, 180, 196 *ff.*
Deutschland, 188
Deutschland, Ein Winter-
 märchen, 12, 176
Devrient, 48
Dichter Firdusi, Der, 86, 234 *f.*
Dieffenbach, 201
Dingelstedt, 189

INDEX

Disputation, 237 *f.*
Droste-Hülshoff, Annette von, 1, 33
Dumas, 163, 209, 228
Dümmler, 50

Eichendorff, 68
Elementargeister, 139, 141, 160, 162
Elsasser, F. A., x
Elsasser, J., x
Elster, 71 *f.*, 136, 222, 251
Embden, Baron Ludwig von, 17, 174, 220
Embden, Moritz, 49
Empress Elizabeth of Austria, 2
Enfantin, Père, 137 *f.*
Englische Fragmente, 71, 75 *f.*, 98, 103, 112, 115, 231
Ernst August of Hanover, King, 4

Faust, Goethe's, 146
Februarrevolution, Die, 211
Fichte, 143
Fichtenbaum, 83, 89
Florentinische Nächte, 160 *f.*
Fouqué, 33, 45, 172
Franz, 83
Französische Bühne, Über die, 162 *f.*
Französische Maler, 129
Französische Zustände, 122, 125, 129, 137, 169
Frau Rat Goethe, 9
Frederick the Great, 189
Frederick II., Grand Duke of Baden, 144
Frederick William III., 126, 189
Frederick William IV., 188, 241
Friedländer, John, 42
Für die Mouche, 244

Gans, Eduard, 48, 62, 111
Gassen, Gottlieb, 2
Gassen, Ludwig, 97
Gathy, 239
Gautier, 209, 228

Gedanken, 10
Gedichte, 49 *f.*, 57 *f.*, 79, 83
Gedichte 1853 *und* 1854, 239
Geldern, Joseph van, 7
Geldern, Peira van (Betty Heine), 7, 9, 15 *f.*, 20, 102, 132, 173, 180, 202, 218
Geldern, Simon van, 7
Geschichte der neueren schönen Litteratur in Deutschland, Zur, 139
Geschichte der Religion und Philosophie in Deutschland, Zur, 138 *f.*, 162
Gesellschafter, Der, 49, 57, 61
Gespräche mit Heine, x
Geständnisse, viii, 9, 19, 120, 215 *f.*, 218, 221, 259
Goethe, 8, 10, 32, 44 *f.*, 57 *ff.*, 79, 89, 91, 93 *ff.*, 99, 109 *f.*, 116, 118, 128, 130, 134, 141, 146 *ff.*, 152, 161, 167, 214, 217, 252, 254 *f.*
Gollancz, Sir Israel, x
Götter im Exil, 141, 216 *f.*
Göttin Diana, Die, 216 *f.*
Gottschalk, 68
Grabbe, 3, 48
Grenadiere, Die, 22, 40, 84
Grillparzer, 52 *f.*, 58
Grimm, Jakob, 95
Grimm, Ludwig, 13, 95, 183
Grimm, Wilhelm, 95
Gruby, 207, 228
Grupello, 3
Gubitz, 57, 61
Gulliver, 22
Gumpel, Lazarus, 107
Gutzkow, 148, 157, 166, 182

Halle, Adolf, 97, 197 *f.*
Hamann, 3
Hamburger Wächter, Der, 35, 41, 49
Hardy, Thomas, 152
Harzreise, Die, 40, 55, 57, 61, 65 *f.*, 68, 71, 91, 106, 131, 171
Hasselriis, 229

288

Hauptmann, Gerhart, 191
Hebbel, 252
Hebräische Melodien, 230, 234, 237
Hegel, 43, 149, 214
Heimkehr, Die, 45, 55, 57, 61, 66, 90
Heine, Amalie, 29 *ff.*, 37, 42, 54 *f.*, 72, 90, 95, 223
Heine, Betty (see Peira van Geldern)
Heine, Charlotte, 10, 16, 42, 194, 218, 220, 222, 224 *f.*
Heine, Gustav, 10, 16 *f.*, 218, 222, 228
Heine, Heymann, 4
Heine, Karl, 29, 194 *ff.*, 200, 209, 221 *f.*, 243
Heine, Mathilde (Crescentia Mirat), 2, 152 *ff.*, 162, 168, 171, 173 *ff.*, 179 *f.*, 185, 193, 196, 207 *f.*, 219, 222, 225, 228 *f.*, 233, 242
Heine, Max, 10, 16 *f.*, 19, 95, 98, 206, 213, 221
Heine, Salomon, 4 *f.*, 16, 27 *ff.*, 38, 41, 50, 54, 72, 97, 107, 119, 159, 173, 180, 190, 194 *f.*, 201, 235, 243, 254, 258
Heine, Samson, 4, 7, 9, 16 *f.* 20, 26, 37, 101, 131
Heine, Therese, 29, 55, 72, 90, 93, 98, 183, 185, 194, 222
Herder, 3, 230, 255
Herwegh, 188, 241
Hesse, Hartwig, 134
Hillebrand, Karl, 209
Hiller, 121
Hindermans, Frau, 19
Hirth, Friedrich, ix
Historien, 234
Hoffmann, 33, 48, 68
Hoffmann und Campe, 95, 239
Hohenhausen, Elise von, 46
Houben, H. H., x, 56
Hugo, Victor, 163
Humboldt, Alexander von, 198, 227

Immermann, 3, 53, 56, 69, 71, 109 *f.*, 112, 125, 132
Irving, Washington, 245
Italienische Reise, Goethe's, 70

Jan Wellem (Elector Johann Wilhelm,) 3
Jean Paul, 18, 147 *f.*
Jehuda ben Halevy, 237 *f.*
Jizzo di Novis, Graf, 17
Jungblut, Emil, 1
Junge Deutschland, Das, 148
Junge Leiden, 50, 83, 95

Kahldorf über den Adel, 117
Kant, 149
Karl Philipp of Jülich-Berg, 7
Kerner, Justinus, 165
Kleist, Heinrich von, 58
Klopstock, 91, 120
Krinitz, Elise von (see " Camilla Selden ")

Lafayette, 127
Lamentationen, 232, 234
Lassalle, 199, 210, 231
Laube, 148, 155, 157, 172, 195, 198, 202
Lavater, 3
Lazarus, 232, 240
Le Grand, Monsieur, 22 *f.*, 72, 84
Lessing, 15, 143, 146, 255, 258
Letzte Gedichte und Gedanken, 239
L'Europe Littéraire, 138, 148
Lewald, August, 154 *f.*, 163
Lewald, Fanny, 218
Lichtenberger, 250
Lieder, 83
Lindner, 96
Liszt, 83
Lorelei, Die, 55, 90
Lots, 223
Louis Philippe, 122 *f.*, 129, 158, 163, 169, 204, 211
Ludwig I, King, 96 *f.*, 188
Ludwig, Otto, 252

INDEX

Ludwig Börnes Urteil über H. Heine, 167
Ludwig Marcus, 216
Lumley, Benjamin, 217
Lutetia, 169, 216
Luther, 141, 143
Lyrisches Intermezzo, 50, 80, 88, 90

Marcus, Ludwig, 48
Marx, Karl, 177
Massmann, 241
Mathilde, Lady, 106 *f.*
Maurer, 49
Mayer, Karl, 165
Mein Kind, wir waren Kinder, 11
Meissner, Alfred, 168, 202 *f.*, 207, 212, 222, 224, 227 *f.*, 244
Memoiren, vii *ff.*, 5, 7, 15, 18 *f.*, 21, 37, 216, 220 *ff.*, 249
Mendelssohn, Moses, 15, 48
Mendelssohn-Bartholdy, Felix, 3, 83
Menzel, 95, 157, 160, 165
Merckel, 79, 114, 121
Metternich, 39, 123 *f.*, 126, 157, 255
Meyerbeer, 200, 241
Monckton Milnes (Lord Houghton), 223
Mond, Frida, x
Morgan, Lady, 99
Moser, Moses, 47 *f.*, 51, 53 *f.*, 58, 60, 62, 65, 69, 73, 93, 102, 117, 130, 134, 159
Müller, Wilhelm, 89
Müllner, Adolf, 46, 52
Mundt, Theodor, 159

Nachtgedanken, 173, 190
Nachträge zu den Reisebildern, 103
Napoleon, 2, 13, 20, 22 *ff.*, 27, 38, 59, 71 *f.*, 75 *f.*, 86, 103 *ff.*, 127, 169
Neuer Frühling, 12, 97 *f.*, 103, 183

Neue Gedichte, 98, 131, 182, 187, 190, 218, 230, 239
Neue Politische Annalen, 94, 97*f.*,
Nibelungenlied, 147
Nicholas, Emperor, 105 *f.*
Nordsee, Die, 61, 66, 69 *f.*, 76, 91, 236
Novalis, 147, 161

Ollea Zur, 187, 239

Paganini, 161
Pariser Zeitung, 159
Pauline, 155
Pfizer, 165
Philarète, Chasles, viii
Platen, 71, 102, 108 *ff.*, 165, 232, 254
Popper, Isidor, 180
Premiers Lundis, 148
Prinzessin Sabbat, 237
Pückler-Muskau, 199

Quixote, Don, 22, 107, 114, *f.*, 164

Rabbi von Bacharach, Der, 27, 49, 62, 162 *f.*, 237
Rahmer, 207
Ratcliff, 50, 52, 75
Reinhart, Richard, 209, 224
Reisebilder, viii, 55, 61, 66 *f.*, 70, 75, 79, 94, 97, 103, 109, 112, 115 *f.*, 128
Reise von München nach Genua, 98, 101, 104, 127, 134
Revue de Paris, viii
Revue des Deux Mondes, viii, 139, 160, 217, 221, 223
Richelieu, Duc de, 17
Robert, Frau, 71, 185
Rocca, Principessa della, 10, 17 *f.*, 28
Roccamora, Isaak, 107
Romantische Schule, Die, 59, 61, 138 *f.*, 144, 148, 165
Romanzen, 83 *f.*, 186

Romanzero, 187, 190, 205, 217 *f.*, 230 *f.*, 238 *f.*, 245
Romanzero, Nachwort zum, 214, 230 *f.*
Rothschild, Baron James, 198
Rothschild, Meyer Amschel, 16, 26
Rousseau, Jean Baptiste, 39
Rousseau, Jean Jacques, 8, 68, 142, 253
Rückert, 109
Ruge, 214

Sainte-Beuve, 149
Saint-Just, 140
Saint-Simon, 138
Saint-Simonism, 117, 133 *ff.*, 138 *ff.*, 144 *ff.*, 151, 169, 177, 185, 212, 256
Salon, Der, 62, 128 *f.*, 131 *f.*, 137, 139, 160, 162, 186, 217
Sartorius, 40
Schadow, 3
Schallmeyer, 19 *f.*
Scheible, 217
Schelling, 213
Schenk, Eduard, von 97, 99 *ff.*
Schenkendorf, 33
Schiller, 60, 146
Schlachtfeld bei Hastings, 234
Schlegel, August Wilhelm von, 38 *f.*, 145, 147
Schlesier, Gustav, 148
Schmiedings, Adolf, 2
Schnabelewopski, Aus den Memoiren des Herrn von, 131 *f.*
Schriftstellernöten, 166
Schubert, 83
Schumann, 3, 35, 83
Schwab, 165
Schwabenspiegel, Der, 147, 165 *f.*
Scott, 22, 53, 56, 71, 75 *f.*
Sefchen, 21, 32 *f.*, 221, 234
Sethe, 30 *f.*, 34 *f.*, 65
Shakespeares Mädchen und Frauen, 164
Sharp, William, 253
Shaw, Bernard, 258

Sketch of Life, viii, 9
Solms, Princess, 66
Sonette, 83, 88
Soult, Marshall, 19
Spanische Atriden, 230, 234 *ff.*
Spinoza, 142
Stadt Lucca, Die, 101, 104, 112, 115, 164, 190
Staël, Madame de, 99, 122, 144, 149
Stahr, Adolf, 218
Stein, Frau von, 44
Steinmann, 41, 50
Sterne, 22, 67 *f.*, 106
Stolbergs, 3
Straube, Heinrich, 41
Strauss, Salomon, 168
Strodtmann, Adolf, 228, 251
Stuttgarter Morgenblatt, 101, 157, 160

Telegraph, Der, 199
Tieck, 56, 147
Tragödien nebst einem lyrischen Intermezzo, 50, 57 *f.*
Traumbilder, 33, 83
Treitschke, 189, 191, 250
Trittau, Alphonse, 221

Über Polen, 49, 66
Uhland, 79, 89, 147, 165
Unparteiische Korrespondent, Der, 213

Varnhagen von Ense, August, 44, 73 *f.*, 78, 93 *ff.*, 102, 107, 111 *f.*, 117, 121, 128, 134, 138, 159, 172, 178, 199, 200, 202, 210
Varnhagen von Ense, Rahel, 16, 43, 45, *f.*, 56 *ff.*, 70, 101
Venedey, Jakob, 241
Verein für Kultur und Wissenschaft der Juden, 62, 256
Vermischte Schriften, 169, 216, 218, 239
Vernet, Horace, 129

INDEX

Verschiedene, 98, 133, 136, 151, 184
Vitzliputzli, 230, 234 *f.*
Vorwärts, 190, 199
Vulpius, Christiane, 152

Wagner, Richard, 83, 131
Waldenburg, Mathilde von, x
Weber, Die Schlesischen, 190 *ff.*
Wedekind, Eduard, 56
Weidmann, 165
Wellington, 75 *f.*
Werner, Zacharias, 52
Wesselhöft, Robert, 117
Wieland, 3

Wienbarg, Ludolf, 131, 148, 157
Wihl, 166
Wisetzki, Wilhelm, 233
Wohl, Frau, 168 *f.*
Wohlwill, 35, 49
Wolf, F. A., 43, 58
Wolfram von Eschenbach, 260
Wunderhorn, Des Knaben, 183

Zeitgedichte, 136, 177, 187, 190
Zeitschrift für die Wissenschaft des Judentums, 48
Zippel, 33
Zunz, Leopold, 48, 62